The Best American

sex

Writing 2004

2007

THE BEST AMERICAN

sex

WRITING 2004

EDITED BY DANIEL O'CONNOR

THUNDER'S MOUTH PRESS
NEW YORK

THE BEST AMERICAN SEX WRITING 2004

© 2004 Avalon Publishing Group

Published by
Thunder's Mouth Press
An imprint of Avalon Publishing Group Incorporated
245 West 17th St., 11th Floor
New York, NY 10011-5300

AVALON
publishing group incorporated

Library of Congress Cataloging-in-Publication Data is available.

ISBN 1-56025-598-6

9 8 7 6 5 4 3 2 1

Designed by Maria Elias
Printed in the United States of America on recycled paper
Distributed by Publishers Group West

Contents

THE BEST AMERICAN

sex

WRITING 2004

Is the Pope Crazy?

By Katha Pollitt
The Nation / October 16, 2003

There are many things to be said against condoms, and most people reading this have probably said them all. But at least they work. Not perfectly—they slip, they break, they require more fore-thought and finesse and cooperation and trust than is easy to bring to sex every single time, and, a major drawback in this fallen world, they place women's safety in the hands of men. But for birth control they are a whole lot better than the rhythm method or prayer or nothing, and for protection from sexually transmitted diseases they are all we have. This is not exactly a controversial statement; people have been using condoms as a barrier against disease as long as rubber has been around (indeed, before—as readers of James Boswell's journals know). You could ask a thousand doctors—ten thousand doctors—before you'd find one who said, Condoms? Don't bother.

But what do doctors know? Or the Centers for Disease Control, or the World Health Organization, or the American Foundation for AIDS Research (Amfar)? These days, the experts on condoms are politicians, preachers and priests, and the word from above is:

Condoms don't work. That is what students are being taught in the abstinence-only sex ed favored by the religious right and funded by the Bush administration—$117 million of your annual tax dollars at work. The theory is that even mentioning condoms, much less admitting that they dramatically reduce the chances of pregnancy or HIV infection, sends a "mixed message" about the value of total abstinence until marriage. How absurd—it's like saying that seat belts send a mixed message about the speed limit or vitamin pills send a mixed message about vegetables. Anti-condom propaganda can backfire, too: True, some kids may be scared away from sex although probably not until marriage; others, though, hear only a reason to throw caution to the winds. According to a 2002 Human Rights Watch report on abstinence-only sex ed in Texas, a condoms-don't-work ad campaign led sexually active teens to have unprotected sex: "My boyfriend says they don't work. He heard it on the radio." Why is the Bush administration giving horny teenage boys an excuse to be sexually selfish? You might as well have high school teachers telling them using a condom during sex is like taking a shower in a raincoat.

Now it seems the Vatican is joining fundamentalist Protestants to spread the word against condoms around the globe. "To talk of condoms as 'safe sex' is a form of Russian roulette," said Alfonso Lopez Trujillo, head of the Vatican's office on the family. On the BBC *Panorama* program "Sex and the Holy City," Lopez Trujillo explained, "The AIDS virus is roughly 450 times smaller than the spermatozoon. The spermatozoon can easily pass through the 'net' that is formed by the condom." That latex has holes or pores through which HIV (or sperm) can pass is a total canard. A National Institutes of Health panel that included anti-condom advocates examined the effectiveness of condoms from just about every perspective, including strength and porosity; according to its report, released in July 2001, latex condoms are impermeable to even the smallest pathogen. Among STDs, HIV is actually the one condoms work best against. "We're all a bit stunned by Lopez Trujillo's lack of respect for scientific consensus," Dr. Judith Auerbach of Amfar, who sat on the NIH panel, told me. "Where do his numbers come from?" Is Lopez Trujillo, who even suggests putting warnings on condoms like those on cigarettes, a loose cannon such as can be found in even the best regulated bureaucracies? According to "Sex and the Holy City," in Africa, where HIV infects millions—20 percent in Kenya, 40 percent in Botswana, 34 percent in Zimbabwe—Catholic clergy, who oppose condoms as they do all contraception, are actively promoting the myth that condoms don't prevent transmission of the virus and may even spread it. The *Guardian* quotes the archbishop of Nairobi, Raphael Ndingi Nzeki, as saying: "AIDS . . . has grown so fast because of the availability of condoms." Thus is a decade of painstaking work to mainstream and normalize condom use undone by the conscious promotion of an urban legend.

When the Nobel Prize for Peace was awarded to Shirin Ebadi, the first ever to a Muslim woman, an Iranian and a crusader for women's rights, not everyone was thrilled. What about Pope John Paul II, now celebrating the twenty-fifth anniversary of his election, and possibly near death? "This . . . was his year," wrote David Brooks in his *New York Times* column, a hymn of praise for the Pope as the defender of "the whole and the indivisible dignity of each person." A few pages over, Peter Steinfels said much the same in his religion column: "Is there any other leader who has so reshaped the political world for the better and done it peacefully?" More knowledgeable people than I can debate how much credit the Pope should get for the fall of

Communism—I always thought it was Ronald Reagan with an unintentional assist from Gorbachev plus the internal collapse of the system itself. With the crucial exception of Poland, the countries in the old Soviet bloc aren't even Roman Catholic, or are so only partially. Whatever his contribution to that historic set of events, though, the Pope is on the wrong side of history now. Women's equality, sexual rights for all, the struggle of the individual against authoritarian religion and of course the global AIDS epidemic—the Pope has been a disaster on all these crucial issues of our new century. It's all very well for David Brooks to mock those who critique the Pope for his "unfashionable views on abortion," as if 78,000 women a year dying in illegal procedures around the world was just something to chat about over brie and chablis. But add it up: a priesthood as male as the Kuwaiti electorate—even altar girls may be banned soon, according to one recent news story—no divorce, no abortion, no contraception, no condom use even within a faithful marriage to prevent a deadly infection.

It's bad enough to argue that condoms are against God's will while millions die. But to maintain, falsely, that they are ineffective in order to discourage their use is truly immoral. If not insane.

Letter to the Editor of *New York* Magazine

By Susie Bright
New York magazine / October 22, 2003

Letters to the Editor
New York magazine
444 Madison Av.
NY NY 10022
10/22/03

Dear Editor:

If you could flip a magic switch and turn off every gigabyte of Internet pornography, you would still not stop young men from masturbating every day.

Surely anyone over the age of thirty who read your recent "Generation XXX" articles could think back to their youth and recall that they jerked off (all the time) without any help from the Internet—indeed often without any pictures but the ones in their own imagination.

I agree with your authors that young adults are having less sex today, and that they have more anxiety about the sex they are having . . . I only wish you had ditched this porno-addict canard. Pornography is not the culprit behind such loneliness and isolation.

I have been studying college students' sexual behavior, every year, since the mid-eighties. At the turn of the nineties, I noted that more students were virgins when they entered college, and that more women were ignorant of masturbation and their own orgasm.

In 2000, I had surveyed my first sample group in which a man replied that he, too, had never experienced an orgasm, and I was shocked. On second thought, I decided it must be a joke because I gave this particular survey at Carnegie Mellon, and they tend to have self-deprecating humor about their sex lives. But since that time, I've traveled to other colleges that don't suffer from a geeky reputation, and the male disassociation from sexual satisfaction has continued. It's scary.

There's no doubt about it—as a group, college-age adults delay sex, they have less sex, and worse sex than they did ten, and even more so, twenty years ago.

Here are some reasons I can quantify about the current sexual malaise:

Young people treated with antidepressant and Ritalin-type drugs have sexual problems. Students involved in binge drinking—the current drug craze on campus—have sexual dysfunction, and most of the time, they can't even remember it.

This generation has been raised on abstinence, body shame, and AIDS—cautionary moralism, in which sex is linked to death, poverty, and dissolution. Most explicitly, kids are warned that sex will destroy their career plans, their chance at a decent college and profession. Surely you have seen the public service announcements on television that spell it all out: "Not Me! Not Now!"—"I'm going to be an astronaut, I'm not going to let sex get in the way of my career goals!"

Women in particular are cautioned to wield their virtue like an old fashioned commodity-talk about a feminist backlash. Boy or girl, they are told to wait—and wait—but there is no grad school where someone finally says, "Hey, you should get into sex at some point."

These twenty-somethings are sexually immature, by earlier generations' standards. If you took your articles by Amsden and Wolf, and pretended that all the case histories were fourteen-year-old kids, then the whole thing would have made a lot more sense: boys too scared of real girls to make a move, and girls who judge themselves by other girls, in a vicious social ladder where sexual self-knowledge doesn't exist. Junior High School was a terrible time for sex.

However, when teenyboppers grow up, Playmates and romance novels don't cut it anymore. You yearn for a real, live, warm somebody in your arms. You learn (by trial and error) the sexual pleasures and complications of intimate connection, and how different it is from masturbation's charms.

Porn is changing because of mainstream corporate intervention—that's a great story I'd like to see you tackle. But on another track, sexual dysfunction, infertility, and erotic indifference are epidemic, and it would be worth a trip out of the sandbox to find out what's going on. Stop tugging the porno-addict chain, and find out why actual sex is in decline in America right now, while retail titillation and non-sexual pacification is soaring. It's a trend that someone ought to give more than a wank about.

Susie Bright

Where's Mae West When We Need Her?

An Interview with Camille Paglia

By Ingrid Sischy

Interview / July 2003

INGRID SISCHY: I wanted to start our conversation this month by referencing a show that's already off the air, thank goodness— ABC's *Are You Hot? The Search for America's Sexiest People*, in which contestants were analyzed, deconstructed, and insulted on the basis of what the judges perceived to be their "sex appeal." Did you see it?

CAMILLE PAGLIA: I tried to watch and found it depressing and awful. It didn't have the narrative flair or romance of *The Bachelorette*, which I do like. My students were infuriated by *Are You Hot?*

IS: It's a real intellectual and emotional exerciser. Why did it emerge when it did?

CP: This is the culmination of a long shift towards defining identity primarily through sexuality. My boomer generation began it, but the results are getting alarming. Young women pop artists have to package themselves like strippers or whores. I'm a long defender of strip clubs: erotic dancing is a symbol of liberation to me—not, as old-guard feminists maintained, a form of servitude to men. But athletic moves created by 1990s strippers have been adopted by singers like Britney Spears and marketed to prepubescent girls who want popularity at school. What we're witnessing is an enormous artificial construction of visualized sex—what D. H. Lawrence denounced as "sex in the head," detached from nature. And it's accompanied by cyber sex and the complete triumph of pornography on the Web.

IS: Is the voyeurism in response to the fear of real sex because of AIDS?

CP: When historians look back on this channeling and ritualization of sexual desire, they'll surely think that the mass voyeurism of the nineties and early twenty-first century was partly a reaction of fear and anxiety about sex, which now carries a huge burden of meaning.

IS: A trend of pornography began a few years ago. Movies, art galleries, advertising campaigns—you could see it everywhere. In the late nineties, instead of being a taboo, a reference to pornography was almost de rigueur for the post-Robert Mapplethorpe generation of art photographers. Suddenly, young photographers sanctioned in the hippest new galleries were reenacting porn scenes. It's still going on. Timothy Greenfield-Sanders, who's best known for his photographs of the luminaries of the art world, is now shooting the big machers of porn—pardon my Yiddish. What will happen once all the taboos have been neutralized? I guess it won't happen as long as there's religion.

CP: I've often said the best pornographers were raised Catholic, which gives you an intense sense of taboo. I know I have it, as did

Mapplethorpe and Warhol, and so does Madonna. Without taboo, you can't get the supercharge of porn. But porn today has become a fashion statement. I'm concerned about my students' cultural landscape. Porn has become a total trend, but there's no charge to it for them, no taboo. For them it's like decor—wallpaper. Gradually over the past fifteen years, very young girls have learned to present themselves in public in a highly sexual manner. They don't know it's sexual; they're simply imitating their pop star models. Hence they're sending messages that are misinterpreted by boys or men on the street. In condemning how women were portrayed in the media, feminists sometimes invited government regulation, but the media represent protected free speech. All we can do is change education to make sure that kids get real culture—great paintings, literature, classic films—so that they have an alternative to the tackiness around them.

IS: Censorship is an uninformed and reactionary backlash. All censorship does is cause an under-the-counter culture: in other words, more pornography.

CP: Absolutely. My generation was raised in the repressive fifties, when everything was censored. Television was so bland they couldn't say the word pregnant. All of a sudden there was a revolution, so sex really was avant-garde for a while. But today's brassy sexual display is shallow and empty. There's very little real eroticism in shows like *Are You Hot?*—which was like a meat parade of clunky kewpie dolls. All of this may have started when MTV ended its twenty-four hours a day of fabulous videos and began running wet T-shirt contests. But Spanish-language soaps and French films still know how to generate sexual steam. There's a great moment in *Niagara* [1953] when Marilyn Monroe comes out of this honeymoon cottage at Niagara Falls and lounges on the stoop, her eyes half-closed while she croons along to a song. She's in a sensual haze—it's like she's on fire. She just exudes sensuality, a molten inner state of sexual heat. There was nothing like that in *Are You Hot?*

IS: No, it was cold. In fact, it was like a big Diane Arbus photograph.

CP: [laughs] You're right! It was like a freak show.

IS: And there was no humor. It needed a Mae West figure, for a start. What made someone like Mae West so memorable, and what made you fight for the strip clubs or me for Robert Mapplethorpe's daring photography, is that they were about humanity. Shows like *Are You Hot?* seem inhuman. There's no sense of fantasy, no respect for the imagination.

CP: They're reductive and literalist. Computer animation is sexier these days. When Mae West was pushing the envelope in the 1920s and getting arrested for it, her work was all about innuendo and ambiguity. She had a juicy, luscious, relaxed sexual maturity. She portrayed sexual relations as a warm, forgiving comedy. She would have been bored to tears by today's plastic sex scene!

The Prisoner of Sex.com

By Chris O'Brien
Wired / August 2003

It's a typically sunny day in Rancho Santa Fe, California, and Gary Kremen is standing on the back patio of the mansion that's a monument to his greatest success—and his worst failure.

A sleepy suburb fifteen miles north of San Diego, Rancho Santa Fe is the richest community in the country, according to the U.S. Census Bureau. Even by local standards, Kremen's seven-bedroom home is swank: It has a swimming pool, an in-ground hot tub, a tennis court, and a volleyball sandpit, all set against rolling acres of lemon groves.

Kremen won the house in a lawsuit over the domain name Sex.com. In November 2000, at the end of a three-year legal battle, a federal judge ruled that Stephen Cohen had stolen the domain by forging a letter from Kremen's company to Network Solutions. Cohen was ordered to return Sex.com to Kremen and pay him $65 million in damages. (Cohen appealed, and in June of this year, the U.S. Supreme Court declined to hear his case.) In the meantime, Cohen had fled the country, so all Kremen got as compensation was this California mansion and a derelict house on the U.S.–Mexico border. Even so, Kremen figured he'd found his winning lottery ticket. Under Cohen, Sex.com had been taking in $500,000 a month selling banner ads to other online porn sites.

It takes only a quick peek inside the Rancho Santa Fe house to realize Kremen, thirty-nine, didn't hit the jackpot. The place is an utter mess. The doors have no knobs. Only a few of the rooms have beds, which are rented. The kitchen has thirty-five cabinets and four refrigerators, with Post-it notes on the few that contain food. Sex.com is in similar shape, a marquee property decaying beneath an enticing facade. When Kremen took possession of the porn portal, he figured it would run itself. But by early 2001, the Internet had become saturated with free porn on peer-to-peer networks like Kazaa, and Sex.com's revenue dropped by two-thirds. Kremen compounded his problems with lousy management skills—multiple firings, obsessive litigation—and an addiction to speed. "I'd be lying," he admits, "if I said I wasn't my own worst enemy sometimes."

Most porn sites reacted to the crisis in the industry by getting more extreme—bombarding visitors with spam, hawking herbal sex-enhancement products, catering to bizarre fetishistic niches. But "we want to get away from porn's negative aspects," Kremen says. He wants to make Sex.com an advertising middleman, selling sponsored links that would appear on major search engines as well as his own site. "Our pitch is simple" Kremen explains. "We'll deal with the adult industry so you don't have to."

Even if that's possible, Kremen might not be the man for the job. As we talk in an office he keeps in the mansion, a man bounds into the room. Kevin Blatt is an adult-entertainment business consultant who goes by his initials; KB has short, gelled hair, a goatee, and sunglasses he keeps on indoors. He works for HerbalO, a company that sells virility products on adult Web sites. Kremen thinks that's tacky. KB scoffs: "If there's money on the table, I'm going to take it."

By KB's side is his current girlfriend and the star of Girliescam.com, Anna Castro, who's wearing a tank top that barely conceals her breasts. "This is Girlie," KB says by way of introduction. "She's hot. And she sucks cock like you wouldn't believe."

Kremen is speechless. "Well," he says.

Kremen sees himself as an accidental pornographer. But he's best described as a speculator in virtual real estate who bought property on the wrong side of the tracks and toughened up to fit in with the neighborhood. In the early 1990s, when the Mosaic browser was fresh to the Web, Kremen registered dozens of domain names like jobs.com and housing.com while they were still free, figuring they could be worth a lot down the road.

Meanwhile, he focused on a site he already had up and running, Match.com. At the time, online personals were seen as terminally tacky—customers faxed in their photos—and venture capitalists were dubious. In 1994, Kleiner Perkins Caufield & Byers offered to invest in the online classifieds business that Match.com was part of, but the VCs wanted to merge it with Architext, which would become Excite.com. Kremen said no, because he wouldn't be made CEO of the new company. Instead, he accepted money from a group of investors led by Canaan Partners. As Internet dating became popular, Match.com started to draw media coverage. A typical photo, in the *San Francisco Chronicle*, featured Kremen looking forlorn and holding flowers, alongside a story about how the founder of Match.com couldn't get a date.

His relationships with his financial backers weren't so smooth, either, and Kremen developed a reputation for being smart but tough to deal with. The board wanted him to start developing other classifieds and stop messing around with lonely-hearts ads. "They were embarrassed by it," Kremen remembers. Meetings became shouting matches. "Gary sometimes loses perspective," says Ron Posner, a venture capitalist who was on the Match.com board. "VCs would call me in the middle of the night and say, 'What are we going to do about Gary?'"

Over Kremen's objections, Match.com was sold for $8 million in 1997 to Cendant, a Connecticut consumer services company. (A year and a half later, Cendant sold it to Ticketmaster Online-City-Search for $50 million.) All Kremen got was $50,000 and a lifetime account on the site—his login is "The Founder."

It was around this time that Kremen discovered Sex.com had been snatched by Cohen, and he pursued the epic case through six lawyers, two dismissals, and a host of setbacks. When he finally won three years later, he was on the verge of bankruptcy. He figured Sex.com represented his second chance to build an empire, to show those VCs what they had missed.

Kremen initially wanted someone else to run the business while he invested the profits in more respectable ventures; after all, he had an MBA from Stanford. But from the day he won control of the site, Kremen just couldn't let go. In January 2001, he fired his attorney, Charles Carreon, who had a 15 percent stake in the business, in a dispute over how much power the lawyer would have. In the course of a year, Kremen hired and fired three management teams. Some of the arguments were about his reluctance to pander as much as other porn sites did; he wouldn't allow bestiality, for example. "I'm judgmental about some of this stuff," he told me at the time. "There's a line I won't cross."

When he wasn't firing staffers, Kremen was filing lawsuits.

He filed a claim against Yahoo! (for intimidation), one against Wells Fargo (in its role as Cohen's bank), and a countersuit against Carreon, who had sued him first. Still bitter about the bruising legal battle to recover Sex.com, he hired a private investigator to track down Cohen in Mexico, without success. Before long, litigation was his biggest expense.

Driven, angry, and increasingly reluctant to surrender control, Kremen started pulling all-nighters and got hooked on speed in the process. His weight dropped as his stress level rose. "People used to say, 'You should be in rehab,'" Kremen remembers. "I'd say to them, 'I'm so efficient, you should be in rehab. I can be up for five days in a row—you guys are slackers.'" By Thanksgiving 2001, Kremen had fired more employees, and his friend and attorney, Sue Whatley, left the company to protest his self-destructive behavior. A month later, Sex.com was running out of cash.

It's spring 2002, a few months after he first met with KB, and Kremen's throwing a party at his mansion to jump-start the new business model. A statuesque redhead is soaking in his hot tub, wearing only a thong and pinching her nipples. Men gather round; some snap photos. The woman is Kym Wilde. Her job is to be the porn star who works for Sex.com. "You have to have a porn star on the payroll," Kremen says. "It's all part of the image."

Wilde steps out of the tub and moves over to a nearby table where Kremen is talking to a buddy, a Valley VC he knows from Stanford. Wilde, who also helped Kremen plan today's event, continues to squeeze her nipples as she and Kremen discuss the logistics for the rest of the evening. His friend's mouth hangs open, a shot of Don Julio tequila in his hand. "My God," he says when Wilde walks away. "Where did you find her?"

Kremen grins and pounds a shot. The party, co-sponsored by Python Video, one of the bigger companies in the adult-entertainment industry, is going well. Liquor is flowing. A DJ is spinning house music. And, most important, his friends from the straight business universe are mingling with his contacts from the porn world.

Kremen may want respect from the Stanford crowd, but he needs support from his new pals at places like Python, and to win it, he has to get up close and personal. As his friend Sue Whatley puts it, "These guys want to party with you, take drugs with you, sleep with the same girls, and then at four A.M. sign a deal." Kremen doesn't go that far, but he does try to fit in. He compares himself to Tony Soprano, another man with his own, idiosyncratic moral code who craves acceptance in the legitimate world. "He's like a CEO," Kremen says, "a businessman who's got business problems."

By summer 2002, things are picking up—monthly revenues rise to $200,000. In August, Kremen appears on a panel at the Search Engine Strategies Conference & Expo, a trade show in San Jose, and spends all three days of the convention meeting with search companies interested in using his sponsored adult links. By then he is already stepping over the lines he's drawn for himself. He has started to use pop-up ads. Within months he will make a complicated deal to sell some of the email addresses he's acquired, and link to a fake bestiality site, figuring he can make money from people he considers loathsome but who will be too embarrassed to ask for it back. "People in this industry beat me mercilessly for not doing those things," he says. "I came to a compromise."

It's March 2003, and Kremen is taking a meeting with three sales reps from Qwest, at Sex.com's office in San Francisco's Dogpatch district. Sex.com has had problems with denial-of-service attacks, so Kremen's looking for backup hosting. He leads all of us downstairs, where he shows the guys from Qwest the servers, the Ping-Pong table, and, finally, the S/M dungeon a few of his friends built. Slack-jawed, the Qwest salesmen stare at the chains hanging from the ceiling. A Sex.com programmer peers in. "I think someone came by earlier to pick up the strap-ons," he says.

In a conference room partitioned off from the rest of the floor, the Qwest regional sales manager makes his pitch: Their network is reliable, their pricing structure is fair, their security is strong. Kremen listens with his arms folded.

As talk turns to technical details, a Sex.com staffer explains the site's business model: "So, let's say we're trying to drive traffic to one of our anal-sex customer sites . . ."

The Qwest reps shift in their chairs, but Kremen just sits there smiling. He needs a deal, but he hates the way these guys act like they're above him, like his money is good enough for them but he isn't. He's a businessman just like they are, doing what he needs to do to make a buck in a tough market.

When the Qwest manager asks about "the credibility of your numbers," Kremen can't take it anymore.

"Credibility?" he howls. His arms spring open and slap the table. "Whose stock is trading at seven cents?"

"Actually," the manager says, "we're up over three dollars."

"Well, my business isn't being investigated by the SEC," Kremen exclaims, raising a triumphant finger in the air. "And we're profitable— unlike Qwest!"

The salesmen laugh nervously, and after a few more uncomfortable moments, the meeting breaks up. Kremen may have won a moral victory, but he still doesn't have a deal for a new hosting service.

There is some good news: Sex.com has signed up 2,300 advertisers, Kremen says, and has partnered with 60 search engines, including Lycos Europe, FindWhat, Mamma.com, and Kanoodle. Traffic has doubled. Monthly revenue has ticked up to $300,000.

But every dollar is a struggle, every customer a battle. Having a valuable piece of property is one thing, Kremen says. "Getting it developed is a hell of a different exercise."

The Forbidden Realm

Why Hasn't There Been a Great Movie About Sex?

By Steve Erickson
Los Angeles magazine / July 2003

Americans don't do ambiguity. In America, discussions of ambiguous issues tend to get polarized as a matter of course. When it comes to sex, the argument is framed by choices of promiscuity on the one hand and abstinence on the other. When it comes to movies, as PG-13 films increasingly become the only kind the studios consider financially viable, the subject of sex—that is to say movies about sex, where sex is the central concern—is left to porn, or "transgressive" films that would seem to flirt with porn. Recently a wave of foreign films has left audiences buzzing and newspaper articles brooding over whether the sex in them is simulated; at the same time, more and more porn aspires to higher production values and even traditional concerns of narrative, edging toward some notion of cinematic legitimacy. Presumably porn and non-porn will meet in an ambiguous middle, where it remains to be seen whether there's an audience. Filmgoers think filmmakers make movies about sex just to be provocative, and sometimes that's the case. But it's also true that for the artist, avoiding the most basic of human drives isn't just creatively frustrating, it's a little unnatural.

The Swedish film *I Am Curious (Yellow)* has just been released by Criterion on DVD, so now anyone can watch it. But when it first crossed American borders thirty-five years ago, it was seized by customs agents and banned; this was before the courts, as courts will do, got all hung up on that First Amendment thing and ruled in the film's favor. I was seventeen years old and vividly remember the newspaper ads with blond gamine Lena Nyman's wanton gaze; you had to see the movie to know she was really thinking about socialist politics. *I Am Curious* was the *Tropic of Cancer* of film, not only in its suppression but because, like the Henry Miller novel, it's about almost everything but sex. As with *Cancer*, what was shocking wasn't the sexual obsessiveness but its casualness; when the first hot rendezvous finally takes place an hour in, it's more a comedy of errors. Ironically but predictably the persecution of *I Am Curious* as a sex film—and the public interest that resulted—opened the floodgates for movies that really were about sex. Porn like *Deep Throat* and *Behind the Green Door* became not only acceptable but chic, while serious filmmakers decided it was safe to venture openly onto what was at once the most fundamental and forbidden landscape of human interaction.

In 1973, Italian director Bernardo Bertolucci released *Last Tango in Paris*. The story of an emotionally paralyzed American expatriate who begins an anonymous sexual relationship in the wake of his wife's death, the film exploded notions of what it means for a movie to be about sex or, for that matter, what sex itself means. In so doing *Last Tango* distinguished itself from porn, which probably sounds more judgmental than I intend. But while I believe an artistic, social, even ethical case can be made for porn that involves consenting adults, the whole attraction of porn is the idea of sex without consequence, sex as a sensual pursuit that has no ramifications. This is what Marion Brando's widower in *Last Tango* believes will save him. Instead he finds that there is no such thing as sex without consequence. If anything, sometimes sex that would mean nothing winds up the most meaningful of all. Of course *Last Tango* has since lost some of its shock; but in its day the movie was so monumental—and even now Brando's performance remains so self-lacerating and revelatory—that for a decade or more film had nowhere else to go. In retrospect it doesn't seem an accident that a new age of movies was at hand, a return to more wholesome entertainment in which people weren't devoured by desire but sharks.

Sex was once more left to the fringe. In Europe this meant directors like the French Just Jaeckin, who made a series of very popular and ridiculous pictures about a libertine named Emmanuelle, and cult filmmakers like France's Jean Rollin (*Shiver of the Vampires*), Spain's Jesus Franco (*Vampyros Lesbos*), and Belgium's Harry Kumel (*Daughters of Darkness*), whose movies rendered explicit the most sexually allegorical of pulp subjects, vampirism. In Rollin's dreamy 1979 *Fascination*, Brigitte Lahaie, a famous French porn actress of the day, wandered the misty countryside naked except for a flowing cloak and long-handled bloody scythe, as though searching for her playmate Death from Ingmar Bergman's *The Seventh Seal*. This turned out to be more prophetic and metaphoric than Lahaie or Rollin could have anticipated. It wouldn't be much longer before AIDS reminded people that sex not only did have consequences after all but always had, what with all those millennia of people dying from syphilis and women dying in childbirth; and so in the 1980s sex became repressed again, and sexuality vicarious. When this happened to coincide with the advent of video, and people could bring adult films into the privacy of their own homes rather than make nocturnal forays down into the stickier environs of Hollywood Boulevard, the shadow cinema of porn became an American phenomenon, and the San Fernando Valley the porn capital of the world.

What happened next no one could have foreseen. In the adult film business there was at least the perception—whether or not it was borne out in numbers—of a new, male audience, and as a result, porn developed . . . well, pretentious though it may be, there's no other word for it . . . an aesthetic. Just as with, you know, real movies, a handful of prominent directors became as much marquee names as stars like Traci Lords, Jenna Jameson, and Tera Patrick by paying attention to things they believed a female audience might care about, such as ambience, cinematography, set design, visual style. In the early eighties, collaborating with musician Mitchell Froom (who would produce records for Paul McCartney, Elvis Costello, and Los Lobos) and writer Jerry Stahl (who would write for TV series like *thirtysomething, Northern Exposure,* and *CSI*), and working under the pseudonym Rinse Dream, a director named Stephen Sayadian made two adult movies that didn't look like any porn made before. Surreal, unsettling, even creepy, more David Lynch than *Deep Throat,* neither *Nightdreams* nor *Cafe Flesh* was successful with the hard-core audience, who had, shall we say, a more functional interest in porn and found Dream's films hopelessly arty. But this was porn for people who didn't watch porn, and both films had a huge influence on Andrew Blake, who became the most famous adult director of the late eighties. Then a former CNN director named Michael Ninn strayed into the business as a moonlighting editor paying off an expensive divorce (insert your feminist psychological interpretation of choice here) and, with films like *Latex, Shock,* and *Dark Garden,* became porn's reigning auteur.

Now, several neon caveats are in order before you all run out and buy this stuff and the inevitable tsunami of outraged letters comes crashing down. This is porn, not erotica, and if you don't know the difference, you certainly will when you see it. And just as porn became more ambitious and self-conscious in the hands of directors like Ninn, the dramatic limits of the form became that much more apparent; for most people, the idea of watching hours and hours of it will be as unfathomable as, oh, watching hours and hours of music videos. After a while it's enough to make you long for old Soviet pastorals of tractors endlessly mowing wheat. Nonetheless, what's interesting is that, as the sensibility of avant-porn in the work of Dream, Blake, and Ninn became more "feminized," the sexuality became not more romantic or ideal but in fact darker. Scenes in *Shock* of a woman coupling with stone gargoyles seem to have bubbled up from a primordial and polymorphous subconscious. "[Porn] allowed me to release all the fury I'd felt my entire life," writes Traci Lords in her new memoir, *Traci Lords: Underneath It All* (HarperEntertainment). Having nearly upended the adult industry of the eighties as a sixteen-year-old queen, she may also have been a prophet of a millennial Porn of Ferocity: "I was vengeful, even savage, in sex scenes, fully unleashing my wrath . . . . I was nothing short of a sexual terrorist."

All right, you get the feeling maybe a canny publicist helped Traci with that last bit. But if you've ever seen any of her early performances—and maybe I have and maybe I haven't—the sentiment rings true about not only Lords and the new porn but also the most notorious of the non-porn movies that have taken on sex in the last five years. An almost unwatchable synthesis of carnality and murder, 2000's *Baise-Moi* confirmed for a lot of people everything George W. Bush has recently suspected about the French. *Baise-Moi* was directed by two women, one a former porn actress herself and Traci Lords's kindred sister-in-rage, and in comparison male-directed films like *L'Ennui, Pola X,* last year's *Y Tu Mama Tambien* and *Sex and Lucia,* and the upcoming *Porn Theater* are melancholy, hushed, haunted by love and emotional loss. Whereas the female director who called her movie *Romance* was being ironic, the guy who called his movie *Intimacy* wasn't. That none of these movies is American should surprise nobody in a country where Jack Valenti's MPAA gives an NC-17 rating to two women naked in bed but an R to Anthony Hopkins sautéing human brains in a saucepan.

The obvious conclusion would be that this reflects the openness of European attitudes about sex and the repressiveness of American attitudes. But then you would have to account for the fact that over the last ten years, the most transgressive movies of all haven't come from Europe but Japan, where all evidence suggests people are at least as screwed up about sex as Americans are. Picking up from Nagisa Oshima's 1976 *In the Realm of the Senses* (where it wouldn't have seemed there was anything left to pick up from), films like *The Bedroom, The Dream of Garuda,* and *I.K.U.* have rendered distinctions about what's porn not only worthless but misleading. In a culture that blew into the twenty-first century on the gust of a nuclear wind long before anyone else and long before it ever wanted to, and where impulses of submission and domination are implicitly recognized as natural parts of sexuality, these movies fuse eroticism with a profound, even frightening alienation. They don't so much shine a light on sex as pull the audience farther into the dark, where there are truths that can't be seen but only felt. Screwed up or not, and steeped though it is in centuries of rigid notions about honor, Japanese culture nonetheless shares with European culture (steeped though it is in centuries of Judeo-Christianity) a belief that the truth of human behavior—sex in particular—is found in that same ambiguity to which Americans have such antipathy. Not all truth, to be sure, and not a "situational" truth that precludes right and wrong or good and evil, but a lot of the truth anyway.

The one major film about sex in the last five years—major in the sense of being backed by an American studio—*Eyes Wide Shut* was a thirty-year grail for director Stanley Kubrick, who reportedly wanted to make a porn film and finally found outer space, Vietnam, and the Orwellian future easier thematic territory. After his death, when it was released in America in a bowdlerized form (meaning with an R rating, which star Tom Cruise insisted was just the way Stanley wanted it), *Eyes Wide Shut* so evoked the ambiguous logic of dreams that domestic audiences didn't know what to make of it. When I first saw it in the theater, I didn't know what to make of it, either. It was only over the weeks and months that followed that I realized I couldn't shake it from my head. Well, what do you want? I'm as American as the next person, and maybe I also don't do ambiguity that well, and maybe that accounts for why I think it's highly arguable whether any of these ambiguous explorations of sexuality has made for a truly great movie that fully succeeds as a work of art, whatever the considerable merits of *Eyes Wide Shut* or *Last Tango in Paris*.

In theory there's no reason a great movie about sex can't be made. But whereas the ambiguities of love involve universals to which everyone aspires—watching a great love story on the screen, whatever the characters or their situation, we recognize certain things we've shared or felt when we've been in love ourselves—the ambiguities of sex lie in a subjectivity that resists identification. Every sexual relationship is ultimately unique. Every sexual relationship is so much the calculus of two subjectivities colliding that the sex other people have is too foreign for most of us to even consider, let alone watch, no matter how great the actors look or how well posed their interplay. The paradox is that porn both succeeds in tapping into our sexual dreams and fails as dramatic conflict for the same reason—because its characters are anonymous and freed from consequence—while with non-porn it's the other way around: The sex between defined and distinct characters is so entirely private and their own that the more we're confronted with it, the more it shuts us out of the drama. The more we watch, the less we know, or understand, or feel. In other words, some degree of artistic failure may be built into the very subject of sex. Of course, you might argue that *Eyes Wide Shut* and *Last Tango in Paris* aren't really just about sex. But then, sex itself is never just about sex. Where the body goes, the psyche gets dragged into things, too, not to mention the heart, and that may be the only thing that can be said about sex that isn't ambiguous at all.

The Moral Birds and Bees

Sex and Marriage, Properly Understood

By Roger Scruton
National Review / September 15, 2003

In the England of the forties, when my parents were courting, terms like "moral," "decent," and "clean living" applied primarily to sexual behavior. Immorality meant sleeping around (and how innocent the word "sleeping" now sounds!); indecency meant unsolicited advances; dirtiness meant whatever put the sexual object before the loving subject. Sexual morality issued from two firm and seemingly immovable premises: that the sexual act is innocent only when sanctified by marriage, and that marriage is a commitment between man and woman, to share their life, fortunes, and family, for better and for worse, until death do them part.

The sixties put paid to that vision. Since then sexual freedom has proliferated, to the point where many people treat sexual conduct as though it were outside the scope of moral judgment altogether. It really doesn't matter, it is often said, what people do together, provided they freely enjoy it. Sure, pedophilia is wrong. But that is because real consent requires maturity; anything that adults agree to do in private is morally unimpeachable.

Now you can take that line and still believe in marriage, as a uniquely valuable institution with a distinctive place in the scheme of things. You may recognize that children need families, and that families depend on marriage as their binding principle. You may recognize this, and still believe that there is nothing wrong with extramarital affairs, or intra-marital promiscuity (i.e., orgies, swapping). However, you would also have to believe that marital love can endure without sexual fidelity, that jealousy can be refined away from sexual love and eventually discarded, that marriages can dispense with the kind of existential commitment whereby husband and wife consecrate their lives to each other. You would have to believe that sexual pleasure can be treated as an adjunct to our personal emotions, something that can be tasted in any circumstances and regardless of moral and personal ties. In short you would have to believe that human beings are quite different from those creatures described in our art and literature, for whom sexual desire has taken the form of erotic love and in whom erotic love has generally aspired to marriage.

Many people do believe all that. Persuaded by the "research" reports of the Kinsey Institute, by Margaret Mead's fabricated account of sex in Samoa, by the Reich-Fromm-Norman O. Brown liberationist orthodoxy, and by latter-day antinomians like Michel Foucault, they have come to assume that the attempts to distinguish right from wrong in sexual conduct, to separate legitimate from illegitimate sexual relations, and to surround the sexual act itself with an ethic of "pollution and taboo" (as the early anthropologists described it) are both unnecessary and oppressive. The only correct response to the problem posed by human sexuality, they believe, is to recognize that it is not a problem. It is we who choose, in Foucault's idiom, to "problematize" the sexual act, and we do so in order to fortify hierarchical and oppressive relations that do us no conceivable good. By discarding sexual morality we free ourselves from our "mind forg'd manacles," so as to enjoy the harmless pleasures that the spoilsports have for so long taken pleasure in spoiling.

According to the gurus of sexual liberation, the real purpose of sex is not to express love or to generate children (which is another way of expressing love) but to obtain pleasurable sensations. Sexual initiation, according to their view of things, means learning to overcome guilt and shame, to put aside our hesitations, and to enjoy what is described in their literature (which is rapidly becoming the literature of "sex education" in our schools) as "good sex." This can occur with any partner of either sex, and requires no institutional preparation and no social endorsement.

That picture leaves out of consideration the phenomenon that distinguishes us from the other animals, and that also generates the need for a sexual morality, namely desire. Sexual desire is not a desire for sensations. It is a desire for a person: and I mean a person, not his or her body, conceived as an object in the physical world, but the person conceived as an incarnate subject, in whom the light of self-consciousness shines and who confronts me eye to eye and I to I. True desire is also a kind of petition: It demands reciprocity, mutuality, and a shared surrender. It is therefore compromising, jealous, and also threatening. No pursuit of a mere sensation could be compromising, jealous, or threatening in this way. Here lies the distinction between the erotic and the pornographic. Erotic literature is about wanting another person; pornography is about wanting sex.

The interpersonal nature of desire explains why unwanted advances are forbidden by the one to whom they might be addressed, and why they may be experienced as a kind of contamination. It explains why rape is so grave a crime: for rape is an invasion of the victim's freedom, and a dragging of the subject into the world of things. If you describe desire in the terms used by the advocates of liberation, the outrage and pollution of rape become impossible to explain. In fact, just about everything in human sexual behavior becomes impossible to explain. Which is why our society is now so confused about sex. We advocate a neutral, scientific view of sex, as a kind of pleasurable sensation in the private parts (which are rapidly ceasing to be private). And by teaching this view of things to children, we encourage them to a premature and depersonalized interest in their own sexuality. In effect we are endorsing in our heads a view of sex that we know in our hearts to be evil. For at some level we all recognize what our behavior denies, that true "sex education" consists not in permitting pleasure but in forbidding it, by fostering shame. And as our society loses its sense of shame, we begin to fear for our children, becoming hysterical at the thought of all those pedophiles out there—who are really the pedophiles in here, the very people who are eliciting in their children a depersonalized interest in sex.

Traditional morality did not exist to prevent sexual pleasure, but to assist in the growth of sexual desire, as an individualizing bond between people. Shame was the barrier behind which erotic energy accumulated, to the point where it could overflow as desire. Marriage was seen as the institutional expression of desire, rather than a way of restricting or denying it. The first purpose of marriage was to consecrate the union of the partners, to make holy and inviolable what would otherwise be a merely secular contract of cohabitation. Such was the view of marriage that arose in medieval Europe, and that is enshrined in our own literature of love. Nor have other civilizations really disagreed, despite all the varied customs that distinguish them. Islamic, Chinese, Japanese, and Hindu cultures have all concurred in representing sexual desire as an existential bond rather than a fleeting appetite, to be hedged round with shame and hesitation until socially endorsed and ceremonially accepted.

As with all moral sentiments, however, this one concerning the connection between desire and marriage has both a subjective meaning and a social role. Its subjective meaning lies in the exaltation and ennobling of our sexual urges, which are lifted from the realm of appetite and reconstituted as rational commitments. Its social role is to facilitate the sacrifices on which the next generation depends. Marriage is not merely a tie between man and woman; it is the principal forum in which social capital is passed on. By tying sexual fulfillment to the bearing of children, marriage offers a double guarantee of a stable home: the guarantee that comes from erotic love, and the guarantee that comes from the shared love of offspring. It offers children durable affection, a secure territory, moral examples, and moral discipline.

This is all so obvious as barely to deserve mention. As James Q. Wilson has shown, being born to an unmarried mother is by far the most significant factor disposing children to a life of crime—more significant than IQ, race, culture, or education. All of us therefore have a deep and lasting interest in marriage, as the only known way to reproduce the moral order. We have an interest in ensuring that this institution is not trivialized or abused, not reduced to a Disneyland caricature or deprived of its privileged place in the scheme of things—which is, socially speaking, that of a link between generations.

Marriage in a religious society is a religious event: not a contract between mortals but a vow before the gods. Such a marriage raises the bond between husband and wife from the secular to the sacred sphere, so that whoever breaks the bond commits an act of sacrilege. Civil marriage (as introduced in modern times by the French revolutionaries) has gradually displaced the religious institution, so that marriage is now conducted by the civil authorities, and the change in status is not ontological, like the change from secular to sacred, but legal. In effect marriage has become a contract and has gradually assumed the provisional and temporary character of all merely secular arrangements. This was not the intention of those who invented civil marriage. In taking over and secularizing the institution of marriage the state was hoping to confer fiscal privileges and legal guarantees that would substitute for religious sanctions, and so help to make our commitments durable. It did this from the belief that marriage is vital to the future of society. The state in effect lent its aid to traditional sexual morality, by privileging faithful union between man and wife. And it did so for the very good reason that the future of society depends on this kind of union.

Now, however, the marriage contract is being enlarged to accommodate the permissive morality. Marriage is ceasing to be a sacrificial union of lovers, in which future generations have a stake, and becoming a transitory agreement between people living now. It is from this perspective that we should view the controversy over gay marriage.

This is not really a controversy about the rights, freedoms, and life-chances of homosexuals. It is a controversy about the institution of marriage itself. Can marriage retain its privileged place in our moral thinking when so effectively severed from the process of social reproduction? Already the secularization of marriage has led to easy divorce, serial polygamy, and growing insecurity among children. But marriage in its fundamental meaning is a form of lifelong commitment, in which absent generations have a stake. If marriage can be celebrated between homosexual partners, then it will cease entirely to be anything more than a contract of cohabitation, and the legal and fiscal privileges attached to it will seem both unjustified and dangerous, so many openings to litigation. Lovers' quarrels, exalted into marital disputes, will be endowed with an intransigent bitterness, while transient crushes will be foisted on friends and colleagues as institutional facts. In effect, marriage, as the institution through which society offers its endorsement and support to the raising of children, will have ceased to exist.

The demand to make institutions conform to our desires, rather than our desires to institutions, is one of the great American failings. Thanks to their Puritan heritage, Americans regard hypocrisy as a serious vice, and sin as so lamentable a condition that it must be avoided at all costs. If the only way to avoid sin is to redefine your sins as innocent pastimes, that is what Americans will do. Elsewhere in the world people have learned to extol marriage as the only innocent sexual relation, while nevertheless failing to live up to it. The important thing for normal un-Americans is to keep up appearances, to acknowledge one's own sinfulness, and to be prepared, when the crunch comes, to give up your lover for your spouse. La Rochefoucauld famously described hypocrisy as the tribute that vice pays to virtue. In the sexual mores of today's America, however, hypocrisy is regarded as the only genuine sin. Which is why, in America, sexual virtue gets no tributes at all.

Might and Right in Colorado Springs

By Samantha Dunn
Ms. magazine / June 2003

The first time I saw Colorado Springs I was on a high school trip up to the big city of Denver. I wanted to stop at the U.S. Air Force Academy on the way and notify them of my intention to enroll as soon as possible.

I had weighed the benefits: My mother was an ex-WAF, and by age six I knew how to salute and crisply recite "yes ma'am, no ma'am, no excuses ma'am." The Air Force had given Mom money for college, allowing her to become the first woman in her family to graduate.

My school counselor had arranged a meeting with the admissions officer. It was brief. There was talk of math and push-ups, neither of my strong suits, but what really got me was imagining life as a cadet: My freedom to do anything I wanted to would be quite limited.

So the Air Force Academy was out.

I am thinking of all this as I drive the same stretch of interstate recently to pay a visit. This time as I come upon the entrance to the Air Force Academy, an electronic sign flashes amber letters: VISITOR CENTER CLOSED.

The headlines generated by the academy this year have been enough to make it close ranks: fifty-six reports of sexual assault or rape of female cadets over the last decade, only now being investigated; only three attackers brought to military trial, none found guilty. In eight other cases since 1996, male cadets have been punished "administratively"—restricted at the academy or expelled.

But now, because a few women finally broke the code and went outside the academy walls with their stories, all hell, to use the technical term, has broken loose. The media is all over the story and at least four cadets are being charged with sexual assault.

There have been Congressional hearings and heads have rolled. The former commander, "Taco" Gilbert, was transferred to the Pentagon, replaced by Brig. Gen. Johnny Weida, a former pilot and a "strong Christian leader." Weida put a letter on the academy website promising to kill the virulence of this problem with a three-pronged attack he describes as "culture, communication and commitment."

Cari Davis and Jennifer Bier of TESSA, Colorado Springs' domestic abuse and rape crisis center, work out of a boxy, cement building with small windows behind high chain-link fence, in a lower-to-middle income neighborhood south of downtown. After nearly decades on the front lines, they are heartened by the serious attention to the crimes.

"It seemed to me that the size of the response really spoke to the level of denial there is about sexual violence, says Davis.

Abuse at the academy was well known to TESSA's workers who, in the course of fifteen years, have helped thirty-eight women cadets who reported being raped. "It was old news in the respect that we knew sexual assault was happening there, just like it happens in the rest of the culture at large," says Davis.

And it seems to be old news to other women in town, too. I stop to get a manicure at a shop downtown near the "Holey Rollers" tattoo parlor. After the usual chitchat, I say to the beautician, "This town's sure been in the news lately, huh?"

Still supporting my hand across the manicuring station, she raises her eyebrows. "It's about time somebody said something about what goes on up there. You should see what the civil service puts up with," says the woman, who, it turns out, served in the Naval Reserve before working a civil service post at the academy for eight years. She says she quit to open up her shop.

"Must have been hard to give up those government benefits to become an entrepreneur," I say.

"It wasn't, really," she says, taking my other hand to file the nails evenly. "I loved myself more."

If geography is in fact destiny, I wonder how much of what has happened has to do with this place. Like all of the true West, the Colorado character is libertarian. The social contract states that you do your thing, I do mine, and we don't get in each other's way. "Colorado Springs has always been conservative," says Cara de Gette, editor of the *Colorado Springs Independent*, the local alternative newsweekly.

But in the last twenty years, the town at the base of Pike's Peak became characterized as not just a bastion of Republicanism, but as the "Vatican of evangelical Christianity." De Gette explains: "Essentially, at the end of the 1980s, Colorado Springs was known as the foreclosure capital of the country. Our reliance on defense contracting [nearly 60 percent of the local economy by some estimates] distressed us further when that money went south. So our city's leaders looked to diversify the economy." A few city leaders are credited with attracting Focus on the Family and other religious nonprofits to town as "clean business."

The El Pomar Foundation provided a $4-million incentive grant to Focus on the Family, a moralistic, quasi-political Christian organization, and it relocated to Colorado Springs in 1991. About sixty other national and international Christian nonprofits soon followed, from Compassion International to the Fellowship of Christian Cowboys, each employing anywhere from a handful to thousands of true believers.

"In retrospect," says de Gette, "I think that the new business attracted folks who brought a much more rigid style of Republicanism, which in many ways has altered the local political landscape of the city." Although Colorado Springs seems to have moderated itself in recent years, it became infamous in the early 1990s for being the nucleus of support for the antigay initiative, Amendment 2, that led to boycotts of town business.

I don't know if there's a line connecting the dots between this culture and the military scandal. I do know there is a fundamental belief here in the strength and rightness of the individual. Personal responsibility is the mantra, and it is both liberating and oppressive. I am thinking of the account by a former cadet, Lisa Ballas, reported in the Colorado weekly *Westword*, in which she relates how the then-commander treated her chronicle of being forcibly penetrated by a cadet she had just been kissing in a bathroom at an off-campus party: "[Gilbert told me that I] didn't have to go to that party, didn't have to drink that night . . . and didn't have to follow him back into that bathroom."

In other words, you have the power to make anything happen, and if something bad happens you created the opportunity for it to occur. Basically, as women have always been told, "It was your fault."

On my way out of town, I call my mom and mention where I am. "I love that place," she says. "I was engaged to an officer up there for a while."

"Really?" She's always doing this. Last surprise she sprung on me was the story that Elvis' first cousin tattooed her name on his shoulder blade while she was in basic training in Biloxi. I ask if she's heard about the sexual attacks at the academy. "Did you ever hear about stuff like that when you were in the Air Force?"

"Is New York *big*?" she says, by way of saying yes. Then she tells me about a captain who asked her out while she was in flight school. She wasn't supposed to fraternize with officers but didn't think it would be a good idea to say no to a superior. "On the drive home he pulls over, tells me I look like his ex-wife, and attacks me."

I'm not sure I am hearing her right. Until this moment, all I have ever heard from her was wonderful stuff about the Air Force.

"Attacks you? Like how?"

"Like he was going to rape me. He scared the bejesus out of me."

I pull off to the side of the road and hold my cell phone more tightly to my ear. "What did you do?"

"I fought him off and told him, 'You take me home right now.' He was not pleased but he did it," she says. "I saw him on base a few times after that and we both pretended like nothing had happened."

I have seen my mother slam a man against a wall. She changes her own oil and doesn't break a nail. She drinks scotch like Kool-Aid, and she blows smoke rings out her nose. But those women cadets must have been tough, too, and look at what they were forced to go through. The question goes through my mind, Did you really, Mom? Were you really able to fight him off?

I pull back onto Academy Boulevard toward I-25. On my right is the U.S. Taekwondo Union. Its sign reads, WOMENS SELF-DEFENSE

CLASSES/CALL NOW. In the distance, apart from and above the town of Colorado Springs, the setting sun illuminates the white of the academy, glowing like Emerald City among the pines.

Double Lives
on the Down Low

By Benoit Denizet-Lewis
The New York Times Magazine / August 3, 2003

In its upper stories, the Flex bathhouse in Cleveland feels like a squash club for backslapping businessmen. There's a large gym with free weights and exercise machines on the third floor. In the common area, on the main floor, men in towels lounge on couches and watch CNN on big-screen TVs.

In the basement, the mood is different: the TVs are tuned to porn, and the dimly lighted hallways buzz with sexual energy. A naked black man reclines on a sling in a room called "the dungeon play area." Along a hallway lined with lockers, black men eye each other as they walk by in towels. In small rooms nearby, some men are having sex. Others are napping.

There are two bathhouses in Cleveland. On the city's predominantly white West Side, Club Cleveland—which opened in 1965 and recently settled into a modern 15,000-square-foot space— attracts many white and openly gay men. Flex is on the East Side, and it serves a mostly black and Hispanic clientele, many of whom don't consider themselves gay. (Flex recently shut its doors temporarily while it relocates.)

I go to Flex one night to meet Ricardo Wallace, an African-American outreach worker for the AIDS Task Force of Cleveland who comes here twice a month to test men for HIV I eventually find him sitting alone on a twin-size bed in a small room on the main floor. Next to him on the bed are a dozen unopened condoms and several oral HIV-testing kits.

Twenty years ago, Wallace came here for fun. He was twenty-two then, and AIDS seemed to kill only gay white men in San Francisco and New York. Wallace and the other black men who frequented Flex in the early eighties worried just about being spotted walking in the front door.

Today, while there are black men who are openly gay, it seems that the majority of those having sex with men still lead secret lives, products of a black culture that deems masculinity and fatherhood as a black man's primary responsibility—and homosexuality as a white man's perversion. And while Flex now offers baskets of condoms and lubricant, Wallace says that many of the club's patrons still don't use them.

Wallace ticks off the grim statistics: blacks make up only 12 percent of the population in America, but they account for half of all new reported HIV infections. While intravenous drug use is a large part of the problem, experts say that the leading cause of HIV in black men is homosexual sex (some of which takes place in prison, where blacks disproportionately outnumber whites). According to the Centers for Disease Control, one-third of young urban black men who have sex with men in this country are HIV-positive, and 90 percent of those are unaware of their infection.

We don't hear much about this aspect of the epidemic, mostly because the two communities most directly affected by it—the black and gay communities—have spent the better part of two decades eyeing each other through a haze of denial or studied disinterest. For African-Americans, facing and addressing the black AIDS crisis would require talking honestly and compassionately about homosexuality—and that has proved remarkably difficult, whether it be in black churches, in black organizations, or on inner-city playgrounds. The mainstream gay world, for its part, has spent twenty years largely fighting the epidemic among white, openly gay men, showing little sustained interest in reaching minorities who have sex with men and who refuse to call themselves gay.

Rejecting a gay culture they perceive as white and effeminate, many black men have settled on a new identity, with its own vocabulary and customs and its own name: Down Low. There have always been men—black and white—who have had secret sexual lives with men. But the creation of an organized, underground subculture largely made up of black men who otherwise live straight lives is a phenomenon of the last decade. Many of the men at Flex tonight—and many of the black men I met these past months in Cleveland, Atlanta, Florida, New York, and Boston—are on the Down Low, or on the DL, as they more often call it. Most date or marry women and engage sexually with men they meet only in anonymous settings like bathhouses and parks or through the Internet.

Many of these men are young and from the inner city, where they live in a hypermasculine "thug" culture. Other DL men form romantic relationships with men and may even be peripheral participants in mainstream gay culture, all unknown to their colleagues and families. Most DL men identify themselves not as gay or bisexual but first and foremost as black. To them, as to many blacks, that equates to being inherently masculine.

DL culture has grown, in recent years, out of the shadows and developed its own contemporary institutions, for those who know where to look: Web sites, Internet chat rooms, private parties and special nights at clubs. Over the same period, Down Low culture has come to the attention of alarmed public health officials, some of whom regard men on the DL as an infectious bridge spreading H.I.V. to unsuspecting wives and girlfriends. In 2001, almost two-thirds of women in the United States who found out they had AIDS were black.

With no wives or girlfriends around, Flex is a safe place for men on the DL to let down their guards. There aren't many white men here either (I'm one of them), and that's often the norm for DL parties and clubs. Some private DL events won't even let whites in the door. Others will let you in if you look "black enough," which is code for looking masculine, tough and "straight." That's not to say that DL guys are attracted only to men of color. "Some of the black boys here love white boys," Wallace says.

While Wallace tests one man for HIV (not all DL men ignore the health threat), I walk back downstairs to change into a towel—I've been warned twice by Flex employees that clothes aren't allowed in the club. By the lockers, I notice a tall black man in his late teens or early twenties staring at me from a dozen lockers down. Abruptly, he walks over and puts his right hand on my left shoulder.

"You wanna hook up?" he asks, smiling broadly.

His frankness takes me by surprise. Bathhouse courtship rituals usually involve a period of aggressive flirtation—often heavy and deliberate staring. "Are you gay?" I ask him.

"Nah, man," he says. "I got a girl. You look like you would have a girl, too."

I tell him that I don't have a girl. "Doesn't matter," he says, stepping closer. I decline his advances, to which he seems genuinely perplexed. Before I go back upstairs, I ask him if he normally uses condoms here.

As a recurring announcement comes over the club's loudspeaker—"HIV testing is available in Room 207. . . . HIV testing in Room 207"—he shakes his head.

"Nah, man," he says. "I like it raw."

If Cleveland is the kind of city many gay people flee, Atlanta is a city they escape to. For young black men, Atlanta is the hub of the South, a city with unlimited possibilities, including a place in its vibrant DL scene.

I went to Atlanta to meet William, an attractive thirty-five-year-old black man on the DL who asked to be identified by his middle name. I met him in the America Online chat room DLThugs, where he spends some time most days searching for what he calls "real" DL guys—as opposed to the "flaming queens who like to pretend they're thugs and on the DL." William says he likes his guys "to look like real guys," and his Internet profile makes it clear what he isn't looking for: no stupid questions, fats, whites, stalkers or queens.

I told him I was a writer, and he eventually agreed to take me around to a few clubs in Atlanta. With one condition: "You better dress cool," he warned me. "Don't dress, you know, white."

William smiles as I climb into his silver Jeep Grand Cherokee, which I take as a good sign. Two of William's best friends are in the car with him: Christopher, a thin, boyish thirty-two-year-old with a shaved head, and Rakeem, an outgoing thirty-one-year-old with dreadlocks who asked to be identified by his Muslim name. We drive toward the Palace, a downtown club popular with young guys on the DL.

William doesn't date women anymore and likes guys younger than he is, although they've been known to get more attached than he would prefer. "Yeah, he's always getting stalked," Rakeem says enthusiastically. "The boys just won't leave him alone. He's got this weird power to make boys act really stupid."

It's easy to see why. William radiates confidence and control, which serve him well in his daytime role as an executive at a local corporation. He says his coworkers don't know he likes men ("It's none of their business," he tells me several times), or that after work he changes personas completely, becoming a major player in the city's DL scene, organizing parties and events.

Christopher, who sits in the back seat with me, is the only one of the three who is openly gay and not on the DL (although he won't tell me his last name, for fear of embarrassing his parents). Christopher moved to Atlanta when he was twenty-four and was surprised when black men in the city couldn't get enough of him. "They would hit on me at the grocery store, on the street, on the train, always in this sly, DL kind of way where you never actually talk about what you're really doing," he says. "That's actually how I met my current boyfriend. He followed me off the train."

Rakeem, a roommate of William's, moved to Atlanta five years ago from Brooklyn. He says he's "an urban black gay man on the DL," which he says reflects his comfort with his sexuality but his unwillingness to "broadcast it." People at work don't know he's gay. His family wouldn't know, either, if a vindictive friend hadn't told them. "I'm a guy's guy, a totally masculine black gay man, and that's just beyond my family's comprehension," he says.

While Rakeem and William proudly proclaim themselves on the Down Low, they wouldn't have been considered on the DL when men first started claiming the label in the mid-nineties. Back then the culture was completely under the radar, and DL men lived ostensibly heterosexual lives (complete with wives and girlfriends) but also engaged in secret sexual relationships with men. Today, though, an increasing number of black men who have sex only with men identify themselves as DL, further muddying an already complicated group identity. And as DL culture expands, it has become an open secret.

For many men on the Down Low, including William and Rakeem, the DL label is both an announcement of masculinity and a separation from white gay culture. To them, it is the safest identity available—they don't risk losing their ties to family, friends, and black culture.

William parks the car in a secluded lot about a block from the Palace. As he breaks out some pot, I ask them if they heard about what happened recently at Morehouse College, where one black student beat another with a bat supposedly for looking at him the wrong way in a dormitory shower.

"I'm surprised that kind of stuff doesn't happen more often," William says. "The only reason it doesn't is because most black guys are sly enough about it that they aren't gonna get themselves beaten up. If you're masculine and a guy thinks you're checking him out, you can always say: 'Whoa, chill, I ain't checking you out. Look at me. Do I look gay to you?'"

Masculinity is a surprisingly effective defense, because until recently the only popular representations of black gay men were what William calls "drag queens or sissies." Rakeem takes a hit from the bowl. "We know there are black gay rappers, black gay athletes, but they're all on the DL," Rakeem says. "If you're white, you can come out as an openly gay skier or actor or whatever. It might hurt you some, but it's not like if you're black and gay, because then it's like you've let down the whole black community, black women, black history, black pride. You don't hear black people say, 'Oh yeah, he's gay, but he's still a real man, and he still takes care of all his responsibilities.' What you hear is, 'Look at that sissy faggot.'"

I ask them what the difference is between being on the DL and being in the closet. "Being on the DL is about having fun," William tells me. "Being who you are, but keeping your business to yourself. The closet isn't fun. In the closet, you're lonely."

"I don't know," Christopher says. "In some ways I think DL is just a new, sexier way to say you're in the closet."

Both have a point. As William says, DL culture does place a premium on pleasure. It is, DL guys insist, one big party. And there is a certain freedom in not playing by modern society's rules of self-identification, in not having to explain yourself, or your sexuality, to anyone. Like the black athletes and rappers they idolize, DL men convey a strong sense of masculine independence and power: I do what I want when I want with whom I want. Even the term Down Low—which was popularized in the 1990s by the singers TLC and R. Kelly, meaning "secret"—has a sexy ring to it, a hint that you're doing something wrong that feels right.

But for all their supposed freedom, many men on the DL are as trapped—or more trapped—than their white counterparts in the closet. While DL guys regard the closet as something alien (a sad, stifling place where fearful people hide), the closet can be temporary (many closeted men plan to someday "come out"). But black men on the DL typically say they're on the DL for life. Since they generally don't see themselves as gay, there is nothing to "come out" to, there is no next step.

Sufficiently stoned, the guys decide to make an appearance at the Palace. More than anything, the place feels like a rundown loft where somebody stuck a bar and a dance floor and called it a club. Still, it's one of the most popular hangouts for young black men on the DL in Atlanta.

William surveys the crowd, which is made up mostly of DL "homo thugs," black guys dressed like gangsters and rappers (baggy jeans, do-rags, and FUBU jackets). "So many people in here try so hard to look like they're badasses," he says. "Everyone wants to look like they're on the DL."

As I look out onto the dance floor, I can't help doing the math. If the CDC is right that nearly one in three young black men who have sex with men is HIV-positive, then about fifty of the young men on this dance floor are infected, and most of them don't know it.

"You have no idea how many of the boys here tonight would let me"—have sex with them—"without a condom," William tells me. "These young guys swear they know it all. They all want a black thug. They just want the black thug to do his thing."

While William and many other DL men insist that they're strictly "tops"—meaning they play the active, more stereotypically "masculine" role during sexual intercourse—other DL guys proudly advertise themselves as "masculine bottom brothas" on their Internet profiles. They may play the stereotypically passive role during sex, they say, but they're just as much men, and just as aggressive, as DL tops. As one DL guy writes on his America Online profile, "Just 'cause I am a bottom, don't take me for a bitch."

Still, William says that many DL guys are in a never-ending search for the roughest, most masculine, "straightest looking" DL top. Both William and Christopher, who lost friends to AIDS, say they always use condoms. But as William explains: "Part of the attraction to thugs is that they're careless and carefree. Putting on a condom doesn't fit in with that. A lot of DL guys aren't going to put on a condom, because that ruins the fantasy." It also shatters the denial—

stopping to put on a condom forces guys on the DL to acknowledge, on some level, that they're having sex with men.

In 1992, E. Lynn Harris—then an unknown black writer—self-published *Invisible Life*, the fictional coming-of-age story of Raymond Tyler, a masculine young black man devoted to his girlfriend but consumed by his attraction to men. For Tyler, being black is hard enough; being black and gay seems a cruel and impossible proposition. Eventually picked up by a publisher, *Invisible Life* went on to sell nearly 500,000 copies, many purchased by black women shocked at the idea that black men who weren't effeminate could be having sex with men. "I was surprised by the reaction to my book," Harris said. "People were in such denial that black men could be doing this. Well, they were doing it then, and they're doing it now."

That behavior has public health implications. A few years ago, the epidemiological data started rolling in, showing increasing numbers of black women who weren't IV drug users becoming infected with HIV. While some were no doubt infected by men who were using drugs, experts say many were most likely infected by men on the Down Low. Suddenly, says Chris Bell, a twenty-nine-year-old HIV-positive black man from Chicago who often speaks at colleges about sexuality and AIDS, DL guys were being demonized. They became the "modern version of the highly sexually dangerous, irresponsible black man who doesn't care about anyone and just wants to get off." Bell and others say that while black men had been dying of AIDS for years, it wasn't until "innocent" black women became infected that the black community bothered to notice.

For white people, Bell said, "DL life fit in perfectly with our society's simultaneous obsession and aversion to black male sexuality." But if the old stereotypes of black sexual aggression were resurrected, there was a significant shift: this time, white women were not cast as the innocent victims. Now it was black women and children. The resulting permutations confounded just about everyone, black and white, straight and gay. How should guys on the DL be regarded? Whose responsibility are they? Are they gay, straight, or bisexual? If they are gay, why don't they just tough it up, come out and move to a big-city gay neighborhood like so many other gay men and lesbians? If they are straight, what are they doing having sex with guys in parks and bathhouses? If they are bisexual, why not just say that? Why, as the CDC reported, are black men who have sex with men more than twice as likely to keep their sexual practices a secret than whites? Most important to many, why can't these black men at least get tested for HIV?

The easy answer to most of these questions is that the black community is simply too homophobic: from womanizing rappers to moralizing preachers, much of the black community views homosexuality as a curse against a race with too many strikes against it. The white community, the conventional wisdom goes, is more accepting of its sexual minorities, leading to fewer double lives, less shame and less unsafe sex. (AIDS researchers point to shame and stigma as two of the driving forces spreading AIDS in America.)

But some scholars have come to doubt the reading of black culture as intrinsically more homophobic than white culture. "I think it's unfair to categorize it that way today, and it is absolutely not the case historically," says George Chauncey, the noted professor of gay and lesbian history at the University of Chicago. "Especially in the 1940s and 50s, when anti-gay attitudes were at their peak in white American society, black society was much more accepting. People usually expected their gay friends and relatives to remain discreet, but even so, it was better than in white society."

Glenn Ligon, a black visual artist who is openly gay, recalls that as a child coming of age in the seventies, he always felt there was a space in black culture for openly gay men. "It was a limited space, but it was there," he says. "After all, where else could we go? The white community wasn't that accepting of us. And the black community had to protect its own."

Ligon, whose artwork often deals with sexuality and race, thinks that the pressure to keep homosexuality on the DL does not come exclusively from other black people, but also from the social and economic realities particular to black men. "The reason that so many young black men aren't so cavalier about announcing their sexual orientation is because we need our families," he says. "We need our families because of economic reasons, because of racism, because of a million reasons. It's the idea that black people have to stick together, and if there's the slightest possibility that coming out could disrupt that, guys won't do it." (That may help explain why many of the black men who are openly gay tend to be more educated, have more money and generally have a greater sense of security.)

But to many men on the DL, sociological and financial considerations are beside the point: they say they wouldn't come out even if they felt they could. They see black men who do come out either as having chosen their sexuality over their skin color or as being so effeminate that they wouldn't have fooled anyone anyway. In a black world that puts a premium on hypermasculinity, men who have sex with other men are particularly sensitive to not appearing soft in any way. Maybe that's why many guys on the DL don't go to gay bars. "Most of the guys I've messed around with, I've actually met at straight clubs," says D., a twenty-one-year-old college student on the DL whom I met on the Internet, and then in person in New York City. "Guys will come up to me and ask me some stupid thing like, "Yo, you got a piece of gum?' I'll say, 'Nah, but what's up?' Some guys will look at me and say, 'What do you mean, what's up?' but the ones on the DL will keep talking to me." Later he adds: "It's easier for me to date guys on the DL. Gay guys get too clingy, and they can blow your cover. Real DL guys, they have something to lose, too. It's just safer to be with someone who has something to lose."

D. says he prefers sex with women, but he sometimes has sex with men because he "gets bored." But even the DL guys I spoke with who say they prefer sex with men are adamant that the nomenclature of white gay culture has no relevance for them. "I'm masculine," as one eighteen-year-old college student from Providence, R.I., who is on the DL told me over the phone. "There's no way I'm gay." I asked him what his definition of gay is. "Gays are the faggots who dress, talk, and act like girls. That's not me."

That kind of logic infuriates many mainstream gay people. To them, life on the DL is an elaborately rationalized repudiation of everything the gay rights movement fought for—the right to live without shame and without fear of reprisal. It's a step back into the dark days before liberation, before gay-bashing was considered a crime, before gay television characters were considered family entertainment and way, way before the current Supreme Court ruled that gay people are "entitled to respect for their private lives." Emil Wilbekin, the black and openly gay editor in chief of *Vibe* magazine, has little patience for men on the DL. "To me, it's a dangerous cop-out," he says. "I get that it's sexy. I get that it's hot to see some big burly hip-hop kid who looks straight but sleeps with guys, but the bottom line is that it's dishonest. I think you have to love who you are, you have to have respect for yourself and others, and to me most men on the DL have none of those qualities. There's nothing 'sexy' about getting HIV, or giving it to your male and female lovers. That's not what being a real black man is about."

Though the issues being debated have life-and-death implications, the tenor of the debate owes much to the overcharged identity politics of the last two decades. As Chauncey points out, the assumption that anyone has to name their sexual behavior at all is relatively recent. "A lot of people look at these DL guys and say they must really be gay, no matter what they say about themselves, but who's to know?" he says. "In the early 1900s, many men in immigrant and African-American working-class communities engaged in sex with other men without being stigmatized as queer. But it's hard for people to accept that something that seems so intimate and inborn to them as being gay or straight isn't universal."

Whatever the case, most guys on the DL are well aware of the contempt with which their choices are viewed by many out gay men. And if there are some DL guys willing to take the risk—to jeopardize their social and family standing by declaring their sexuality—that contempt doesn't do much to convince them they'd ever really be welcome in Manhattan's Chelsea or on Fire Island. "Mainstream gay culture has created an alternative to mainstream culture," says John Peterson, a professor of psychology at Georgia State University who specializes in AIDS research among black men, "and many whites take advantage of that. They say, 'I will leave Podunk and I will go to the gay barrios of San Francisco and other cities, and I will go live there, be who I really am, and be part of the mainstream.' Many African-Americans say, 'I can't go and face the racism I will see there, and I can't create a functioning alternative society because I don't have the resources.' They're stuck." As Peterson, who says that the majority of black men who have sex with men are on the DL, boils it down, "The choice becomes, do I want to be discriminated against at home for my sexuality, or do I want to move away and be discriminated against for my skin color?"

So increasing numbers of black men—and, lately, other men of color who claim the DL identity—split the difference. They've created a community of their own, a cultural "party" where whites aren't invited. "Labeling yourself as DL is a way to disassociate from everything white and upper class," says George Ayala, the director of education for AIDS Project Los Angeles. And that, he says, is a way for DL men to assert some power.

Still, for all the defiance that DL culture claims for itself, for all the forcefulness of the "never apologize, never explain" stance, a sense of shame can hover at the margins. It's the inevitable price of living a double life. Consider these last lines of a DL college student's online profile. "Lookin 4 cool ass brothers on tha down low. . . . You aint dl if you have a VIP pass to tha gay spot. . . . You aint dl if you call ur dude 'gurl.' . . . Put some bass in ur voice yo and whats tha deal wit tha attitude? If I wanted a broad I would get one—we both know what we doin is wrong."

The world headquarters of the Web site www.streetthugz.com is a small, nondescript storefront next to a leather bar on Cleveland's West Side. The site's founder, Rick Dickson, invites me to watch one of its live Web casts, which he says feature "the most masculine DL brothers in the world doing what they do best."

Rick opens the door holding a cigarette in one hand and a beer in the other. Inside, a group of young black men sit in a thick haze of cigarette smoke as the song "Bitch Better Have My Money" plays from a nearby stereo. By the far wall, two men type frantically on computer keyboards, participating in thirty chat-room conversations at once. Near the street-front window, which is covered by a red sheet, there are three muscular black men in their early twenties.

Rick sits down and lights another cigarette. A part-time comic who goes by the stage name Slick Rick, he has a shaved head, piercing green eyes, and a light-skinned face with a default setting on mean. Twice a week, Rick's thugs, as he calls them, perform a sex show for anyone who cares to log on. Although less than a year old, the site has developed a devoted following, thanks mostly to chat-room word of mouth. "We're going to be the next Bill Gates of the Internet industry," he assures me. "We got black DL thugs getting it on, and that's what people want to see!"

One of the site's most popular stars is a tall, strikingly handsome twenty-three-year-old former Division I basketball player, who goes by the name Jigga. When I first meet Jigga about ten minutes before the show, he's naked, stretching and doing push-ups in an adjacent room as he peppers me with questions about journalism and sportswriting. "I want to be a sportswriter," he says. "Either that, or a lawyer. I love to argue."

Unlike some of the other streetthugz stars who dropped out of school and hustle for money, Jigga says he comes from a close middle-class family and always did well academically. Considering all that, I ask him how he came to find himself here. "It's some extra cash," he says. "But mostly, it's 'cause I like the attention. What can I say? I'm vain." Jigga says he has sex with both men and women, but he doesn't label himself as bisexual. "I'm just freaky," he says with a smile.

Like many guys on the DL, Jigga first connected to other DL men through phone personals lines, which still have certain advantages over Internet chat rooms. "You can tell a lot right away by a voice," he says later. "There are guys who naturally sound masculine, and then there's guys who are obviously trying to hide the fact that they're big girls."

At 10:07 P.M., seven minutes behind schedule, Rick announces, "It's show time at the Apollo." He unfolds a burgundy carpet that serves as the stage, and Jigga and two thugs take their places. The phone won't stop ringing as viewers call to make requests ("Can I talk to Jigga when he's done?"), and Rick answers each call with an enthusiastic reference to the caller's location. "Hey, we got Detroit in the house! Say wuzzup to Detroit!"

The show temporarily goes "off air" when Chi, a thirty-two-year-old promoter for the site, trips over the MegaCam's power cord. While someone else plugs it back in, he takes a seat on the sidelines. Thin and deceptively strong, Chi looks younger than his age. He has a tattoo on his left arm, which he tells me is a reminder of his gang days. Back then, he says, before he moved to Cleveland, his life was a disaster: he had three kids with three women and spent most of his twenties in jail for drug trafficking.

Chi says he doesn't deal drugs anymore—not since his mother, a heroin addict, died with a needle in her arm. Today he works at a fast-food joint in a shopping-mall food court and is a talent scout for Rick, which means that if he spots a young black man with "the look" (tough, masculine, and preferably with a wild streak), he'll ask him if he'd like to take some pictures for money—or, better yet, act in one of the site's live sex shows. Chi has a fiancée he has been with for four years.

When Rick has seen enough foreplay, he throws condoms at the boys. Rick has been making a big deal to me about how his site promotes safe sex, which he insists is a moral obligation at a time when so many young black men in America are dying of AIDS. But previous viewers of the show told me they didn't see condoms being used, and the site boasts of keeping everything "raw." I ask Rick about the discrepancy. "It's just an expression, man," he says, and explains that the sex is sometimes simulated.

The actors seem somewhat bored, but the point, I gather, is not what they do on camera, but how they look. And these guys look straight—in fact, they look as if they might rather be having sex with women. That, Rick knows, is the ultimate turn-on in much of the DL world, where the sexual icon is the tough unemotional gangster thug.

"Do these guys ever kiss?" I ask Rick.

"Well," he explains, "thugs don't really kiss. Sometimes they stick their tongues in each other's mouths, but it's not really kissing. Gay people kiss. DL thugs don't kiss."

In May 1986, Sandra Singleton McDonald showed up at the Centers for Disease Control in Atlanta, eager to begin her research into diseases affecting blacks in the South.

"Well," said a young research assistant there, "then you'll want to look into AIDS."

McDonald laughed. "Baby, you must have misunderstood my question," she said in her loving, motherly voice. "I'm talking about African-American diseases."

"Yes, I know," the man said. "Like I said, you'll want to look into AIDS."

McDonald did, and what she learned floored her. "This wasn't just a gay, white man's disease like we had all been told from the beginning," recalls McDonald, the founder of Outreach Inc., an Atlanta-based nonprofit organization providing services to those affected by AIDS and substance abuse in the city's black communities. "I went out and told leaders in the black community that we needed to start dealing with this now, and they looked at me like I was crazy. People were outraged that I was even bringing this up. They said, 'Oh, be quiet, that's a white problem.' But why would we think that a sexually transmitted disease would stay within one racial group, or within one geographic area? It made no sense. The public health community made a lot of mistakes and gave out a lot of wrong information. Once we became aware of the impact of the disease, we did a lot of blaming and shaming so that we could feel O.K. and say, 'This isn't about us.'"

Five years later, that fiction ceased to be viable when Magic Johnson told a national television audience that he was HIV-positive. AIDS organizations were flooded with calls from panicked black men and women wanting to know more about the disease. Meanwhile, Magic dismissed the rumors that he'd slept with men during his NBA career, insisting he didn't get infected through homosexual sex, but rather through sex with a woman. Young black men on inner-city basketball courts weren't so sure. They wondered if maybe Magic had men on the side.

That it took Johnson's announcement to introduce the reality of AIDS to the black community goes to the depth of the denial around the disease. By 1991, 35,990 African-American men had been reported with AIDS (roughly half having contracted it through sexual intercourse), accounting for about a quarter of all AIDS cases in America. But while there was a mass mobilization around AIDS in the early eighties among gay white men, there was no similar movement among black men with AIDS, black leaders, politicians, clergy or civil rights organizations. "There was a real sense in black communities that you had to put your best face forward in order to prove that you deserve equal rights and equal status, and that face didn't include gays and IV drug users with AIDS," says Cathy Cohen, author of *The Boundaries of Blackness: AIDS and the Breakdown of Black Politics.* "It's been a very slow process for the black leadership in America to own up to this disease. Not acknowledge it in passing, but own it."

Black churches, which are the heart of many African-American communities, were particularly slow to respond to the crisis, and many still haven't, even despite the disease's ravages within their parishes. In 1999, after female congregants of Cleveland's Antioch Baptist Church told their pastor that they were HIV-positive, the church started an AIDS ministry that has been applauded for its courage and effectiveness. Still, the black church—like many in white America—is careful not to condone homosexual behavior. "Some gays want a flat-out, standing-on-the-tower affirmation from the church that the gay lifestyle, or the lifestyle of whoring around with men, is acceptable," says Kelvin Berry, the director of the Antioch program. "And that's not going to happen."

Combating AIDS in these communities also means confronting popular conspiracy theories that claim that HIV was created by the U.S. government to kill black people. One study in the nineties by the Southern Christian Leadership Conference found that 54 percent of blacks thought HIV. testing was a trick to infect them with AIDS. In the early nineties, the rapper Kool Mo Dee and Spike Lee expressed concern that HIV was a part of a calculated campaign intended to rid the world of gay men and minorities, and as recently as 1999, Will Smith told *Vanity Fair* that "possibly AIDS was created as a result of biological-warfare testing."

Pernessa C. Seele, founder and CEO of the Balm in Gilead, an international AIDS organization that works with black churches, explained, "For the most part, we don't want to get tested, and we don't want to get treatment, because we really believe that the system is designed to kill us." She continued: "And our history allows us, or helps us, to believe that. We have documented history where these kinds of diseases have been perpetuated on us. And that's why it's so important for the church to get involved. Black people trust the church. We don't trust health care. We don't trust doctors and nurses, but we trust the church. So when the church says, 'Get tested,' when the church says, 'Take your medicine,' people will do it."

Other black AIDS organizations are focused on prevention. In some cases, the strategies are straightforward: push condoms, distribute clean needles. But reaching men on the DL is difficult. James L. King, a publishing executive, spoke about his former DL life at a National Conference on African-Americans and AIDS. "I sleep with men, but I am not bisexual, and I am certainly not gay," King said. "I am not going to your clinics, I am not going to read your brochures, I am not going to get tested. I assure you that none of the brothers on the Down Low are paying the least bit of attention to what you say."

Earl Pike, executive director of the AIDS Task Force of Cleveland, agrees that many of the prevention messages aimed at black men have been unsuccessful. "Up to this point, we've failed to make a convincing case to young black men about why they should listen to us when we tell them to put on a condom, mostly because we've had the wrong people delivering the wrong kind of message," he says. "The usual prevention message for all these years can be interpreted as saying: 'Gee, we're sorry about racism. We're sorry about homophobia in your homes and churches. We're sorry that urban schools are crappy. We're sorry that you can't find a good job. We're sorry about lack of literacy. We're sorry about all these things, but you really need to start using condoms, because if you don't, you could get infected tomorrow, or next year, or some point during the next decade, and if you do get infected, at some point, you could get sick and die.'"

Many AIDS organizations now say that frank, sexy prevention messages that use the masculine imagery of hip-hop culture are the only way to reach men on the DL. In St. Louis, for example, a $64,000 federal grant financed a billboard campaign—depicting two muscular, shirtless black men embracing—aimed at raising AIDS awareness. But Mayor Francis Slay called the billboards inappropriate and ordered them taken down.

"I need a beer," Chi says as we drive through downtown Cleveland on a Saturday night, looking for something to do. It's been three months since I last saw him at the streetthugz.com filming. As we stop at a red light, he turns to get a better look at a young Hispanic woman in the car next to us. "That girl is beautiful," he says. "But she needs to lose the car. What a shame—a beautiful woman driving a Neon!"

Chi loves women. He also likes men, although, like many guys on the DL, he doesn't verbalize his attraction to them, even when he's with like-minded people. When I ask him about this, he's stumped to explain why. "I don't know," he says. "Maybe it's because being black, you just learn to keep that to yourself." Anyway, he always had a girlfriend. "Guys were there for sex."

Unlike many other DL guys, who never tell anyone about their private lives, Chi opens up with little prompting. He says that he loves his fiancée but that he doesn't consider the sex he has with men to be cheating. "Guys are a totally different thing."

Unbeknownst to his fiancée, he has been casually dating his male roommate for several months. "I told her that he's gay and makes passes at me," he says, "but she doesn't know we have sex." On some level, Chi says he feels bad about the deception. Right now, though, he isn't feeling guilty. His fiancée just called to tell him that she's going out tonight—and that he needs to come over to pick up their feisty one-year-old son.

"She just wants to go out and shake her groove thing with her friends instead of taking care of him like she said she would," Chi says. "Man, she's selfish sometimes. I love her, but sometimes I hate her, you know what I'm saying?"

We pull up to Chi's apartment, where his fiancée and two of her friends are waiting for him in the driveway. Inside the apartment, the couple argue about whose turn it is to take care of their son while I sit in the dining room and watch him fearlessly attack the four house cats. In the dark living room, Chi's roommate, who is white, lounges on the couch in blue boxers, chain-smoking as he half-watches television.

Chi's fiancée eventually leaves, after which Chi changes out of his work shirt and mixes a drink for the road. "We've been on shaky ground," Chi tells me, referring to his roommate. "He loves me, but I'm committed to someone else. I think he has problems dealing with that. Like I tell him, 'I care about you, but I can't be that guy you want.'" What Chi means, I think, is that he can't be gay.

Chi puts his son in the back seat of the car, and we drive toward Dominos, a black gay bar where we're supposed to meet Jigga. Chi spends most of the ride complaining about his fiancée. His son finally starts crying and kicks the back of Chi's seat. "Yeah, defend yo mama!" Chi says, laughing.

They wait in the car as I walk into Dominos looking for Jigga. The long, rectangular-shaped bar is packed with regulars tonight, mostly middle-aged black men—some openly gay, others on the DL—and a few tough-looking younger guys. Jigga spots me first and waves me over to the bar. He tells me a lot has changed since the first time I met him. He's in law school now and has put aside the sportswriter idea. And while he is still on the DL (his coworkers and most of his straight friends don't know he likes guys), he has a serious boyfriend who is also on the DL.

Four months ago, having a serious boyfriend would have been inconceivable to him. "I think I love this dude," he tells me as we walk to the car. "He's got a lot of attitude, but I kind of like that. We have fistfights all the time, and we don't stop until somebody has blood. Then we have sex." Jigga laughs as he opens the car door. "But I must really love him, because I never got in fistfights with any of my exes."

I'm about to question his definition of love when Chi interjects. "I still need a beer," he says, pointing the way toward a nearby gas station. We pull into a tight parking spot, careful to avoid the young black man with a sideways baseball cap who leans into the car next to us, blocking Chi's passenger-side door. "Move your ass," Chi says, knocking the kid out of the way with the car door. The boy laughs it off, avoiding a possible confrontation.

"I think I hooked up with him," Jigga says, craning his neck from the back seat to get a better look at the kid. "Actually, nah, that's not him. Looks like him, though."

Recently, Jigga told his parents that he's interested in both guys and girls. "I was drunk when I told them," he says. "But I'm glad I did. They've been really cool about it." It takes me a few seconds to process the words. Really cool about it? In six months of talking to young black gay and DL men, I found that Jigga is one of the few who told his parents, and the only one who reported unconditional acceptance. "I'm blessed," he says. "I realize that. Black parents don't accept their gay kids. Black culture doesn't accept gay people. Why do you think so many people are on the DL?"

Jigga is proof that being on the DL isn't necessarily a lifelong identity. He seems considerably more comfortable with his sexuality than he was the first time I met him, and I suspect that soon enough, he may be openly gay in all facets of his life without losing his much-coveted masculinity. I tell him what I'm thinking. "Who knows, man?" he says. "Two years ago, I wouldn't have believed that I'd be having sex with guys." Chi opens the car door, cradling a six-pack of beer. "I love beer," he says, smiling. As we drive away, he checks out a young woman stepping out of a nearby Honda Civic. "Damn, that girl is fine!"

Do Women Need Viagra®?

It Can't Hurt Unless Doctors Start Trying to Standardize Our Sexual Performance

By Barbara Ehrenreich
Time / January 19, 2004

It's almost enough to make you pity Big Pharma: here it is, on the verge of a major new breakthrough—a Viagra-type drug for women—and feminists are in a major snit. One faction is muttering that the drug companies are sexist for taking so long to find a cure for female sexual dysfunction (FSD) while the fix for its male counterpart, erectile dysfunction, has been available for over five years. Others, like sex expert Shere Hite, are already denouncing the drug companies for "cynical money grabbing"—i.e., creating a disease in order to market a pill or a patch.

On the Viagra-envying side of the debate are plenty of women who find their libidos drained by surgery, menopause, crying infants, or overwork. Plus, there is a significant minority still seeking the zipless interaction popularized by Erica Jong in *Fear of Flying:* skip the relationship, the candlelight and the wine, and cut to the chase. I know at least one respectable grandma who is preparing for the advent of a female Viagra by stocking up on batteries for her vibrator.

Of all the sex issues covered in this special issue of *Time*, this one may be the most controversial: Is there really a need for an orgasm-promoting drug for women? The drug companies like to cite a study suggesting that 43 percent of American women suffer from FSD, which would make the disorder more than ten times as prevalent as breast cancer or AIDS, though surely a bit more bearable. But critics point out that in the study, women were judged to have FSD for answering yes to any one of seven questions, such as whether they had experienced difficulty with lubrication or sometimes lacked desire. Perhaps the more amazing conclusion is that 57 percent of American women seemed to be ready to party at the drop of a hat.

You might also wonder, if FSD is so widespread, why Viagra is now about as popular as vitamin C among all those male sex partners. To judge from the billion-dollar market for Viagra, no man can count on slipping peacefully into impotence. Who's behind the massive use of Viagra, if not an army of FSD-free girlfriends and wives? And thanks to the influence of *Sex and the City*, even reliably potent men are now indulging, says the *New York Times*, because of "the Samantha complex, a fear of wilting in the face of a new wave of sexually empowered women." Or are the drug companies trying to promote an arms race between pumped up Viagra poppers and chemically Samantha-ized women?

This wouldn't be the first time that the medical profession was caught inventing a disease to go with the cure in hand. In the 1990s plastic surgeons discovered "micromastia," a syndrome characterized solely by small breasts and conveniently curable with silicone implants. A century and some years ago, doctors detected an epidemic of "hysteria" among affluent women, manifested by hundreds of unrelated symptoms and requiring constant medical attention. Or we may reflect on the case of hormone-replacement therapy, which doctors promoted as a cure for the "disease" of menopause, only to discover, after millions of women had been snookered into taking them, that the pills increased the risk of far nastier diseases like breast cancer.

Furthermore, the feminist critics point out, it's not clear that FSD, to the extent it exists, can be vanquished with a pill. Unlike male sexuality, female sexuality isn't just a matter of plumbing. Context matters more than it seems to in men—along with emotion, fantasy, and, yes, candlelight—so that anyone afflicted with FSD might do better to claim some leisure in her life and work on rekindling the romance. Of course, the same may be true for the Viagra-taking sex, a surprising 50 percent of whom fail to renew their prescriptions.

Finally, as psychiatrist Leonore Tiefer argues, there's something deeply creepy about the medicalization of sexuality, male and female. Once there's a drug to prescribe, doctors will feel the need to establish "norms"—say two orgasms a week—and women who fall short are bound to feel inadequate, unfeminine, even pathological. Better, Tiefer thinks, for them to seek more satisfying relationships or more inspiring partners than rely on a pill for their thrills.

Still, if there's a possibility of a female version of Viagra, I say, Get it to the market fast. Only make that the black market, or at least over the counter. Let's circumvent the medical profession with all its profoundly off-turning talk about disorders and norms, and appropriate the new drug for purely recreational use, just as men are doing with Viagra. Sure, we need dashing partners and the leisurely evenings in which to enjoy them, but these improvements could be years in coming, if ever. In the meantime, my feminist guru is Cyndi Lauper, with her revolutionary dictum: Girls just wanna have fun. If Big Pharma comes up with something to advance that agenda, bring it on.

Times Up

Times Square's Sin and Vice and Squalor Helped Define the New York Experience. They Still Do. In Our Minds.

By Mark Jacobson
New York magazine / April 7–14, 2003

THE STREETS 1980

In 1980, Carl Weisbrod, then head of the fledgling Times Square cleanup, peered out his office window in the old McGraw-Hill Building. Below were the usual Forty-Deuce Street hookers, junkies smoking Kools in front of Al Shark's bodega, a row of blinking XXX signs. "I'm not against local color. But look at this crap," said Weisbrod. "We can't leave it like this: It's Times Square, the center of the city."

That was the beginning of the end for Times Square as a self-determining, sleazological biosphere. Gone are the grind runs of *Scream, Blacula, Scream!*, pushers selling bogus "smoke," "Ts and Vs" (Tuinals and Valiums), "'ludes," and "dust" (Q: If a dope pusher pushes dope with no dope in it, what's he guilty of?), and the mid-operation transsexuals hitting no-account boyfriends with pocketbooks outside Church's Chicken.

It is debatable whether the current Vegasization model, with the Toys 'R' Us Ferris wheel and theme restaurants (the Condé Nast Frank Gehry lunchroom fits right in with the WWE and ESPN

Zone), is really an improvement. But really, what was supposed to happen? As Carl Weisbrod said, you couldn't "leave it like that." Not every package-deal tourist sees the charm in having his feet stick to the floor at the old Selwyn (or Harris, or Lyric) during the eye-gouge scene from *The Good, the Bad and the Ugly* as some balcony denizen shouts, "You're sorry? You piss on my date and you say you're sorry?"

Still, I retain a prurient wistfulness for the Deuce of my youth. It was at the long-gone Hubert's Museum and Flea Circus that I saw my first naked breast. Upstairs, Hubert's was a pinball parlor, but down the wide flight of linoleum-covered stairs, "the museum" was another world. Along with the fleas pulling tiny covered wagons was the Atomic Man—radiation grew a crêpe-paper nose on the back of his head. Here, also, were the ancient flip-card machines. You put a nickel in a slot, pressed your eyes to the rubber cup, and turned the crank.

Inside was a woman by the seashore. She smiled and took off her blouse. Turn the handle backward, she put it back on again.

Hubert's disappeared, and I didn't think much about it until the early eighties, in the time of Koch, when the Deuce was at its foulest. It was one of those little encounters that happen in the Big City. I was riding on the RR, and a woman in her early twenties, pretty but weary-looking, sat across from me holding a book. Every once in a while she'd doze off. Her book, an astrological tome called *Making the Future Your Friend*, fell out of her hand. I picked it up and gave it back. Her smile was sweet, if ravaged. "Thanks," she said.

That seemed to be that, except that we both got off at Times Square, and there she was again, walking west on 42nd Street. Halfway down the block, she turned and went into Peepworld. I knew about Peepworld. My cousin Irv, the family smutmeister, once ran the XXX Peeps down the street. Bragging that he'd had his arm personally broken by reputed porn mobster Matty "the Horse" Ianello, Irv once offered to teach me the business.

So I knew Peepworld. I knew the video booths were upstairs, and below, as the barkers put it, were "the Live Girls." The woman on the subway was a "Live Girl." For a quarter, you could look through a window and see her naked; for a dollar, you could touch her breasts.

As I walked down the steps, it dawned on me: I'd been here before. This was the same linoleum staircase I once strode with my horny junior-high-school buddies. Peepworld was Hubert's Museum, home of the Atomic Man, where I'd seen my first-ever naked breast. The realization stopped me; in this place of however misremembered innocence, I didn't feel like shoving a sweaty dollar through a slot to touch the breast of woman who read a book about making a friend of the future.

In the new Times Square, the former Hubert's/Peepworld is occupied by Easy Everything, the Internet café where tourists come to send e-mail home. In keeping with the Deuce's full circle, firewalls block out the porn. Next door is Madame Tussaud's, which, like Hubert's, bills itself as a museum. Recently, I came here with my family, something you never did in the Travis Bickle days. In the new Times Square, New Yorkers can be dim tourists for a day. In addition to a waxy Hitler and Elton John, Tussaud's has got Rudy, screwed down to the floor, the way he should be. Still, it's eerie being around those dummies, and for a moment, you can almost hear the ghosts of Times Square past. "Smoke . . . smoke," they say.

American Torture, American Porn

By Alessandro Camon
Salon.com / June 7, 2004

Twice in the last few months torture and its graphic representation has been at the center of public discourse. The first time had to do with *The Passion of the Christ,* a film that features more violence than any big Hollywood movie before it. The second time—now—has to do with the events at Abu Ghraib prison. The two spectacles reveal disturbing truths about American politics, sexuality, and spirituality.

It's easily observed that torture has a highly developed aesthetic dimension. Medieval instruments of torture are gathered in dedicated museums and traveling exhibits all over the world. Those very instruments, of course, were often used in public. Torture, despite its need for secrecy, also needs its own representation. It's usually meant not only to inflict pain but to instill terror. It's sometimes meant to please the torturer. Therefore, the ritualistic, fetishistic, "spectacular" aspects of torture are an integral part of the practice. As a spectacle, torture is akin to porn—S/M being the obvious shared territory. It elicits voyeurism and a morbid fascination.

The Passion of the Christ was accused by many detractors of being "pornographic." The torture of Iraqi prisoners is pornography in a very direct and complete sense. It's not just violence but sexual violation— what is more, it's sexual violation staged and captured on camera, made into a spectacle readily available for future and expanded viewing. It's sexual violation fixed into an essential symbolic image to be preserved like a trophy. Just like conventional porn, it's completely self-conscious and deliberate yet morally unimpeded.

In a recent cover story in *The New York Times Magazine*, Susan Sontag criticizes George W. Bush and his administration for their initial profession of shock and disgust at the Abu Ghraib pictures, "as if the fault or horror lay in the images, not in what they depict." This is, of course, richly deserved criticism, yet there's another point to be made: The horror that was depicted was largely designed for the depiction itself. It was conceived and executed as pornography.

Several of the pictures we have seen show both victims and torturers posing for the camera. There's a naked man kneeling in front of another man as if performing oral sex. A naked man on a leash held by a female American soldier. Naked men in chains. Naked men stacked up in a grotesque pile, half gangbang and half mass grave. Other alleged tortures, which may be documented by the hundreds of pictures we haven't yet seen, included forced masturbation. Whether the sexual acts were performed or simulated, the prisoners were forced into the position of pornographic "actors." Significantly, the hundreds of pictures seen by Congress after the scandal erupted included not only acts of torture upon prisoners, but acts of sexual intercourse amongst the guards themselves. The soldiers who took the pictures knew that, in both instances, they were making porn (albeit in different sub-genres.) There was no other reason to record the tortures; it was, in fact, self-incriminating and stupid by all practical standards. Except that the idea of recording the acts of torture was, to a significant extent, the inspiration to commit them.

You can sense the sexual disturbance in the minds of the soldiers responsible for this. It's a disturbance exacerbated by the months away from home, but created by a lifelong familiarity with porn—its cynical humor, cheap patriotism, crude vocabulary of submission and prevarication. The president and his inner circle said, "This is not the America that we know." But it is. The pictures from Abu Ghraib are American "gonzo porn." They reek of frat-house hazing and gang initiation rituals, of *Jackass* and *Bumfights*. They encode racial hatred and fetishistic allusions to slavery.

New York Times columnist Frank Rich points out that the right is using the "pornography made them do it" excuse to scapegoat liberal attitudes, invoke censorship, and exonerate the Bush administration. This may be true, but it's no reason to gloss over the sexual nature of the torture. The torturers were enabled by specific political decisions. They were also inspired by broad cultural influences.

The torture/pornography connection is deep and inescapable. Mark Bowden, of *Black Hawk Down* fame, wrote a well-informed, compellingly readable article in October's *Atlantic Monthly* about "the dark art of interrogation" (which was promptly optioned for movie development). He makes a strong case for the effectiveness of torture as a means for acquiring intelligence—which of course is not an unchallenged notion, and not necessarily a justification. But torture is not the mere application of pain to the task of extracting information. Much of what we identify as torture is actually gratuitous, like the ear-severing in the film *Reservoir Dogs*. "I believe you," says Mr. Blonde (Michael Madsen), "but I'm gonna torture you anyway." This is, arguably, the real "point" of torture—the assertion of power over the law, over pity, over logic. I'll torture because I can. I don't need a reason, I don't need a goal—the arbitrary nature of the act is in fact its very essence. You cannot understand it except by internalizing the absolute fact that I have all the power and you have none, and our very identity as human beings is defined by this fact. You can conclude that I am not human because I lack pity. But that's an abstraction. The concrete reality of the situation is that you are not human because you lack all freedom and all dignity.

The torturers of Abu Ghraib had both a reason and a political sanction to do what they did. Yet the nature of the tortures and their recording suggests a casual licentiousness, the arbitrary indulgence of mean appetites. The two aspects—rational justification and gratuitous sadism—are superficially at odds but deeply inextricable from one another. I must inflict pain on you because you and your associates are terrorists, evildoers to be stopped for the greater good of mankind. But because you are an evildoer, enemy of mankind, I can also abandon myself to the pornographic voluptuousness of total control. In fact, not only can I, I must. In order to torture you, it is important that I see you as less than human, and so I will use torture to reinforce that image.

When power is exercised in such an extreme, absolute form as torture, it literally dehumanizes those it's exercised upon. And they know it. Stripped of rights, of the ability to trust a fellow human being, and most importantly, of self-respect, they lose the very sense of who they are. The identity of the torture victim can never be the same again. That's why sexual torture is central to the experience. The emasculation of men, the degradation of women, turns them into something they no longer recognize as themselves. Torture is largely the business of creating shame, indelible memories of one's own impotence which serve as warnings to a whole society. An instinctive understanding of this task can be evinced by the acts of the American torturers. They were aiming to hurt the Arab man where it counts the most—in his masculine pride. There was hardly a more explicit way to do it than to strip him naked and capture him in effigy as the perverse negation of his own self—as a pathetic loser, writhing on the floor or engaging in simulated sexual acts on command, while American men and women pose next to him with a grin and a thumbs-up. This instinctive understanding was further refined by the superior education in pornography that is typical of the contemporary American man (and to some lesser extent, woman.)

Pornography shares with torture an inherent ability to dehumanize. It reduces the individual to a sexual function, flattens identity to a physical act performed for somebody else's ultimate pleasure. As a performer of pornography, you relinquish your dignity going in. You adopt a vulgar, ludicrous stage name and sell yourself by the pound—or more to the point, by the orifice. Pornography records acts of degradation to be perused, collected, lusted over by anonymous customers. A pornographic image is a trophy: the record of somebody's submission to the base needs of a customer, exercised as "power" through the laws of the market.

It is noteworthy, of course, that at least three of the alleged torturers are women. This inspires two opposite conclusions: One, that extreme situations such as war produce aberrant behavior, and a woman may occasionally go against her feminine nature and behave like the worst of men (still, that being the exception that proves the rule). Two, the participation of several women in the tortures is consistent with larger social trends, and therefore it belies the idea that pornography, rape, and sexually predatory behavior are the exclusive domain of men. If we follow this hypothesis, we may conclude that porn has so deeply corrupted the female psyche that women have become willing to endorse an enterprise that is largely directed at their own degradation.

There is ample evidence in our culture to corroborate this second scenario. Women have been co-opted into watching porn, shopping at the Hustler store, patronizing strip bars. "Porn star" is a label of cool. It's routine to see actresses and singers showing every allowed inch of skin (and "suggesting" the rest) on the cover of mainstream magazines. Fashion dictates that thongs must peek out of low-rider jeans. Pamela Anderson and Paris Hilton illustrate the willingness of a generation of women to ply themselves into camera-friendly sex objects. Much too much scandal was made out of the Janet Jackson Super Bowl exploit, but few people seemed to object to its most insidious aspect—not the baring of a nipple, but the pantomime of sexual aggression without reprisal: a man rips off a woman's clothes, she pulls a funny face and keeps on singing. And as far as violence goes, it's interesting that women are now victimized not only by men but, with statistically increased frequency, by other women. The Glenbrook North High School hazing incident, featuring junior-class girls forced to sit while drunken senior girls doused them in feces, urine, paint, animal guts, and blood, followed by punching and kicking—much of which captured in yet another infamous video—was a chilling example of this trend.

This is the sad state of affairs that is, to the Islamic mind, the dark side of our much-touted freedom. And it is exactly this dark side that we are rubbing their nose in. The torture at Abu Ghraib says: Our pornography will conquer you.

In contrast, Islamic terrorists divulged the recording of a bloody execution. The victim, an American civilian: a sacrificial lamb whose blood was spilled with the declared intention to restore Arab pride. This is, as much as ever, a war of symbols, and the symbol of Arab emasculation couldn't but inspire somebody to create a symbol of absolute and terrifying Arab supremacy over a Western man. The American government reacted with proclamations of horror for such barbarity. But such barbarity is a direct reflection of our own dehumanizing ways. A beheading (a forty-second beheading with a knife) undoubtedly represents a more extreme form of cruelty than to strip somebody naked, beat him, sexually humiliate him, and put ever saw *Salo*, Pasolini's allegory about the last days of fascism in Italy, you know his thesis that separating the exercise of power from the fear of consequences—whether because of granted impunity, or because of already certain doom—is the true test of one's nature. The power of an individual over another will naturally tend to speak the language of sexual sadism, a language that articulates and celebrates it. Sadism will be implicit in every situation of captivity. It will be explicit in situations where the fear of consequences is reduced. It may become extreme where such fear is removed altogether.

It may seem ironic that a war fought in the name of principles and imbued with religious ardor should degenerate to such sordid lows. While in America people flock to see Christ tortured, in Iraq we torture our own prisoners—for information, for deterrence, but also—as the pictures document—for the sheer fun of it. And yet, perhaps "irony" is not quite the right concept. Perhaps the relationship between a U.S.-made blockbuster about Christ's pain and the pain inflicted by our soldiers abroad is closer and more inevitable that the notion of "irony" would suggest, because many of the torturers are no doubt heartland Americans, many of them surely devout Christians—the core audience of *The Passion of the Christ*. They are the people Bush directly addressed when he characterized the war as a crusade, a fight against evil in the name of the God. The aptitude of Christians for delivering pain draws on a rich, millennial tradition—a tradition built on certainty and a Manichean worldview. The ability to torture somebody both requires and confirms this certainty; the torturer's exhilarating privilege is to feel right by God while doing what is normally forbidden.

The Passion of the Christ is, not unlike an exploitation movie from the seventies, saturated with ultra-violence to the point of ridiculousness. Yet the representation of this violence is unobjectionable to the audience because the violence is inflicted upon the Christ. There seems to be no limit to the amount of violence you could show in this context (provided you could root it in the Scriptures). The torturers themselves are not the ultimate culprits: those are the Jews, as architects of the deicide. By assigning blame to "them," we can watch an hour of torture entirely guilt-free. In fact, the more severe the torture, the more godlike and awesome Christ's endurance. Which means we have a moral incentive to welcome the sight of torture, to wish for more and more punishment to be administered and exhibited on screen. The amount of butchery is directly proportional evidence of our own worth: look what Jesus, the extreme athlete of pain, chose to endure in order to save us! This is the fundamental perversion of the movie—that it encourages us to fetishize and get high on the horror of the martyrdom.

Sacrifice is perhaps the most ancient form of religious devotion. It goes back to pagan times, when it was meant to placate the gods. It is at the heart of our notion of justice, which focuses its previously random nature onto a "culprit" whose death will placate the aggrieved party. Christian sacrifice is rather meant to educate. It comes as the culminating point of a vast body of teachings. By choosing to emphasize the sacrifice outside the context of those teachings, Christianity (Mel Gibson's version of it) harks back to the most primitive, bloodiest aspect of religiosity. *The Passion of the Christ* repositions pain, blood, sacrifice, at the heart of the religious experience.

Why is this exercise so relevant and so powerful right now? The answer takes us straight to 9/11. As much as we loathed the terrorists, we couldn't help being affected by their conviction. When Bill Maher disputed the assertion that they were cowards, the hysterical outrage that met his remark was a symptom of a raw nerve being tweaked. Because this kind of conviction is precisely what we couldn't be further from. The question is not whether their conviction justifies their action—it doesn't (and I tend to believe a case for the fundamental cowardice of attacking any defenseless person, regardless of whether or not one commits suicide in the process, could be convincingly made). The question is how we respond to the sheer intensity of the conviction. Because as much as this intensity horrifies us, it may also be something that, in some dark recesses of our psyche, we (some of us, anyway) envy. And so we may want to remind ourselves that our own God performed the ultimate act of self-abnegation, exonerating us from doing the same as long as we maintain and worship the memory of it. You can fly into the building in the name of Allah? We can reenact the torture and crucifixion of Jesus Christ in the name of our own God. The effort to distill every ounce of sacrificial pain from this representation, and the uplift that the audience gets from it, can be read as a response to the suicidal fury of the 9/11 terrorists. Our guy's sacrifice was not only purer, because he didn't bring any innocents along for the death trip, but it was also more painful. We can reach back into our spiritual history and find our own, superior certitude.

It's not simply demagogy that the war against terrorism, or against Iraq, has been cast in religious terms, as a crusade, a fight against evil and for God-given freedom. September 11 shook us to the core because if an act like that can be executed not in the name of profit, power, or the traditional motivations we understand, but in the name of religious ideals (however aberrant), our own beliefs—or lack of them—are called into question. We suddenly realize we live in a spiritual vacuum, where no comparable degree of conviction can be easily summoned forth.

The Passion came to fill this profound need. Paradoxically, the fervor it inspires is directly proportional to the distance we have accrued from any kind of spiritual authenticity in our life. The more our culture obsesses about fad diets, plastic surgery, Paris Hilton's sex video, Donald Trump's hair, or Jennifer Lopez's butt, the more fervent our response to *The Passion* has to be.

And so we come full circle. While frivolousness and pornography saturate our culture, *The Passion* offers us redemption, all the more effectively for pushing the limits of graphic representation that porn itself has irrevocably stretched. And while at home we feast our eyes on the torture inflicted upon the Christ, abroad we vindicate ourselves by torturing the infidel with the same righteous abandon, in the way we know best—a pornographic way. Two faces of torture. Two faces of porn.

In Search of Erotic Intelligence

Reconciling Our Desire for Comfortable Domesticity and Hot Sex

By Esther Perel

Psychotherapy Networker / September–October 2003

A few years ago, at a psychology conference, I heard a speaker discuss a couple who had come to therapy in part because of a sharp decline in their sexual activity. Previously, the couple had engaged in light sadomasochism; now, following the birth of their second child, the wife wanted more conventional sex. But the husband was attached to their old style of lovemaking, so they were stuck.

The speaker believed that resolving the couple's sexual difficulty required working through the emotional dynamics of their marriage and new status as parents. But in the discussion afterward, the audience was far less interested in the couple's relationship than in the issue of sadomasochistic sex. Some people speculated that motherhood had restored the woman's sense of dignity, and now she refused to be demeaned by an implicitly abusive, power-driven relationship. Others suggested that the couple's impasse illustrated long-standing gender differences: Men tended to pursue separateness and control, while women yearned for loving connection.

When after two hours of talking about sex no one had mentioned the words *pleasure* or *eroticism*, I finally spoke up. Their form of sex had been entirely consensual, after all. Maybe the woman no longer wanted to be tied up because she now had a baby constantly attached to her breasts—binding her better than ropes ever could. Why assume that there *had* to be something degrading about this couple's sex play?

Perhaps my colleagues were afraid that if women *did* reveal such desires, they'd somehow sanction male dominance everywhere—in business, politics, economics. Maybe the very ideas of sexual dominance and submission, aggression and surrender, couldn't be squared with the ideals of compromise and equality that undergird couples therapy today.

As an outsider to American society—I grew up in Belgium and have lived in many countries—I wondered if these attitudes reflected cultural differences. I later talked with Europeans, Brazilians, and Israelis who had been at the meeting. We all felt somewhat out of step with the sexual attitudes of our American colleagues. Did they believe such sexual preferences—even though they were consensual and completely nonviolent—were too wild and "kinky" for the serious business of maintaining a marriage and raising a family? It was as if sexual pleasure and eroticism that strayed onto slightly outré paths of fantasy and play—particularly games involving aggression and power—must be stricken from the repertoire of responsible adults in committed relationships.

What struck us was that America, in matters of sex as in much else, was a goal-oriented society that prefers explicit meanings and "plain speech" to ambiguity and allusion. Many American therapists encourage clarity and directness, which they tend to associate with honesty and openness: "If you want to make love to your wife/husband, why don't you tell her/him exactly what you want?" These professionals in large part "solve" the conflict between the drabness of the familiar and the excitement of the unknown by advising patients to renounce their fantasies in favor of more reasonable "adult" sexual agendas.

Whereas therapists typically encourage patients to "really get to know" their partners, I often say that "knowing isn't everything." Most couples exchange enough direct talk in the course of daily life. To create more passion, I suggest that they play a bit more with the ambiguity that's inherent to communication. Eroticism can draw its powerful pleasure from fascination with the hidden, the mysterious, and the suggestive.

Ironically, some of America's best features—the belief in equality, consensus-building, fairness, and tolerance—can, in the bedroom, result in very boring sex. Sexual desire and good citizenship don't play by the same rules. Sexual excitement is often politically incorrect; it often thrives on power plays, role reversals, imperious demands, and seductive manipulations. American therapists, shaped by egalitarian ideals, are often challenged by these contradictions.

In Europe, I see more of an emphasis on complementarity—the appeal of difference—rather than strict gender equality. This, it seems to me, makes European women feel less conflict about being both smart and sexy. They can enjoy their sexual power, even in the workplace, without feeling they're forfeiting their right to be taken seriously. Susanna, for example, is a Spanish woman with a high-level job at an international company in New York. She sees no contradiction between her work and her desire to express her sexual power—even among her colleagues. "If compliments are given graciously, they don't offend. We're still men and women who are attracted to one another, and not robots," she says.

Of course, American feminists accomplished major improvements in women's lives in many ways. Yet without denigrating their achievements, I believe that the emphasis on egalitarian and respectful sex—purged of any expressions of power, aggression, and transgression—is antithetical to erotic desire for men and women alike. (I'm well aware of the widespread sexual coercion and abuse of women and children. Everything I suggest here depends on getting clear consent and respecting the other's humanity.) The writer Daphne Merkin writes, "No bill of sexual rights can hold its own against the lawless, untamable landscape of the erotic imagination." Or as filmmaker Luis Buñuel put it more bluntly, "Sex without sin is like an egg without salt."

Many therapists assume that the fantasy life that shapes a new relationship is a form of temporary insanity, destined to fade over a long-term partnership. But can sexual fantasy actually enhance the intimate reality of relationships? Clinicians often interpret the desire for sexual adventure—ranging from simple flirting and contact with previous lovers to threesomes and fetishes—as fear of commitment and infantile fantasy. Sexual fantasies about one's partner, particularly those that involve role-playing, dominance, and submission, are often viewed as signs of neurosis and immaturity, erotically tinged idealizations that blind one to a partner's true identity. Here's an example from a client I worked with (the name changed, of course):

Terry had been in therapy for a year, struggling with the transition from being half of an erotically charged couple to being one-quarter of a family with two children and no eroticism at all. He began one session with what he deemed a "real midlife story" that began when he and his wife hired a young German au pair. "Every morning she and I take care of my daughters together," he said. "She's lovely—so natural, full of vitality and youth—and I've developed this amazing crush on her. You know how I've been talking about this feeling of deadness? Well, her energy has awakened me. I want to sleep with her and I wonder why I don't. I'm scared to do it and scared not to."

I didn't lecture him about his "immature" wishes, or explore the emotional dynamics beneath this presumably "adolescent" desire. Instead, I tried to help him relish the awakening of his dormant senses without letting the momentary exhilaration endanger his marriage. I marveled with him at the allure and beauty of the fantasy, while also calling it just that: a *fantasy*.

"It's great to know you still can come to life like that," I said. "And you know that you can never compare this state of inebriation with life at home, because home is about something else. Home is safe. Here, you're on shaky ground. You like it, but you're also afraid that it can take you too far away from home. And you probably don't let your wife evoke such tremors in you."

A few days later, he was having lunch in a restaurant with his wife and she was telling him of her previous boyfriend. "I'd been thinking hard about what we talked about," he told me, "and at the table I had this switch. Normally, I don't like hearing these stories of hers—they make me jealous and irritated. But this time I just listened and found myself getting very turned on. So did she. In fact, we were so excited we had to look for a bathroom where we could be alone."

I suggested that perhaps the experience of desiring a fresh young woman was what enabled him to listen to his wife differently—as a sexual and desirable woman herself. I invited Terry to permit himself the erotic intensity of the illicit with his wife: "This could be a beginning of bringing lust home," I said. "These small transgressions are acceptable; they offer you the latitude to experience new desire without having to throw everything away."

It amazes me how willing people are to experiment sexually outside their relationships, yet how tame and puritanical they are with their partners. Many of my patients describe their domestic sex lives as devoid of excitement and eroticism, yet they are consumed by a richly imaginative sex life beyond domesticity—affairs, pornography, prostitutes, cybersex, or feverish daydreams. Having denied themselves freedom of imagination at home, they go outside to reimagine themselves, often with random strangers. Yet the commodification of sex can actually hinder our capacity for fantasy, contaminating our sexual imagination. Furthermore, pornography and cybersex are ultimately isolating, disconnected from relations with a real, live other *person.*

A fundamental conundrum is that we seek a steady, reliable anchor in our partner, at the same time we seek a transcendent experience that allows us to soar beyond our ordinary lives. The challenge, then, for couples and therapists, is to reconcile the need for what's safe and predictable with the wish to pursue what's exciting, mysterious, and awe-inspiring.

It's often assumed that intimacy and trust must exist before sex can be enjoyed, but for many women and men, intimacy—more precisely, the familiarity inherent in intimacy—actually sabotages sexual desire. When the loved one becomes a source of security and stability, he/she can become desexualized. The dilemma is that erotic passion can leave many people feeling vulnerable and less secure. In this sense there is no "safe sex." Maybe the real paradox is that this fundamental insecurity is a precondition for maintaining interest and desire. As Stephen Mitchell, a New York psychoanalyst, used to say, "It is not that romance fades over time. It becomes riskier."

Susan and Jenny came to see me about their sexual relationship. Susan, a longtime lesbian, set out to seduce Jenny right after they met. Jenny responded, though it was her first lesbian relationship. They moved in together just as Susan was waiting for the arrival of her adopted baby. Once they were a threesome, Jenny thought they were a wonderful family, but completely lost any sexual interest in Susan. Jenny, already in some conflict about her lesbianism, couldn't be a second mom to the new baby, family builder, companion, and passionate lover all at once.

The transition to motherhood can have a desexualizing effect. I reminded them that the mother isn't an erotic image in our culture. Mom is supposed to be caring, nurturing, loving, but, frankly, rather asexual. "Being new parents can be pretty overwhelming," I said. "But can you try to add making love to the list of all the other things you enjoy doing together to unwind and relax? The idea is to make each other feel good, not to solve the fate of your relationship. That's an offer you can't refuse."

At the next session, Jenny reported: "That really loosened us up. We can talk about it, laugh and not be instantly scared."

So many couples imagine that they know everything there is to know about their mate. In large part, I see my job as trying to highlight how little they've seen, urging them to recover their curiosity and catch a glimpse behind the walls that encircle the other. As Mexican essayist Octavio Paz has written, eroticism is "the poetry of the body, the testimony of the senses. Like a poem, it is not linear, it meanders and twists back on itself, shows us what we do not see with our eyes, but in the eyes of our spirit. Eroticism reveals to us another world, inside this world. The senses become servants of the imagination, and let us see the invisible and hear the inaudible."

The Right to Party

By Neal Pollack
The Brooklyn Rail / June 2003

A few years ago, when I was a reporter in Chicago, I did a story on a phenomenon I called "The New Prohibition." The city, for various reasons, was shutting down neighborhood bars. In poor black neighborhoods, taverns were the targets of moralistic church crusaders. In gentrifying neighborhoods, they were the bête noire of noise-averse yuppies. What was wrong with Mayor Daley? I asked. Didn't he want Chicago to be fun anymore?

The article garnered a bit of local attention. I appeared on an episode of a nightly public-affairs show. For once, a piece of mine actually got a few letters to the editor. And I decided to take it further. I did a local NPR radio commentary in which I called, tongue-in-cheekly, for a new political party, "The Party Party," that would campaign to make Chicago the freewheeling town I imagined it had once been.

Oh, how naïve I was then, and how foolish I feel now! Those little tavern raids and precinct vote-dry initiatives were nothing, a little internecine tap-dance, compared to the assault on fun currently being waged by the federal government. Our right to party is being attacked by forces far more powerful, more sinister, and more organized than Mayor Daley's liquor-law enforcement bureaucracy. Everything fun about America is under serious threat.

Let's review the evidence of the last few months.

In late February, DEA and Department of Justice officials arrested fifty-five people and seized thousands of dollars of drug paraphernalia during "Operation Pipe Dreams." The arrests mainly targeted online bong dealers, who attorney general John Ashcroft claimed had "invaded the homes of families across the country without their knowledge." But also included in the arrests were employees of several head shops in Pittsburgh, where the investigation was centered. The feds even raided the California home of Tommy Chong, who in mid-May pleaded guilty to conspiring to sell drug paraphernalia. The most stunning quote from the whole affair came from acting DEA chief John Brown, who said, "People selling drug paraphernalia are in essence no different than drug dealers. They are as much a part of drug trafficking as silencers are a part of criminal homicide."

The government is equating Tommy Chong with murderous criminals. Perhaps next they'll haul in Rodney Dangerfield and the inflatable pilot from *Airplane!* Something is wrong. Very wrong.

In March, Senator Joe Biden of Delaware managed to sneak the RAVE act through as an attachment to a bill establishing a national warning system about child abductions. RAVE stands for, amazingly, Reducing Americans' Vulnerability to Ecstasy. But its main targets are concert promoters and club owners, who the act holds to an absurd standard. According to the law, it is illegal to "manage or control any place, whether permanently or temporarily, either as an owner, lessee, agent, employee, occupant, or mortgagee, and knowingly and intentionally rent, lease, profit from, or make available for use, with or without compensation, the place for the purpose of unlawfully manufacturing, storing, distributing, or using a controlled substance."

This definition was derived from a twenty-year-old federal law that permitted raids on "crackhouses." The law is so broad that you could have ten people over for dinner, put on some loud music, and you've got yourself a rave. If someone lights a joint at your "rave," and the neighbors complain about the music, and the police are in a bad mood that night, you face decades in prison. Suddenly everyone is a potential drug criminal and it's doubly dangerous if there's dancing involved. Keep in mind that these are Democrats pushing these laws. This War On Fun is not single-party.

That said, the Republicans seem to have a serious problem with sex. The federal government's financial commitment to "abstinence education" reached a new high this year. When I say a new high, I mean $120 million. This is not the sex education we received in high school. According to federal guidelines for applying for abstinence education grants, a federally funded program must, among other things, teach "abstinence from sexual activity outside marriage as the expected standard for all school age children," and that "a mutually faithful monogamous relationship in the context of marriage is the expected standard of human sexual activity."

From personal experience, I will agree with certain tenets, such as the fact that "drug use increases vulnerability to sexual advances," and I cannot argue with the fact that "sexual activity outside of the context of marriage is likely to have harmful psychological and physical effects," but is this really something that needs to be legislated? Can you imagine being a teenager today in this context? Teen pregnancy and STDs are a problem, for certain. But is the answer really organizations like Pennsylvania's Silver Ring Thing, which, in exchange for twelve dollars and a pledge of abstinence until marriage, offers high-school students a silver ring and a Bible? Sounds like a bad trade to me. Couldn't they at least throw a couple of condoms into the gift pack, just to make sure?

Lest we think that these phenomena, which seem to be loosely linked, are just the usual mix of anti-drug nonsense and hypocritical fundamentalism, we should think again. Journalist Eric Schlosser, in his excellent new book *Reefer Madness*, drops the stunning statistic that more than 20,000 Americans are in prison for marijuana-related "crimes." But the current trend in policy goes far beyond that. Under the RAVE act, you're guilty by association with marijuana smokers. Abstinence education had a foothold during Bill Clinton's America, too, but now there's an extra moral force, and lots more money, behind the preaching. When Pennsylvania Rick Santorum made his controversial remarks in April about not approving of homosexual "acts," he also said, "the idea is that the state doesn't have rights to limit individuals' wants and passions. I disagree with that. I think we absolutely have rights because there are consequences to letting people live out whatever wants or passions they desire. And we're seeing it in our society."

What is he talking about? What consequences? As far as I'm concerned, that phrase, from a leading Republican senator, is an official government declaration of a War On Fun. What exactly would be Rick Santorum's idea of a good party? One where nobody got drunk or high, where nobody hooked up, and where nobody danced with abandon? Why, that doesn't sound like a party. It sounds like church. I've had enough.

This time, for real, I'm calling for the establishment of a Party Party, or, at the very least, for a Party Party attitude. I'm issuing a call to arms for those of us always in need of, as the great Jeff Spicoli once said, tasty waves and a cool buzz. Of course there are many issues in the world that are more pressing, and we should continue to press them. But Saturday night eventually comes even for the most politically committed. These are tense times. People want to loosen the steam valve a little bit. They want to participate in culture outside of the jurisdiction of federal "morality" educators. We don't want the government telling us how to spend our free time, sussing out and prosecuting casual drug users and harassing nightclub owners. And for heaven's sake, give the kids some condoms.

Sex and drugs and live music make life great. These are the kinds of things that were outlawed in Taliban-run Afghanistan. If they can't be legal and easy in America, then I don't want to live here anymore. I want to live in a place where drugs and sex are tolerated, where the government provides a sane level of social services, where religion isn't always threatening to take over the state. Amsterdam. It always comes back to Amsterdam.

Americans, we have to party. It is our right. And we have to fight for that right. Yes, you heard me. We have to show the moralizers that they cannot win.

We have to fight for our right to party.

Up Close and Personal

Sex, Power, Money, and Babies

By Niles Eldredge
from *Why We Do It: Rethinking Sex and
the Selfish Gene*

One thing that makes the television soap opera *The Sopranos* so
appealing is the stark contrast between the violently sociopathic life
of a mobster and his perfectly conventional upper-middle-class
home life in the suburbs of northern New Jersey. There they are:
Tony, his wife, Carmela, their daughter, Meadow, and younger son,
Anthony Jr. ("AJ"), living in a large, fairly new McMansion, replete
with swimming pool and vanity SUV. There's even a shrink in Tony's
life as he wrestles with the conflicts of living in two incommensu-
rate worlds.

The four members of the Soprano family are stereotypically
American: mom and dad, sister and brother—as in the old cereal box
scene of a surreally calm mother pouring out cornflakes for her brood
while mild-mannered dad looks on with a goofy grin on his face.
There it is: food, love, procreation—with the kids about to go off to
school and dad to his work as accountant, paleontologist, or hit man.
The families—especially the "nuclear families" of parents and
kids—are the smallest of human social systems. They are also the
only units that combine all three: economics, sex, and baby making.

Most families these days do not conform to the stereotype of dad, mom, and a couple of kids—and probably never did. Fifty percent of American marriages end up in divorce, and single-parent households are rife. Then, too, many marriages remain childless throughout their duration, whether by choice or infertility. The assumption that all humans are driven to make babies to leave copies of their immortal genes to the next generation is nicely countered by the existence of same-sex liaisons and heterosexual couples—such as the famous Madison Avenue–named DINKS, "double income no kids" unions in which husband and wife (or both unmarried partners) pursue careers in the world—and a home life free of the responsibilities and costs of raising kids. And though it is true that some homosexual couples may indeed raise children—sometimes the offspring of a previous marriage of one or perhaps even both, sometimes through artificial insemination, sometimes collateral kin, and sometimes pure adoption of totally unrelated children—for the most part, gay and lesbian couples do not have children, whether their own or someone else's, in their day-to-day lives. Leaving aside the nature/nurture issues of the basis of homosexuality (i.e., whether homosexuality is ensconced in the genes or is instead a behavioral choice, or a mixture of both), gay and lesbian couples can procreate and rear children should they want to, and most appear not to.

So not all families are alike by a long shot. Even if we restrict the term "family" to the kind where kids are a part of the scene (or were—though it increasingly has seemed that they never will leave, most eventually do), families differ markedly in size, age spacing between children, ratios of girls to boys (not always a matter of chance), and patterns of allocations of resources to the kids.

All that being said, it is obvious that the family in the restricted sense of mom, or dad, or mom and dad—and the kids—reflects a pretty tight integration of economic, sexual, and reproductive behavior. The Sopranos are a good case in point: Tony is the sole breadwinner—not perhaps the most common situation in married family life in northern New Jersey these days, where the present generation typically needs to have two incomes to maintain standards equivalent to the suburban life today's parents knew as children themselves. Carmela's economic activities are, however, prodigious, for she is the one who maintains the house, shops for and prepares the food (except for the cannolis that Tony sometimes brings home), tends to the kids, pays the bills—and badgers Tony for an economic plan to cover herself and the kids "should, God forbid, anything ever happen" to Tony.

Then there is their sex life, depicted as off and on, and easily disrupted by depression (Tony's), household spats (often, but not always, over the kids), and other downers. Tony conducts a sex life outside the house, whether vicariously, surrounded by bare-breasted women at the Bada Bing, or directly with his current girlfriend. Like everything else in Tony's life, the fun outside-the-house sex life also presents its problems. Carmela, meanwhile, literally flirts with extramarital affairs, but so far, at least, has not acted on them. Meadow starts having sex—intercourse—in college and takes measures to protect herself. Her younger brother, AJ, has yet to show much of an interest in sex, though (as I write) that seems about to happen.

And, of course, Tony and Carmela had sex at least twice to produce their children. The money goes to keeping hearth and home, body and children, alive and to sending them to college. The kids, more often than not, are the apples of their parents' eyes, and seem somehow to be worth all the aggravation and financial outlay.

There is thus a close association between sex, baby making, and economics, nowhere closer than in a nuclear family. The Sopranos might be fictitious, but they reflect reality very well indeed.

ALL IN THE FAMILY

Long before evolutionary psychologists, in their search for human universals, arrived on the scene, other people had been wondering how universal nuclear families really are. The anthropologist Melford E. Spiro once asked just that question; he thought that Israeli kibbutzim—where children are raised communally by surrogates, with most of the jobs of child rearing usually handled by biological parents now taken over as a task by community specialists—to be one of the comparatively rare examples of non-nuclear-family structure, the exception that "proves" the rule. Other anthropologists, of course, disagreed with the claim that the kibbutz represents a significant departure from the nuclear family.

More recently, we have reports of the Na people, one of China's ethnic minorities living in Yunnan Province. The Na know no marriage; instead, "visits" by males to the bedrooms of females go on supposedly *ad libitum*. Children know their mothers, but do not know the identities of their fathers. Thus the typical household arrangement seems to consist of women and their children—including daughters old enough to have "visits"—and male relatives of the women in the house. Only on rare occasions, reportedly, will a man used to having visits with a woman in a house actually move in—only when there are not enough men already around the house to perform the essential economic labors that keep things going.

So "marriage" and the "nuclear family" are not completely universal, but they are nearly enough that exceptions are few. And even when some apparent exceptions crop up that are sufficiently credible and compelling that some analysts, at least, are willing to say "this is not the usual way of doing things," the basic integration of sex, reproduction, and economics is still present in whatever social structure is there in its stead. There is a mix of sex, reproduction, and economic life in kibbutzim—bonded-pair sex, extramarital sex, baby making among the married—but the nurturing is now expressly recognized for what it is: an economic activity directed to the physical (and, presumably, emotional) well-being of the children, conducted by specialists as part of their kibbutz work, rather than by the biological parents.

The Na also present a mix of sex, reproduction, and economics in their lives—though with the focus in the reports so heavily on the sexual "visits," less seems to be known about the economics of village life. Yet males do in fact seem to be involved in the daily economic pursuits of household compounds, there is plenty of sex, and babies are reared by their mothers in an economic environment in which both men and women of the household participate. In a kibbutz, you get married and have kids, but someone else raises your kids. With the Na, you don't get married, but the children are raised in a home that is itself an economic cooperative among close relatives—and the occasional male who is allowed to move in.

However much such alternatives deviate from the nuclear family, they all present the familiar theme of interlocking economics, sex, and reproduction. How did this tight integration of economics, sex, and baby making come to be?

THE SEX-FOR-FOOD, FOOD-FOR-SEX SCENARIO

How did sex come to be decoupled from reproduction, and at the same time to be so closely tied to economic human behavior? Recall that bonobos, the most humanlike of our closest living ape relatives, indulge in a great array of sexual activities, much of which have nothing to with pregnancy. Couplings (often missionary style) take place at all ages, female-female genital contact is common, and a variety of other noncoupling sexual behavior goes on between all ages and gender combinations. The decoupling of sex from reproduction obviously started a long time ago and, like other aspects of biologically imbued human behavior, goes way back in primate evolution and is not evolved only within our species or even our closest evolutionary ancestors back on the Pleistocene savannas of Africa, as evolutionary psychologists commonly suppose. Frans De Waal and other close observers of bonobo behavior believe that much of the flamboyant and incessant sexual behavior of bonobos has far more to do with reducing tensions, such as those arising over competition for food. Sex among bonobos is not only decoupled from reproduction; it seems also to have overt economic implications.

Human females are continually sexually receptive and can conceive twelve months of the year, albeit only for a few days each month. Though there may well have been some reproductive adaptive value for being able to make babies year round, I have no idea what that advantage would be. All but the largest families on record could just as easily have been produced with a single seasonal period of estrus, given the nine months it takes for a human fetus to develop fully.

It makes more sense to think that access to continual sex in humans evolved not for reproductive purposes but rather as a kind of "food for sex, sex for food" arrangement that led to the creation of more stable pair bonds than are found, for example, among bonobos. It's an arrangement with clear reproductive advantages, since such pair bonds would presumably have led to a more protracted and stable "family" life, in which economic necessities were looked after by both parents and care of offspring particularly (if not exclusively) was the domain of the mother.

Humans are notoriously helpless at birth; walking doesn't come for about a year, and speech usually takes two or more years. Kids simply cannot fend for themselves until, as a rule, well into their teens or (in some situations in some societies) even later. To provide the economic support for such a labor-intensive job as raising a human child, stability of the support system is crucial. Sexual gratification is the carrot on the stick (so to speak), not just to keep the guys around (as has most commonly been supposed, since guys are supposedly the main breadwinners) but also to keep women interested in the arrangement. Obviously, women often work while in the midst of their childbearing careers. In hunter-gatherer societies, women collect much of the food (chiefly plants) and tend to most of the other domestic economic chores, while the men hunt for animal protein. Hunter-gatherers, of course, are not infallible guides to ancestral hominid life of the African savannas, but theirs are the only preagricultural societies still with us (though just barely), thus our only living signposts to what human behavior might have been like prior to the agricultural revolution that started ten thousand years ago.

So food for sex has deep implications for successful baby making. But food for sex also means sex for pleasure rather than just sex for babies. If food is an economic commodity, so now is sex, as any item in a barter arrangement is by definition something of value, something that can be bought and sold. For the first time in the 3.5 billion years of life on Earth, sex has acquired a use and a meaning that transcends the pure production of babies.

It is thus not the reproductive imperative, but rather the diffusing influence of taking sex away from its strictly reproductive function, that creates the human triangle and really drives human existence. Sex is now free to have its own life in human affairs—a life that exists in and of itself and has special "relations" with the economic side of human life. And, oh yes, we still have sex to make babies.

SEX FOR ITS OWN SAKE

My personal favorite theory for why there is sex at all—and why although the majority of us prefer partners of the opposite sex, some of us prefer same-sex partners—comes from an ancient Greek story recounted in the playwright Aristophanes' comedy *The Clouds.* We were all doubles once (so goes the story), physically connected to our twin half, who was usually, though not invariably, of the opposite sex. Some epochal event severed all the doubles of the world, and now all of us spend all our time running around looking for our double—which means most of us are looking for someone of the opposite sex. But sometimes, some of us, because our double was of the same sex, are looking for *that* person.

Not right away, however. Sexual maturity comes after a period of infancy, and whereas sexual latency is there from early infancy, overt sexual behavior is generally muted until adolescence. Adolescence comes at different times for different sexes, is changeable in history, and varies between cultures. But just ask a young American teenager whether life is different from what it used to be before his or her hormones started to rage. It is very much as if old August Weismann's distinction between the germ line and soma were played out in striking, very personal ways as a kid grows up.

Then sex intervenes. For almost everyone, this is a shock. Priorities change. On the plus side, there's the thrill and pleasure of surging hormones, of discovering orgasms—usually, though not invariably, on one's own, abetted only by gossip from friends, and soon pulsating to the ubiquitous sex stimuli that were there surrounding them as preteen-agers all along. There is the heady success of being attracted to someone else, maybe even of becoming "popular" and doing pretty well from the get-go in the embryonic phases of sexuality. And, last but not least, there's puppy love.

But just as often there is utter doubt and uncertainty. Rejection both real and imagined—with pure fear of rejection itself, or simply the feelings engendered by unfamiliar hormones. Worries about acne, weight, breast size—a million extra worries that simply hadn't clouded life until sex came along.

If ever there were a graphic example—the literal proof—of the fundamental apartness of one's simple existence, one's fundamentally *economic* life, from one's sexual and (possibly also) reproductive life, this is it: human adolescence. There you are, a young human being, eating, sleeping, defecating, urinating, breathing, growing. Sex only vaguely intrudes from time to time on your consciousness— and though you might be acting as a surrogate to help raise younger sibs, baby making per se is something, like being a fireman sometime, that lies some vague and distant time in the future. We can see and feel in our own selves the practical consequences of that germ-line/soma distinction that Weismann drew so long ago: all organisms live both economic and reproductive lives. And nearly all live at least for a while as purely economic entities before they "mature" and start making babies on their own.

In the United States, girls tend to begin menstruation and to develop breasts and pubic and underarm hair on the average around the age of twelve, and boys somewhat later (again, on the average) start growing facial, pubic, and other secondary sexual hair and having far more erections than ever before—erections that now can lead to explosive ejaculations. Eighteen- and nineteen-year-old boys are said to have an erection on the average every ten minutes, think explicitly about sex at least that often, and produce sperm in quantities their fathers can barely remember. In contrast, there is no comparable physiological or psychological sexual peak for girls, since interest in sex continues, even strengthens, in women up through the start of menopause.

From a purely physiological point of view these are, or should be, the prime baby-making years. Frequently, of course, they are not, as schooling and early career development for both young women and men—in the middle, upper middle, and upper classes—more often than not intrudes. It takes an economic life to support a family—a reality that has much to do with relative success in spreading genes in all human societies, and a theme that also is closely tied to the human population explosion that is threatening environments, ecosystems, species, and human life, virtually everywhere on this planet.

So why is adolescence typically as painful as it is thrilling? Barnacles settle out as larvae, metamorphose on a bit of shell or piece of rock, and feed and grow until the time comes when their gonads ripen and they start making eggs and sperm (many barnacle species are hermaphroditic). There is a metabolic cost to sperm and egg production; some of the energy derived from food intake now must go to this new activity. But most barnacles seem to be able to absorb this cost and go on living, not overly traumatized by the sudden onset of sexual maturity and the additional burdens of baby making.

Why, then, do humans find adolescence so typically rough? And not just American adolescents but kids virtually everywhere? Why are there elaborate rituals, like male and female circumcision, or shutting girls up when they first menstruate (or even throughout their entire lives as menstruating women)? Why, if it is no big deal for barnacles (and perhaps not even for bonobos, which show a rudimentary form of disentanglement of sex and reproduction) to simply take on the added functions of sperm and egg production, mating, and perhaps some forms of child nurturing, is it such a big deal for humans?

The answer almost surely is that sex *means* more in the average human life than in the lives of any other sorts of organisms that have ever graced the earth. Sex is fraught with meaning, from the hidden symbolic to the explicitly overt. As the only truly conscious animals on the planet, we are naturally in a position to invest meaning in anything that strikes us about our lives—and that is surely what we have done with sex.

Sex has come to symbolize personal worth and personal power. It ranks right up there with money in that respect—and sometimes even higher. As we shall soon see, the two are sometimes inseparable.

SEX FOR PLEASURE, AND *NOT* FOR MAKING BABIES

Adolescent sex is not generally about baby making. Yes, there's a lot of out-of-wedlock pregnancy among teenagers in the United States, and in many other places around the world. In some circumstances, teenagers deliberately do seek pregnancy and babies to enhance their social and economic status. For the most part, though, babies are as unwanted as the social diseases that are still rampant. Condoms are routinely sold in men's bathrooms in bars and restaurants around the United States—marked "sold for the prevention of disease only," a sop to the ambient cultural forces (read conservative Protestant and Catholic interests) still adamantly opposed to birth control. In truth, condoms are sold in such venues every bit as much for the prevention of pregnancy as for the prevention of the spread of syphilis, gonorrhea, and now AIDS.

The connections between sex, power, and baby making run deep, and it is especially difficult to tease apart the motives and forces acting on any person's behavior—be that person an adolescent, young adult, mature adult, or older member of society (terms themselves defined only partly biologically and, in any case, differently from culture to culture). Teenagers are notorious for following the perceived dictates of their immediate peers first and foremost, and those dictates are further shaped by standards of behavior in other groups of teenagers, increasingly easy to find out about through electronic media. (Think of Tipper Gore's crusade against what she and many others perceive as encouragement of bad behavior encapsulated in the lyrics of rock, hip-hop, and rap recordings.) Coming in last in the competition for effective influence on the behavior—sexual and otherwise—of adolescents are the norms preached by their parents, schools, and churches, should any of these categories of supervening power be present in their lives.

So it is difficult to look at the "typical" sexual behavior of anybody, let alone of any group of people defined by age and sex, and explain exactly why they do the things that they do. Biology—rampant hormones—is obviously a strong motivating factor in teenage sex. But so is peer pressure (What? Still a virgin??), and I am aware of only a very few reported instances where making babies per se is part of the social mix that underlies sexual exploits (for example, in the boasting of out-of-wedlock fatherhood of some inner-city young men in the United States).

Tough as it is to separate larger-scale cultural forces, especially the all-important defining factors of economic (class) status, from the biological and psychological factors underlying everyone's sexual behavior, from adolescence into old age, there is still plenty to be said about individual sexual practices that are not overtly connected to either economics or the production of offspring.

Masturbation and bestiality are obviously forms of sex that cannot result in pregnancy. So are the various forms of "sodomy." These sexual practices are pursued strictly for pleasure—and sometimes, of course, for money. The list of sexual behaviors that have absolutely nothing to do with baby making is very large and potentially endless, limited only by the bounds of the human imagination and anatomical realities—which is to say hardly limited at all.

SEX AND POWER—AND NOT BABIES

Sex has a lot to do with one's self-esteem. There is a common desire to associate with someone glamorous: for men, a beautiful woman; for women, perhaps a handsome man, but perhaps as well an older, powerful man—someone with lots of money, prestige, *power*. Even people who are not especially motivated to seek out a chain of progressively more glamorous or powerful partners are nonetheless not uniformly immune from consuming the often tawdry details of famous people who publicly do live such lives.

For men, it may well be that simply proving, over and over, that you are still able to attract a desirable woman leads to so many affairs and divorces. Even if it were strictly true that the initial urge to find and "acquire" an attractive woman was for the express purpose of setting up a nuclear family arrangement and having children, one more fling at handing down those precious genes, the repeated search for the same heady feelings of infatuation, and the often desperate attempt to prove that you can still make it in the competitive world of beautiful women—all this is for the most part not about making still more babies.

Affairs, for either sex, are rarely about gene spreading and baby making. Extramarital sex, whatever its complex motivation (trouble at home, perhaps trying to create trouble at home, or just looking for excitement), seldom leads to the production of still more children.

Serial marriage is another matter. Often, for both men and women, periodic divorce and remarriage is about acquiring "trophy" spouses. A woman dumps a guy to get another one richer or more famous. She may or may not give him children, either as part of the "deal" or perhaps because she wants to, regardless of his intentions. On the other hand, if a guy dumps his wife to marry a woman younger than the previous wife, that can be purely all about trophy collecting, but kids do often enter into the picture.

High school is the place where all the accoutrements of power through sex are first explored, in the form of connections with the economic world. The cute little Honda, or the bright chrome muscle car (depending on time and place, of course), whether or not bought by mom and dad, are status symbols that fall neatly into place. Not that preadolescent kids can't be snobs to one another about their possessions, but women and fast cars tend to go with one another in a guy's mind like ham and eggs in a somewhat more prosaic context. "Cock cars" need not be limited to old Corvettes, nor are they limited in their appeal to the very young. It was in the pages of *Playboy* that a full-page cartoon depicted the stages of a man's life, from youth to old age, through his cars: a banged-up runabout for starters, a new, modestly small car at marriage, a station wagon when the kids come along, and progressively bigger cars as he moves up the corporate ladder—until, at the pinnacle of his career, he becomes chairman of the board and buys an expensive sports car the size of the car he started out with. Big smile in his face, a cigar clenched in his teeth as he races down the road, the air blowing what hair he has left.

Power. What person you are with, what car you drive (could be construed as purely economic power, but there is that connection with sex), how long your penis is. Women worry about how slim they are and how curvy. Women do tend to worry about the size of their breasts, but apparently not nearly to the degree to which men tend to worry about penis size. The Internet now has as many ads for penis-enlarging products as for lower-rate mortgages and computer printer ink cartridges.

And now we have Viagra, latest in an unbroken string of "male potency" nostrums that extends back to the dawn of human history. Viagra has been an amazing hit. The former senator Bob Dole, one of America's current crop of elder political statesmen, has enthusiastically and very publicly endorsed this product.

Viagra is emphatically not about making babies. It is selling like mad (and through the Internet) mostly to men in their fifties, sixties, seventies, and eighties—men whose most vibrant days are long past, but men with memories and with wives or girlfriends who still want sex lives. Sure, some of them might have younger wives where the issue is perhaps more pressing, and some of these younger wives may be intent on having a baby or two. But most of Viagra's use is of the "à la recherche du temps perdu" variety of experience, a recalling of youthful vitality, strength, potency—power. Surely a significant amount of the pleasure Viagra brings comes from the simple fact of erection as much, perhaps, as from the actual sexual experience that presumably follows.

Women, too, crave sex far beyond their reproductive years. Menopause, the official and internally very noticeable end of the reproductive years, can be a physical challenge as well as a manifestation of aging and decline of power that is often emotionally difficult to deal with. A silver lining not missed by many women, though, is that birth control devices are no longer required (though concerns about disease never go away). But no more pill, and never again the specter of abortion or RU-486 (for women with access to such modern chemicals and the desire to use them). Whether or not one has reproduced, once the fertile days are over, sex can be, and usually is, still very much in the picture. Sex symbolizes power and success to American women as much as to American men, perhaps even more so.

But there is a downside to everything, and the psychological dangers of having so much of one's feelings of success, well-being, and power wrapped up in sex is that there is an awful lot that can (and routinely does) happen in life that upsets the applecart.

For one thing, sex itself is risky. There are the risks of disease. There is the risk of pregnancy: for when pregnancy raises the specter of loss, the costs are immediately seen as too great. The continual stories of babies dumped in bathrooms and garbage disposals—babies born of upper-middle-class as well as of poor mothers—are graphic reminders that even when there is plenty of money for child support, the reality of a child's existence can represent such a drastic threat to the future already planned that the child simply has to go.

Even when babies are wanted—at least in the abstract, "eventually" —their arrival is commonly planned (sensibly enough) around the economic needs of career building and establishment, and often, if conception occurs prior to the planned moment, that pregnancy will be terminated for reasons of convenience and economic necessity. Sometimes, of course, those delayed pregnancies never do happen; the biological clock simply runs out, or career turns out to be more compelling than baby making.

The connections between sex, health, and psychological well-being run deep. At the physical level, it is notorious that women athletes who train rigorously will sometimes stop menstruating; sex can go on, but there is temporarily no chance of becoming pregnant. It is very much as if excessive stress to the economic side of one's body comes at the expense of the reproductive side.

Male athletes do not face that issue, but just as sex can lead to drowsiness in both men and women (even postcoital "tristesse"), there is a persistent sense that sex successfully completed results in a temporary loss of power. While some coaches of male teams have been known to encourage at least some members of their teams to enjoy as much sex as possible, more of them have reportedly tried to temper their players' sex lives so as to save their strength and concentration for the game or event that lies ahead.

But if sex helps convey a sense of power, anything else that brings about a loss of power, whether real or imagined, can have devastating effects on anybody's sex life: the vector, in other words, is reversible. Illness can do it, even if the illness itself does not technically prevent sex from happening. Depression, whether of internal origin or caused by external events—or the more usual combination of the two—is a notorious anti-aphrodisiac.

This is especially true when it comes to the links between one's economic and sex lives: loss of job, career reversal of any sort, any kind of financial disaster can very quickly undermine one's sense of well-being and power. And there, usually, goes the sex life right along with financial security. A sort of cultural analog to the depression of reproductive functions (if not libido per se) in overexercised female athletes, economic loss at the level of individual human beings is at least as graphic a symbol of loss of power as is sexual dysfunction— and can lead to loss of sexual appetite every bit as quickly as economic success can stimulate one's sex life.

SEX, MONEY, AND POWER—BUT NO KIDS

The connections between economics and sex run very deep. As we already noted, both are commodities (as babies can be as well). When sex leaves the house and enters the world of economics, it immediately becomes difficult to distinguish the needs, drives, and behaviors of individuals pursuing their sex lives for fun, power, and profit from the cultural dictates arising from social norms and economic exigencies of class. Though it can be fairly easy to separate the acts of individuals from the larger-scale social patterns of infanticide, rape, and slavery, the more subtle and arguably less destructive acts of individuals indulging in sex at the office, visiting prostitutes, or consuming some of the vast quantities of ubiquitous pornography have both individual motivations and social overtones (including social sanctions that at once discourage and abet such behavior) that are frequently hard to tell apart.

Take office sex. No doubt the office is a great place for conducting an active dating or sex life, and much of this behavior involves the core search for a mate suitable for pairing off and settling down and, in the case of heterosexual couplings, eventually marriage and production of offspring. Yet, despite the great inroads women have made in American economic life—to the point where many more women than ever before hold positions of power in corporations (including that of CEO) and in the professions— "sleeping up the ladder" has seemingly not been abandoned as a strategy for success in the economic world. Sex will not stop being a medium of exchange as long as there is a perceived payoff in terms of job advancement. Men, on the other hand, seem to pick on women with lower status at the office (not difficult in any case, since women remain at lower levels of remuneration and status in the workforce), so when already married males pursue women at work, their motives seem to be largely the power and fun of an extramarital fling, possibly enhancing their reputations among peer males, rather than direct economic gain—or the production of children. But all permutations and combinations take place, and women higher up the corporate ladder are also known to select a male of lower status.

Nowhere is extramarital sex more closely linked to power and even glamour than in the realms of show business and politics. The extremely visible attempts to bust Bill Clinton for his escapades with women as governor of Arkansas and, especially, as president of the United States (where his article of impeachment boiled down to his allegedly having lied about his sex life, rather than to the fact he was conducting one) made the United States a laughing stock of the rest of the world (especially in Europe, where such behavior is recognized as the norm). When François Mitterrand, the president of France, died, both his wife and his mistress (and assorted children) attended the funeral. As a young man, Bill Clinton was inspired by John F. Kennedy, whose extramarital sex life was discreetly ignored by the Washington press corps, though well known to all. Gary Hart was another ambitious politician who thought it was all right to engage in various sexual high jinks; like Clinton, he mistakenly assumed that the same rules that had applied to powerful politicians in the recent past (and, stories have it, off and on pretty much throughout the history of the American presidency) continued to apply even when the political and "moral" climate shifted toward the right. If it weren't so traumatic, it would be downright hilarious that some of Clinton's biggest political enemies on the Hill, including House Speaker Newt Gingrich, were also found out to be conducting clandestine extramarital affairs. No stranger to hypocrisy, American political life nearly absorbed the impeachment of a sitting president while his enemies were carrying on much the same way: Kenneth Starr's beady gaze caught Clinton with his pants down and produced a parade of women eager to tell of similar previous encounters, while the others thought they were safe. The whole messy episode shows how closely associated sex is with power, especially with the sort of heady power conveyed by high positions in national politics. Clinton's "crime" was in misjudging the political climate, far more than in being a unique departure from the typical shenanigans of high-power political life.

Then there is Hollywood. However straitlaced, goody-two-shoes the American public seem to consider itself, it has a collective fascination for the tawdrier, sexual side of our movie stars. I have no idea whether the starlet sleeping-up-the-credit-line days are over (it seems unlikely that those days will ever be forever gone); in any case, starlets and their male counterparts are endlessly, publicly active. It's like high school gone mad. You can't go through a supermarket checkout line without seeing sexy tabloid headlines (not, of course, unfailingly accurate). If there is a general human triangle of economics, sex, and reproduction, here we find triangles of the old familiar variety—someone is always out screwing around with another, at times more famous partner, leaving the purportedly confused and certainly betrayed spouse at home (or off on his or her own escapade), there to suffer public humiliation.

It's all about publicity, for it has long been a public relations axiom that public notoriety for whatever reason is good for the career—so long as they spell your name right. Sex is probably the easiest way to keep your name in the gossip columns. Much better than drug busts, and less of a threat to your overall health. It can even help overcome flops and bad reviews.

Nor is Hollywood the only locus for nonstop sexual news. You might think that a hit record or two is the ultimate goal of a rock musician, but most bands are still heavily into sex, drugs, and rock and roll—to the point that no tour is going well unless it has its full complement of groupies for postconcert partying. This is not a new phenomenon: when big-band "swing" music was the popular music of the nation (especially from the mid-1930s into the early 1950s), musicians on the road lived a life fraught with sex, and often with drugs, and with the boredom and loneliness that comes to the lives of all who are forced to spend much of their days away from home.

Sports, too. For every story of a (recently retired) Joe DiMaggio hooking up with a Marilyn Monroe (a famous celebrity marriage that ended in divorce and no children), there are countless episodes of athletes, married or not, with active sex lives in every port of call. Though it must be admitted that efforts are here generally made to stay out of the newspapers (not always successful—the famous Copacabana brawl involving Mickey Mantle, Billy Martin, and other Yankees included women as well as booze and other male brawlers). Yet it is the glamour and power that is the lot of famous athletes that gives them access to women (and a host of other things that threaten to mess up their lives). Let us never forget that Wilt Chamberlain—he who boasted that he'd had ten thousand women as sexual partners over his sexually active lifetime—was an incredibly successful athlete, a famous basketball star who once scored 100 points in a single game.

Sex is about pleasure. Sex is about baby making, some small percentage of the time. But sex is also about power, symbolically and even financially. Sex confers and conveys power—and power in the form of fame, fortune, or simply a sense of well-being in the more humble lives that most of us lead. Sex and power feed off one another in an endless dance.

But sex is also for sale.

LOVE FOR SALE: SEX AS A COMMODITY

The world's oldest profession? That was probably the hunting-gathering amalgam that kept people alive as ancestral humans, though if there is anything to the "food for sex" scenario of early hominid pair bonding, sex has been an economic commodity since the earliest days of hominid existence.

But if by "profession" we mean the things people do in exchange for material goods (food, manufactured items, eventually money) and services after the invention of agriculture and the sedentary life that came with it, then there is little reason to doubt that prostitution—sex for sale—was there from the get-go. Amply documented in the Bible (which is, after all, one of the oldest written records shedding light on what life was like thousands of years ago), sex for shekels goes back to a time long before Mary Magdalene's.

Sex for hire is no laughing matter. For every college girl who works at a topless bar for kicks and spending money, and maybe throws a few tricks more or less as a lark, there are hundreds of thousands of women who sell their bodies as the absolute last resort for their survival—and frequently their children's survival as well. Even worse (if possible), there is the rampant sexual slave trade—ranging from families selling their daughters to work in the brothels of Southeast Asia to the importation of European, African, and Asian women to serve as sex slaves right here in the United States. These are sweeping social issues, and especially because they often involve the production and support of children, I'll get back to the dark social-issues side of sex for hire in the next chapter. For the moment, though, it is worth taking a look at the commercial side of sex strictly for the connection between money and sex—to the patent exclusion of baby making, at least insofar as the sexual partners are concerned.

The sex industry is worth billions of dollars a year to the American economy alone. Prostitution might be the oldest component of this ancient business, but pornography is probably the most lucrative.

Prostitution, it seems clear, will never go away. Beyond the hard fact that there will always be women who need to support themselves, their kids, or, sadly, their drug habits, there is the equally hard fact that there will always be men willing to pay for sex. The anonymity of it—the very real sense that paying money removes any sense of obligation and thwarts any propensity toward emotional entanglement (though men through the years have, of course, fallen in love with prostitutes)—is apparently a potent draw. Sex can be enjoyed (or not) on its own; the only thing the guy owes is his money. No guilt (at least not toward the prostitute) and no further obligations.

So guys visit prostitutes while they're on the road, or while they're at work (New York City cops have been busted for frequenting whorehouses within their precincts while supposedly on "active" duty). What is not accomplished on the street or in (sometimes state-sanctioned) red-light districts is supplied the world over by "escort services." Massage parlors provide a not very cryptic cover for otherwise frowned-upon prostitution. They are everywhere, and if some of them are no more than what they profess to be, the "no hand jobs" notice on a massage parlor ad seen recently in a tourist newspaper in Shanghai is otherwise the exception once again proving the rule. And if sex clubs like New York's Plato's Retreat are at the moment dormant in the United States, others like them will pop up again as soon as the moral climate and economic conditions again become conducive to such ventures.

Pornography in the United States alone is a multibillion-dollar industry. Peep shows, sex shops, nude dancing, even pornographic bakeries, abound. Evolutionary psychologists will insist that much of this sex business, like rape, is an epiphenomenon of the *real* deal, which is, of course, having sex to make babies. Conversely, feminists are just as likely to maintain that pornography is misogyny, representing often violent exploitation of women by men. A sex shop owner, however, will say that sex sells and that he (or she) is in business to make a living and is in any case not getting rich. Just trying to eke out an existence, pay the rent, stay married, and, yes, possibly, as part of the picture, have some kids. The customers who buy the dildos, vibrators, and graphic video tapes will most likely say—when cornered—that what they do to take their pleasure in the privacy of their own homes is no one else's business. Some will turn out to have kids; others won't. Sex goes on, all the time, independently of the reproductive imperative, and some forms cost money for the practitioners.

Sex is by far the biggest economic item on the Internet, encompassing pornography, sales of sexual nostrums, penis and breast enlargers, relief for the erectily challenged—as well as direct personal connections, which in a few cases have led to tragedy. The Internet, as we already noted, is a nonstop purveyor of all things sexual—testimony not only to the power of the Internet in modern life but also to humanity's seemingly unquenchable thirst for pornography, sex toys, and sex aids.

So much for the obvious, direct connections between sex and the marketplace. But anyone who has ever perused a Victoria's Secret catalog for the pure titillation of it knows, too, that soft-core images of scantily clad women (and guys in other catalogs) is a powerful marketing strategy for clothes, jewelry, perfume, cars—any and all objects associated with the good life—with power. The message is "Buy this lingerie, this necklace, or this car, and you will feel great and have all the sex you are looking for." It's the power message, put to use to further the economic goals of those who want to sell you their material wares.

The connections between sex and economics run deep—and to

the near exclusion of the production of babies. Neither the man nor the prostitute he visits wants a child as the outcome of their encounter. The woman buying a necklace to enhance her beauty and sense of self-worth is not necessarily thinking that this necklace is going to help her get pregnant. The guy buying the sexy car might think it will help him pick up babes, but as a rule he isn't thinking that the car will help him make babies.

If anyone's "fitness" (propensity to produce and care for babies) is enhanced by the sex industry, it is the people who are making the money off of it. And though this includes prostitutes, all too often they are sharing their fees with pimps or are, worse, slaves forced to have sex simply to eke out a bare, bleak existence. Mostly it is the entrepreneurs who make the money: the madams of the glitzier bordellos, the massage parlor and sex shop owners, and the pornography publishers.

And here, with those making (sometimes) handsome profits from the sex industry, there is indeed a connection between economic success and, at times, the production of offspring. A recent television documentary profiled a mother/son team in Los Angeles who specialized in purveying pornography centering on anal sex. They were shown making a good living (though being occasionally hassled by the powers that be). I have no idea whether the mother was able to have her son in part because of income derived from some earlier foray into pornography (more likely she was a relative newcomer to the game, just helping sonny boy out in his business venture).

But there can be little doubt that pornographers and other purveyors of sex in the marketplace use their incomes the way people everywhere, in all walks of life, use their incomes: to provide food, clothing, and shelter to themselves, to their spouse (should there be one), and to children (should they have them). The triangle of sex, economics, and reproduction is intact among the people who run the sex businesses. It is the customers who are buying their products who are committed to a 100 percent disconnect between sex and baby making as they pay their money to take their pleasures.

So sex is pursued on its own, for its own intrinsic, private pleasures. Sex is intimately linked to human self-esteem—to feelings of power (or lack thereof). And sex and money go hand in hand. Babies are incidental to all this. Humans have sex for lots of reasons, only some of which have to do with making babies and thereby passing along their genes.

For a Promising but Poor Girl, a Struggle Over Sex and Goals

By Nina Bernstein
The New York Times / March 8, 2004

The framed poster in the nurse practitioner's office lists "101 Ways to Say No to Sex." But Tabitha F., a seventeen-year-old high school senior, wants to say yes without apology.

"I guess I'm a feminist, because I don't believe having sexual freedom is bad, dirty," she declared during a break between Spanish and A.P. Lit, where she was reading *The Awakening*, an 1899 novel about a woman's emancipation. "I think it's all about being ready, and not to go there without a helmet."

The modern armory of contraception is inventoried on another poster in the clinic, an outpost of Montefiore Medical Center that is tucked inside DeWitt Clinton High School in the Bronx. But despite her brave words, real protection eludes Tabitha, who travels two hours to her honors program at DeWitt Clinton from a homeless shelter in Queens.

As she first told it, she chose the birth control patch when she fell in love. Later, she confessed: "I got off the patch because it was a lot of money. I couldn't go on asking my mother for fifteen dollars." Eventually, over a semester when she embraced Dickens and grasped physics, Tabitha revealed the darker reality of the romance that had claimed her virginity.

On a winter night in 2002, after her family was evicted from their Bronx apartment, there was no room for her with relatives who had taken in her mother and four younger siblings. For two nights she rode the subway to keep warm. Then a young man she knew gave her a place to sleep.

"I guess I loved him, but on the other hand there was this depressing moment of, like, nothing's going right in my life," she said. "He was there for me. I felt, well, it's the least I can do."

Tabitha's journey through high school, so full of promise and peril, illustrates why no one is yet declaring victory in the national crusade to prevent teenagers from conceiving. Though teenage pregnancy rates have declined for more than a decade, to historic lows, they could rebound at any time, experts say.

If fear of AIDS instilled more sexual caution in a generation of adolescents, that fear may be waning, as upbeat subway ads promote HIV drugs and younger siblings engage in riskier behavior. If a religious revival and an influx of immigrants have brought stricter attitudes toward sex, the teenagers from such backgrounds who stray are less likely to use contraception or seek abortion. And if the growth in opportunities for poor women depressed birth rates in the 1990s, the economic downturn and rising college costs could have the opposite effect—tightening the persistent link between low income and high rates of unintended birth.

Those large forces reverberate in the daily lives of individual teenagers like Tabitha. Born to a seventeen-year-old in 1986, when teenage childbearing began its most alarming spike, she is now a tall, striking girl with a radiant smile and a yearning to succeed.

At times it seems that nothing can stop her. She is part of DeWitt

Clinton's Macy Scholars program, which helps low-income minority students qualify for competitive colleges. Last summer, she organized a literacy class at her homeless shelter. This semester, she stuffed her copy of *Great Expectations* with scribbled Post-it notes, parsing the book's strange words and strangely familiar themes: childhood hardship, heartbreak and redemption.

"She's smart, articulate—she has so much spunk," said Phyllis McCabe, the coordinator of the Macy program and one of Tabitha's fiercest advocates. "She's poised, she's compassionate."

But after their warm embrace in front of a photographer, Ms. McCabe pulled her aside for a stern private lecture. The teenager had missed so much school during her junior year, after her family's eviction, that she was still struggling to bring her average back up to the 85 required to remain a Macy Scholar. And now, with her long commute, she was arriving late. Colleges would excuse her checkered junior year only if she could prove she had overcome her troubles, the coordinator warned her.

"We have kids with terrible, terrible situations," Ms. McCabe said later. "They're hanging on by a thread, and sometimes when we're asking them to do it, you wonder how they can."

Tabitha's next stop was the Montefiore clinic, which like many pregnancy prevention programs is threatened with cutbacks. It has been her only reliable source of health care since her mother left welfare and lost family Medicaid benefits three years ago.

Tabitha would never be caught, she said, like her childhood friend Rasheeda, the shy girl with high grades who wanted to be a nun—and ended up pregnant at fifteen by her first boyfriend, seeking an abortion when it was already too late. She would not follow in the footsteps of her mother, who had five children and a church wedding to the father of her youngest three, despite his drug addiction and domestic violence.

But at the clinic it emerged that Tabitha had missed her last appointment. Embarrassed by her poverty, she had not mentioned dropping the patch. Nor did she disclose that a new man had entered her life—an adult with a car, money and his own apartment.

A stray remark revealed the stakes.

"I was glad," Tabitha told the nurse, "when I got my period two weeks ago."

PERILS IN EVERY CASE

The decline in teenage pregnancy is a statistical abstraction to Margaret Rogers, forty-nine, who has been a nurse practitioner at the clinic for seven years.

"I see them one on one," she explained before Tabitha's visit, excusing herself to speak with an angry mother whose daughter, fifteen, had tested pregnant.

An enduring myth of teenage pregnancy is that affluent adolescents get pregnant as often as poor ones, but have more abortions. In fact, national surveys show that poor women of all ages have much higher rates of abortion and unintended births than the better-off. And though government studies typically display results by race, ethnicity and geography, the most dramatic and consistent differences in each category are by income.

At DeWitt Clinton, where more than 75 percent of the 4,600 students live below the federal poverty line, Ms. Rogers sees case by case how disadvantage can stack the deck.

As the "101 Ways" poster in her office suggests, Ms. Rogers often counsels students about how to refuse or avoid sex. Some people believe that is the only message she should deliver. Ms. Rogers, a mother of two and the daughter of a Presbyterian minister, disagrees.

"The majority of the tests are negative, thank God," she said. "But that's a kid we know is sexually active, we know is taking some chances, who needs to be screened for sexually transmitted diseases, to be counseled about condoms and contraceptives."

Like many in the field, Ms. Rogers is not convinced that lower pregnancy rates are here to stay. Adults, she said, forget how quickly one wave of teenagers gives way to the next. For an earlier generation, the safe-sex message may have come home when Magic Johnson announced he was infected with HIV and retired from basketball in 1991. "This generation already doesn't know who Magic Johnson is," she said.

The average teenage girl has a nearly 90 percent chance of getting pregnant during a year when she is having sex without contraception, a study by the Alan Guttmacher Institute shows—a rate that condoms cut to 15 percent and the most effective birth control methods reduce to less than one in 200.

But there are mothers who find and throw out their daughters' birth control pills in an effort to stop them from having sex. There are girls who reject Depo-Provera, a long-lasting hormonal contraceptive shot, not because it causes bone loss but because it stops menstruation, and they know their mothers check the garbage for their used sanitary napkins. Other girls, the nurse said, are engaging in anal sex "not just as a pregnancy prevention, but to maintain their virginity."

Ms. Rogers finds it particularly difficult to counsel needy girls whose sexual partners are adults—as are most males who father babies born to teenagers. "I consider them predatory," she said, noting that older men have higher rates of sexual disease and lower rates of condom use than teenagers. "But the girls consider it a great relationship—a guy with some money and a car."

After Tabitha mentioned getting her period, the nurse scheduled another appointment for counseling and screening, wrote a new prescription for the patch and offered to arrange a waiver of the fee. Tabitha said she could afford to pay now: she had started a weekend job at a McDonald's near her shelter.

But would she follow through with the patch? If not, would she derail her life? Those who work with young people like Tabitha say they are constantly asking such questions as they strain against the force field of poverty.

"Welcome to the club," said Michael Carrera, a New York doctor recognized nationally for his health and social services program for poor children, which beats back the odds of pregnancy through the kind of day-to-day support taken for granted in more affluent families. "I and all the people who work with us have the same sense of crossing our fingers, falling to our knees in desperation and frustration sometimes.

"This is so fragile, this is so on-the-edge, that the least little thing could move us back."

REBELLING AGAINST THE ODDS

During a long subway ride back to the Queens shelter, run by the Salvation Army, Tabitha recalled the day she started high school. Her father, who lives in Virginia with his wife and two children, had marked the occasion with a rare telephone call.

"He said, 'These four years determine where you go in life,'" she remembered, imitating his deep voice and lecturing tone. She gave a short laugh. "I sometimes think my father has been expecting me to be another statistic. He was expecting me to fall like my mother did."

Tabitha was not a statistic. She was a senior facing college applications, and the task of finding a narrative arc in her life story that could produce a happy ending. Sometimes she recounted her experiences in a way that fit that expectation. Sometimes she revealed the painful contradictions.

This day had started at five A.M., searching for clean clothes for school as though through a shipwreck. Her younger brothers and sisters—Malik, fifteen, Isaiah, eight, Akilah, seven, and Kierra, two—were still sleeping. For nine months the family of six had been living in the shelter, a former hotel surrounded by chain-link fencing, in two small rooms with no telephone.

Riding two buses and two subways, Tabitha had made it to her first class in time for her big test in American history. Later, she would apply her understanding of the Bill of Rights like balm to the humiliation of unannounced room inspections at the shelter.

"It's like the ultimate violation of the Constitution, the Fourth Amendment, the right to privacy," she complained after a social worker walked in on Isaiah, naked in the bathroom. "Their excuse? 'Oh, we just want to teach everybody good housing skills.' People think you're poor, they think you're dumb or you're a barbarian."

In some ways, Tabitha knew, her mother had fulfilled the public's worst expectations of teenage mothers in the late 1980s: She dropped out in eleventh grade, had a second baby at nineteen and turned to welfare to support two more born out of wedlock.

But she had also followed every current prescription for protecting her children from the hazards of poverty, including the risk of early pregnancy. She continued her education, with help from a city child care program for mothers in high school. Eventually, she earned a two-year associate's degree as a physical therapy assistant. She joined a church, left welfare for work and married.

"Marriage is not something obsolete," Tabitha's mother, thirty-four, declared later over a Sunday lunch at her Pentecostal church in East

Harlem, with Kierra in white crinoline beside her. "It's to be held up as a standard."

Yet in Tabitha's experience, poverty itself made work, religion and marriage double-edged. On welfare, her mother had managed to provide food for a family of six or seven, including an orphaned cousin, and kept a one-bedroom apartment a short subway ride from DeWitt Clinton. But when she went to work, "they took everything away from her," Tabitha recalled, citing a rent subsidy, Medicaid and food stamps that vanished along with welfare, making it harder than ever for the family to make ends meet.

Her mother's proud church wedding to the father of Isaiah and Akilah in 2000 did nothing to improve a troubled relationship that Tabitha said was shaped by his beatings, growing drug problem and failure to share his pay—at best $5.75 an hour when he worked.

Until her junior year, Tabitha had been a God-fearing, churchgoing girl, as she put it. Now she was unsparing as she challenged the pieties of her childhood. "God wants you to wait," she said sarcastically. "And do you think your husband will have waited? What about him? What if you wait for him and he cheats on you, he beats you up?"

"I guess I'm a rebel," she added. "During that period when I was really homeless, I began questioning a lot. I was like, if you're so loving and forgiving, why is this happening to me?"

On this school day, Tabitha had stayed late for an extra-help physics class with Mr. Strasser, an Austrian teacher with a ponytail. She was the only student without a calculator, and she had to squint to read formulas on the blackboard since there was no money to replace her broken glasses. But she loved the way Mr. Strasser explained a problem about acceleration in free fall, by dropping a piece of paper through her outstretched fingers before she could catch it.

Maybe Tabitha had caught herself just in time. She had made an appointment with Ms. Rogers to be screened for everything: HIV, chlamydia, and other sexually transmitted diseases. She had vowed to organize her homework better, to find school clothes the night before, and never again to have sex without protection. And just in case, she had asked Ms. Rogers how to apply for emergency Medicaid if she ever needed an abortion.

Now, waiting in the dark at a bus stop on the last leg of her journey back to the shelter, she pointed out the place where she had met her mysterious new beau, Mike, twenty-four. He had offered her a ride in his car, and assuring herself that it would be all right, she had stepped in.

It was nearly 7:30 P.M. when she trudged up the hill to the shelter's security post. Even outside the fence, a reporter's presence provoked the guard to threaten Tabitha with expulsion because shelter rules bar the news media. Tabitha argued with him politely. "Imagine," she finally said, "threatening someone with homelessness like that!"

AN ATTACK, AND AN ESCAPE

In Tabitha's high school journey, even the lack of a small sum—for laundry, a cab—has sometimes had far-reaching consequences that have raised the odds against her.

One hot day late in her freshman year, she and her stepfather argued over her attempt to dry a blouse in the oven. As she told it, he punched her in the face. Tabitha, who had just turned fifteen, grabbed a kitchen knife and stabbed him. The charges against her were dropped after she spent a night in jail. But when she returned home, her stepfather was there, too—awaiting the birth of another baby that Tabitha would have to tend.

"Mom, stop having kids!" Tabitha said she begged.

Some experts think reactions like hers help explain the decline in teenage pregnancy. But others say such experiences can cut both ways: Some girls forced to baby-sit while their mothers work seek escape in adult romance and early motherhood.

Early in her sophomore year, a cute twenty-three-year-old man from her grandmother's neighborhood in Harlem befriended Tabitha. She was fifteen and a virgin, and she thought it would be safe to go to his place because she had warned him beforehand, "'I'm not doing anything with you.'"

It was not safe. "He kept turning out the lights, trying to force me to touch him," she said. "I knew if I was to run away, I would have to call a cab. My mom would be, 'Why was you there?' I'd be in trouble."

She was in trouble anyway. Haunted by a hip-hop music video that warned about AIDS, she went to the school clinic to be tested. The counselor who heard her full account had no doubt that what had happened was a sexual assault. School officials called the police.

Two officers came to her house, Tabitha said; she had been napping and was still dazed when they drove her around the corner in their squad car in the dark.

"I'm here crying and crying," she recalled. "They shine a flashlight at me, and they're like, 'Are you sure you want to pursue this?' Making me tell it over and over, and then: 'There are so many inconsistencies in your account. It's your word against his. Do you want to just take this as a learning experience?'"

Her choked "yeah" was an agreement not to press charges. In retrospect, what she hated most, she said, was seeing the way the two white policemen looked at her family's apartment. "Our house, O.K., it was never the best, but that day it was so dirty, roaches and everything," she recalled, her voice growing thick. "It gave them more reason to think I wasn't worth it."

Far from teaching greater sexual caution, such experiences can be precursors to depression, risky teenage sex and early pregnancy, studies in recent years have shown. What protected Tabitha?

One camp might point to religion, another to counseling. But the key factor may have been DeWitt Clinton's strong theater program, the kind of extra that schools cut when budgets tighten. It sent her downtown to audition at La MaMa, an experimental theater in the East Village. Cast in an Elizabeth Swados production called *The Violence Project,* Tabitha found a new community where she felt valued and challenged.

That summer, traveling between Manhattan and the Bronx, she noticed "the invisible line of poverty" on Park Avenue at Ninety-sixth Street. As the economy soured, she watched her mother, now separated, fall further behind on the rent. More than ever, Tabitha dreamed of going away to college. A scholarship was possible, her guidance counselors had told her. But her junior year would be crucial.

IN SEARCH OF SHELTER

As that school year began, marshals evicted the family with one day's notice. Efforts to secure an apartment in Newark failed. And a crisis hit during Christmas break.

Her mother and the other children had taken refuge with Tabitha's grandmother. Tabitha, then sixteen, had been shuttling between aunts and friends, working at a McDonald's in Midtown after school to pay her own way. Then she was laid off, and temporary living arrangements ran out. Tabitha asked her grandmother to make room for one more.

Her grandmother refused: The teenage girl could not share close quarters with her male cousin, seventeen, and fourteen-year-old brother. Her mother did not insist. That hurt, but Tabitha understood.

"My mother was real desperate," she explained. "She didn't want any problems with my grandmother, because she could throw them all out." Tabitha volunteered that she had another place to stay. Then the weeks of being "really homeless" began.

For two nights, she rode the subways—or, as she wrote in a draft of her college essay, "From Woodlawn to Crown Heights and then from Inwood to Far Rockaway Beach, I sat on stone-hard train seats, thinking . . . planning . . . what train to ride next."

On the third night, she asked Dayvon, a twenty-year-old friend of two weeks' standing, if she could stay with him. When he agreed, the "101 Ways to Say No to Sex"—My parents are waiting up for me, I don't know you very well, Love isn't just about sex—no longer seemed to apply.

"We girls tend to think sex is going to be the most wonderful feeling," Tabitha observed later. "But it hurt at first. It wasn't what I expected."

Even among the 93 percent of young women ages fifteen to twenty-four who report that their first sexual intercourse was voluntary, a quarter say it was unwanted, according to a 1998 analysis of data from the National Survey of Family Growth that suggests the "decision" to start sex is far more ambiguous than imagined by policymakers.

Eventually Tabitha would wonder if what she had felt for Dayvon was gratitude, love, obligation or envy. "He was in college, he had a job, he had a life," she said. "He lived at his stepfather's—a nice home, decorated, with couches. I never had that."

When Dayvon's mother called and found her there, Tabitha felt too uncomfortable to stay. "It was like charity," she said.

For one night, she stayed with a church friend. The next day, she joined her family as her mother turned to the city's Emergency Assistance Unit to apply for shelter.

"Everywhere we went we had to take our belongings," Tabitha recalled of the two weeks they shuttled between the unit and various overnight shelters until they were found eligible. "Sometimes I'd come with my comforter to school. Mainly, I was not making it in. I hated coming to school and seeing all these kids with homes."

Yet as she looked around at the other homeless families, school seemed her only escape hatch. "The EAU was all black and Hispanic people," she said. "I realized the only way I'm going to get out is education. I don't have a singing talent. I don't rap. I act, but I'm not going to be a Broadway star. My goal is just to be stable."

THE MOMENT OF TRUTH

This school year, all of Tabitha's goals hinged on her taking the SAT's on Saturday, November 1. But at the shelter, she had never received the letter telling her where to report for the test. Her student identity card was lost. It was Friday, Halloween, and no regular replacement I.D. would be available until Monday.

At the last minute, Ms. McCabe, the honors program coordinator, improvised. A few calls unearthed Tabitha's assigned place for the test. A guidance counselor remembered the principal's Polaroid camera, which had film for one more picture. They typed up her description and an explanation on a DeWitt Clinton letterhead and pasted on the snapshot.

This time, it worked. "You can't put your fingers in the holes fast enough," Ms. McCabe said later. "Just with this one child you see how many pieces there are —the emotional, the academic, the physical. She's not being negligent in her behavior; it's just too much for her."

In the weeks that followed, Tabitha teetered between vulnerability and resilience, buoyed or brought low by her relationship with Mike. At first she stayed up late talking to him on a borrowed cellphone about her school day, details that no one else cared to hear—like her acceptance into a Manhattan theater youth group. But later he was always talking to someone else when she called. He would promise to call back, then not do it.

Tabitha had grown up on a seesaw of love and rejection. Her father, now a salesman, left when she was four, but he had sent her presents of money over the years. Then when she visited him the summer before high school, he compared her unfavorably to Southern girls. Rejection from Mike seemed to reinforce paternal disapproval.

But by mid-December, Tabitha sounded upbeat when she answered her cellphone in the shelter. "I'm in the Shakespearean competition—Lady Macbeth," she said, chattering on about theater excursions and new writing projects before revealing why she was so giddy: After a monthlong disappearance, Mike was back, and he was taking her to *The Lord of the Rings.*

First, though, he took her to his apartment.

As Tabitha described the place later, it was a studio in Jamaica, Queens, with "a leather white couch, white towels and a white comforter, a dresser drawer, a computer, a microwave."

She had bought the birth control patch. Her tests for diseases had all been negative, and she had made a vow to use protection. But when she suggested he use a condom, he reacted with disdain. "He was like, 'You really know how to ruin a moment.' I was like, 'It's not about ruining a moment, but now that I know you're talking to someone else. . . .'" She trailed off.

Did she stick to her vow, or give up? "I gave up," she said sadly. "I'm a little weakling."

Later she remembered the funny ad she had seen on the bus: Ninety-two percent of women carry lip protection, 10 percent carry HIV protection. Because she wasn't carrying a condom herself, she said, "I couldn't speak my mind."

There seemed to be a politics to it, an ebb and flow of self-esteem. At one point in her eight-month relationship with Dayvon, she herself had felt offended when he insisted on using a condom, as though she was unclean. She had told him, "We don't need to have sex at all," and that time they did not. On another occasion, she had been the one to insist that Dayvon use protection.

But with Mike, she just cared too much to insist. And after that weekend, he dropped her anyway.

"They're just little girls," Ms. McCabe had said, reflecting on her student mothers, in words that could apply to Tabitha as well. "There's such a need for human contact. They try to get it where they can, and lots of times, there's a price to pay."

EXPECTATIONS, BIG AND SMALL

As Tabitha plunged into *Great Expectations*, a dictionary beside her in her shelter bunk bed, she found another framework for her feelings: the story of the poor boy who suffers the contempt of the wealthy and beautiful, and for the first time sees himself as "a stupid, clumsy, laboring boy."

"I identified with Pip," she said, "when he runs away and starts to cry because he realizes his position in life."

Last month, the family was still in the shelter—one of a record 9,000 homeless families in city shelters, including 16,000 children. Her brother, turning sixteen and failing in school, was sleeping with a twenty-eight-year-old shelter resident, a mother of three. "The worst thing in the world would be if he gets her pregnant," Tabitha said.

Her mother did not want her to go away to college, she said. Tabitha still longed to go, but she was uncertain whether her SAT scores—520 verbal, 470 in math—were good enough. She was struggling with her applications. And she still missed Mike terribly. At least, she said, she wished she knew his last name.

At the theater group, she tried out the monologue she had chosen, from Karen L. B. Evans's play *My Girlish Days*. Stephen DiMenna, the director, was impressed. "I thought Tabitha was this sort of quiet, shy girl," he said. "Her monologue is stunning, and it sort of blew everybody away."

The character was Gertie, a smart, ambitious black woman relegated to factory work after her dream of college is broken by poverty, pregnancy and abuse. She cries out, "Why am I stuck, frozen?"

"It's like me," Tabitha said later. "What is keeping me from, like, soaring? 'Cause I just want to soar."

Have Yourself a Horny Little Christmas

Looking at the Abercrombie & Fitch Catalog Makes Me Want to Buy Their Clothes, but I'm Too Exhausted from Self-Abuse

By Cole Kazdin
Salon.com / November 26, 2003

Nothing says "Christmas" like a good old-fashioned circle jerk by the fire.

For all you squares who don't know what a circle jerk is, turn to page 88 of the Abercrombie & Fitch Quarterly, under the picture of wet, naked college kids and the heading "Group Sex." (It's difficult to figure out where you are in the book since most pages aren't numbered.) It reads: "Sex, as we know, can involve one or two, but what about even more? . . . A pleasant and supersafe alternative to this is group masturbation."

The challenge for me, when masturbating with my friends to the nubile nudies in the Abercrombie & Fitch catalog, is trying not to think about serious things like racial diversity; it tends to kill the mood. But because most of the models in the catalog are white and because a lawsuit has been filed against the clothing retailer for allegedly discriminating against a black woman who applied for a job at the store, it's hard for the issue not to rear its nonsexy head.

Part *Barely Legal*, part vapid teen magazine, the Christmas issue of the A&F Quarterly is unparalleled in the amount of naked frolicking it uses to sell clothing. And considering the demographic it is trying to reach, it's downright risqué. Besides the couples seemingly in the throes of sexual intercourse, there are subtler seductions. If you look very, very closely, somewhere around page 100, you can find not-quite airbrushed male pubes on a well-cut frat guy, as he slides in the buff down a wet rock into crashing waves. It's beyond anything our parents saw in *Playboy*.

"It's very healthy to be free and be honest about it," says Sam Shahid, an A&F board member, and head of Shahid & Co. in New York, the firm that designs the racy ad campaigns. The cover of the Christmas issue promises "280 pages of moose, ice hockey, chivalry, group sex & more." There wasn't a whole lot of ice hockey or chivalry, unless, by "ice hockey" they mean bare asses, and by "chivalry" they mean nipples.

One layout is of four giggling topless coeds, tanned and blond, sprawled across a plaid blanket in the woods, pulling down the boxer shorts of a freshly scrubbed muscular guy, with a Cheshire cat grin revealing Tom Cruise-like pearly whites. And his ass.

Then there's a completely naked couple, making out, or having sex, on wet rocks. There's Tom Cruise-guy again, naked by the fireplace, but for a strategically placed gift with a bow. And look! Two naked men (can eighteen-year-olds be called men?) in the river, standing barely far enough away from each other not to be construed as gay—though that's how I construed it.

"There's no such thing as being too sexy," Shahid says. "You're speaking to the kids. Everybody talks about sex all the time." He says none of the sexual content in the catalog is meant to shock—though this comes from the same man who gave us the borderline kiddie porn ads for Calvin Klein years ago.

The A&F catalog regularly evokes plenty of outrage and numerous boycotts from Christian, conservative and parent groups all over the country. "Everyone has their own hang-up," he says. "We think it's beautiful and gorgeous and we're not offending [anyone]." And he adds that most of the ideas come from the models themselves. "They have a great time and we don't do anything that they don't want to." The "kids," as he refers to them—almost parentally—pair up, form friendships, and sometimes have tears in their eyes at the end of the shoot.

But maybe that's because they can't find their clothes. In the catalog, the first sweater doesn't show up until page 122 and by then, you're too tired from masturbating to shop. But I'm missing the point. The catalog isn't about the clothes. Huh?

"How many plaid shirts can one have?" Shahid asks. He explains that they are selling the "aspiration and the idea." He says Abercrombie & Fitch is "cool and sexy and very Eastern seaboard," and when you buy the clothes, "your image in your head is: I'm one of those kids. I put one of those shirts on and, Oh!—I'm one of those kids. It denotes a particular feeling. There's nothing wrong with it."

There is something wrong with it, according to Brandy Hawk, the nineteen-year-old college student who filed the recent lawsuit in U.S. District Court in Camden, N.J. Hawk went to prep school and describes the A&F style as virtually her uniform; it was always a place she wanted to work. "It never really occurred to me that I'd be the only black person working there," she says. She had an interview this past May, where the assistant manager explained that they were looking for their employees to represent "casual lifestyle, American youth, athletes, sorority girls," says Hawk. When Hawk—an athlete with previous retail experience and a wide-open schedule—never heard from them again, she was mystified. She says a security guard at the store found out from the manager that she wasn't hired because she wouldn't represent the company well.

Hawk couldn't believe that being black had anything to do with it, but when she found out about a similar lawsuit filed in California by a young Mexican-American man, she was heartbroken. This free and casually fabulous lifestyle that she and her friends had so loyally bought into suddenly didn't want her. "I really took it as a slap in the face," she says. "It's knocking the wind out of me. It's like your best friend doing something . . ." she pauses, looking for the right word, but can't find one to convey the severity, "like your best friend doing something really bad to you."

Hawk filed a complaint with the Equal Employment Opportunity Commission in June, and then, just last Wednesday, filed suit in U.S. District Court. When we spoke on Saturday, she said there had been no response yet from the company.

The cult of Abercrombie & Fitch clearly has some power over the youth of America. The store started in 1892 selling sporting goods. Ernest Hemingway bought hunting gear there in the 1950s. The brand had lost its way until Shahid and current CEO Mike Jeffries entered the picture in the 1990s. It emerged as the elite, young WASP, country club brand it continues to be today. The same kind of country club that perhaps doesn't admit people of color. Today, it has more than 650 stores, which include Abercrombie & Fitch, Abercrombie for kids, and another store for teenagers, Hollisters. It's less of a genuinely elite brand like Ralph Lauren, and more of a Middle American-mall version of what prep school is like.

The A&F models look like the rich kids at boarding school who drink too much and crash their parents' expensive cars and, worst crime of all, wear those obnoxious "Co-ed, Naked Lacrosse"-type T-shirts. Or "Abercrombie & Fitch Ski Patrol," or some vague

"Athletic Department." When I visit the store in downtown Manhattan, the salespeople look identical to the kids in the catalog—the same contrived cool, almost Stepford-hipness to them. I feel incredibly out of place. I suspect it's because I'm over thirty. I notice another suspiciously old person—a bald guy, alone. Maybe an abandoned dad. ("You're embarrassing me! Stand by the sweaters!") Or perhaps another reporter.

The A&F drones remind me of the group in high school of which I was never a part. While I was rehearsing *The Crucible*, they were at lacrosse practice. They threw wild, crazy parties while their neglectful, wealthy parents were out of town skiing. Maybe with the Abercrombie Ski Patrol. Years later, I developed an enormous prejudice and decided these kids were lame and often lazy and their successes were usually owed to their parents' connections and legacies. For some reason that made me think of George Bush.

I look around the store. I notice two girls and a guy giggling in a corner. A surfer-type guy—or "dude," as I believe they're called—stands awkwardly by a display, holding a pair of pants. No one's folding anything. They're bad folders. Their dads totally got them in here.

I see an enormous poster of the Tom Cruise look-alike from the catalog. I place my hand on his waxed chest and say hello to his giant teeth like he is an old friend, or a guy I hooked up with during New Student Week. I have seen him naked, after all.

For all the suggestive images on the walls (PG-13 versions of the catalog's R- and X-rated photographs), the store doesn't feel sexy or erotically charged in any way. It feels like the gift shop for the sexy world you visited in the catalog. I felt as if I was in some guy's messy dorm room.

I feel conspicuous so I decide to go into the dressing room to take some notes—not before picking out a pair of meticulously rumpled camouflage pants, red flannel pajama pants (if the catalog is any indication, no matching top exists; it must look better topless), and a tank top. I ask Surfer Dude where the dressing rooms are and he looks confused. He begins to point me in one direction, but then changes his mind and gives me overly elaborate directions simply to the other side of the store. Still not folding, I might add. I find the dressing room. The three gigglers, it turns out, are in charge, but they don't notice me with my armful of clothes, so I walk past them and into the room where I write down my observations: useless popular kids . . . no folding . . . George Bush . . . no one really seems to work here, everyone is just posing.

I try on the clothes. The fatigues are way too big on me, as are the pajamas. But then again I suppose the pants are intended to be worn around the ankles. I think of the old pickup line: "I like your pants—they'd look great on my floor." The shirt doesn't fit well either, and I realize that these are poorly made clothes. They're cheap.

When I call the Abercrombie & Fitch corporate office I run into more incompetence. I'm transferred incorrectly three times and finally put on hold. The song "Another Brick in the Wall" plays as the hold music. I hum along, enjoying the irony: "We don't need no education . . ." I get through the entire first verse by the time the company spokesperson, Hampton Carney, picks up the phone. The name is so perfect that I wonder if it's real or if it's a character the company's developed to talk to the press. Carney's not so chatty and won't answer any of my questions. He won't comment on any of the current litigation. Nor will he comment on the company's hiring practices, or a recent suit it settled for $2.2 million brought by employees who said they were forced to buy and wear A&F clothes.

I find my conversation with Hampton Carney as unsatisfying as the thin, faux-faded and rough-to-the-touch sweatshirt I pass on my way out of the store. The only thing Hampton Carney does say is that, though there have been complaints from various groups, customers have "responded overwhelmingly positively" to what he calls "adult material" in the catalog.

The catalog is popular. Circulation of this year's Christmas catalog is 400,000. I see young women lined up at the cash register waiting to purchase it. It's seven dollars and you have to be over eighteen to buy it. Carney told me a photo I.D. with proof of age is required, but no one was asking for it at the store I went to.

Perhaps more shocking and offensive than the teen orgies in the catalog is the bad writing. At the beginning of the catalog is a letter with a somewhat facetious apology list to all of the groups who've complained in the past. Among them, Mothers Against Drunk Driving, who, in 1998, protested a Back-to-School issue that featured a "Drinking 101" section complete with cocktail recipes. Also, to Asian American organizations that protested a 2002 line of T-shirts with slant-eyed faces and slogans like "Two Wongs Can Make it White"—referring to a laundry business. Abercrombie & Fitch received so many complaints that the company eventually pulled the T-shirts from the shelves.

The apology reads like the courtroom remorse of a frat guy-date rapist who gets off scot free and is then seen that night at the campus bonfire, drunk on his ass, high-fiving his friends and seducing some freshman girl. I think it's supposed to seem clever and intelligent and spontaneous, but the rest of the catalog seems to me like it was written by a slightly drunk seventeen-year-old—or perhaps a fifty-five-year-old who is trying to sound like a drunk seventeen-year-old.

A&F's Hampton Carney says the writers are all in their twenties. There are interviews with Paris Hilton and cast members of the Fox teen soap opera *The O.C.*—a program whose substance, or lack thereof, merits a story credit at the top of the show, "Inspired by the board shorts of Abercrombie & Fitch." There are film and music reviews. Words like "sex," "pussy," and "masturbate" get pulled out and bolded in the middle of the page.

I leaf through the J. Crew catalog I just got in the mail to see what words it pull outs and bolds: "shearling," and "bright stripes." Which one would you rather masturbate to?

"I don't think we're used to seeing it [sex] commercially in a catalog," says ad creator Shahid. He talks about his past work for Calvin Klein. "Calvin was a genius—in a fragrance ad, you couldn't smell it, [but] he gave you a sense of what it is—sexy."

Could it work for any brand? "L.L. Bean shouldn't show a guy shirtless," says Shahid. Then he changes his mind. "No, maybe it could. Maybe it would help! It would have to be the right L.L. Bean guy, with his wife, on the phone. Ed Burns. It's got to look real and fabulous and everyone wants to be that."

Brandy Hawk works at Old Navy now. She notices diversity among the employees there, where she didn't really think about it before. She talks about other stores in the mall selling clothes like Rocawear, Ecko and other hip-hop-inspired lines. "I notice even though the models may be black, they still have white people working in the store."

Lawyers for the nine plaintiffs in the California suit did not return calls, but according to a June press release, the plaintiffs, all people of color, were denied jobs, fired or allocated to the stockroom rather than the sales floor. Before this happened, Hawk thought that if she didn't get a job, it was the company's prerogative not to hire her. "Now I see how much of an injury it is," she says. When you look at the catalog, or when you go into an Abercrombie & Fitch store, "it's almost like an army—everyone looks the same, everyone dresses the same."

Though she liked the clothes, she never understood the A&F catalog. "I wondered what they were trying to advertise," she says. "It was like soft-core porn. I didn't see the point." She would rather have looked at the clothes, which don't appear until much later in the catalog, and they are pictured on the page without anyone wearing them. Models without clothes followed by clothes without models. "I guess it's supposed to be artistic," she says. "Maybe it's over my head."

I look at the pictures in the catalog again, searching for a deeper, artistic meaning. Tom Cruise-guy just smiles back at me, his big, toothy, charming smile. He looks like he's having too good a time to care.

The Girls Next Door

By Peter Landesman
The New York Times Magazine / January 25, 2004

The house at 1212 1/2 West Front Street in Plainfield, N.J., is a conventional midcentury home with slate-gray siding, white trim, and Victorian lines. When I stood in front of it on a breezy day in October, I could hear the cries of children from the playground of an elementary school around the corner. American flags fluttered from porches and windows. The neighborhood is a leafy, middle-class Anytown. The house is set back off the street, near two convenience stores and a gift shop. On the door of Superior Supermarket was pasted a sign issued by the Plainfield police: SAFE NEIGHBORHOODS SAVE LIVES. The store's manager, who refused to tell me his name, said he never noticed anything unusual about the house, and never heard anything. But David Miranda, the young man behind the counter of Westside Convenience, told me he saw girls from the house roughly once a week. "They came in to buy candy and soda, then went back to the house," he said. The same girls rarely came twice, and they were all very young, Miranda said. They never asked for anything beyond what they were purchasing; they certainly never asked for help. Cars drove up to the house all day; nice cars, all kinds of cars. Dozens of men came and went. "But no one here knew what was really going on," Miranda said. And no one ever asked.

On a tip, the Plainfield police raided the house in February 2002, expecting to find illegal aliens working an underground brothel. What the police found were four girls between the ages of fourteen and seventeen. They were all Mexican nationals without documentation. But they weren't prostitutes; they were sex slaves. The distinction is important: these girls weren't working for profit or a paycheck. They were captives to the traffickers and keepers who controlled their every move. "I consider myself hardened," Mark J. Kelly, now a special agent with Immigration and Customs Enforcement (the largest investigative arm of the Department of Homeland Security), told me recently. "I spent time in the Marine Corps. But seeing some of the stuff I saw, then heard about, from those girls was a difficult, eye-opening experience."

The police found a squalid, land-based equivalent of a nineteenth-century slave ship, with rancid, doorless bathrooms; bare, putrid mattresses; and a stash of penicillin, "morning after" pills and misoprostol, an antiulcer medication that can induce abortion. The girls were pale, exhausted, and malnourished.

It turned out that 1212 1/2 West Front Street was one of what law-enforcement officials say are dozens of active stash houses and apartments in the New York metropolitan area—mirroring hundreds more in other major cities like Los Angeles, Atlanta, and Chicago—where under-age girls and young women from dozens of countries are trafficked and held captive. Most of them—whether they started out in Eastern Europe or Latin America—are taken to the United States through Mexico. Some of them have been baited by promises of legitimate jobs and a better life in America; many have been abducted; others have been bought from or abandoned by their impoverished families.

Because of the porousness of the U.S.–Mexico border and the criminal networks that traverse it, the towns and cities along that border have become the main staging area in an illicit and barbaric industry, whose "products" are women and girls. On both sides of the border, they are rented out for sex for as little as fifteen minutes at a time, dozens of times a day. Sometimes they are sold outright to other traffickers and sex rings, victims and experts say. These sex slaves earn no money, there is nothing voluntary about what they do, and if they try to escape they are often beaten and sometimes killed.

Last September, in a speech before the United Nations General Assembly, President Bush named sex trafficking as "a special evil," a multibillion-dollar "underground of brutality and lonely fear," a global scourge alongside the AIDS epidemic. Influenced by a coalition of religious organizations, the Bush administration has pushed international action on the global sex trade. The president declared at the UN that "those who create these victims and profit from their suffering must be severely punished" and that "those who patronize this industry debase themselves and deepen the misery of others. And governments that tolerate this trade are tolerating a form of slavery."

Under the Trafficking Victims Protection Act of 2000—the first U.S. law to recognize that people trafficked against their will are victims of a crime, not illegal aliens—the U.S. government rates other countries' records on human trafficking and can apply economic sanctions on those that aren't making efforts to improve them. Another piece of legislation, the Protect Act, which Bush signed into law last year, makes it a crime for any person to enter the U.S., or for any citizen to travel abroad, for the purpose of sex tourism involving children. The sentences are severe: up to thirty years imprisonment for each offense.

The thrust of the president's UN speech and the scope of the laws passed here to address the sex-trafficking epidemic might suggest that this is a global problem but not particularly an American one. In reality, little has been done to document sex trafficking in this country. In dozens of interviews I conducted with former sex slaves, madams, government and law-enforcement officials and anti-sex-trade activists for more than four months in Eastern Europe, Mexico and the United States, the details and breadth of this sordid trade in the U.S. came to light.

In fact, the United States has become a major importer of sex slaves. Last year, the CIA estimated that between 18,000 and 20,000 people are trafficked annually into the United States. The government has not studied how many of these are victims of sex traffickers, but Kevin Bales, president of Free the Slaves, America's largest anti-slavery organization, says that the number is at least 10,000 a year. John Miller, the State Department's director of the Office to Monitor and Combat Trafficking in Persons, conceded: "That figure could be low. What we know is that the number is huge." Bales estimates that there are 30,000 to 50,000 sex slaves in captivity in the United States at any given time. Laura Lederer, a senior State Department adviser on trafficking, told me, "We're not finding victims in the United States because we're not looking for them."

ABDUCTION

In Eastern European capitals like Kiev and Moscow, dozens of sex-trafficking rings advertise nanny positions in the United States in local newspapers; others claim to be scouting for models and actresses. In Chisinau, the capital of the former Soviet republic of Moldova—the poorest country in Europe and the one experts say is most heavily culled by traffickers for young women—I saw a billboard with a fresh-faced, smiling young woman beckoning girls to waitress positions in Paris. But of course there are no waitress positions and no "Paris." Some of these young women are actually tricked into paying their own travel expenses—typically around $3,000—as a down payment on what they expect to be bright, prosperous futures, only to find themselves kept prisoner in Mexico before being moved to the United States and sold into sexual bondage there.

The Eastern European trafficking operations, from entrapment to transport, tend to be well-oiled monoethnic machines. One notorious Ukrainian ring, which has since been broken up, was run by Tetyana Komisaruk and Serge Mezheritsky. One of their last transactions, according to Daniel Saunders, an assistant U.S. attorney in Los Angeles, took place in late June 2000 at the Hard Rock Cafe in Tijuana. Around dinnertime, a buyer named Gordey Vinitsky walked in. He was followed shortly after by Komisaruk's husband, Valery, who led Vinitsky out to the parking lot and to a waiting van. Inside the van were six Ukrainian women in their late teens and early twenties. They had been promised jobs as models and baby sitters in the glamorous United States, and they probably had no idea why they were sitting in a van in a backwater like Tijuana in the early evening. Vinitsky pointed into the van at two of the women and said he'd take them for $10,000 each. Valery drove the young women to a gated villa twenty minutes away in Rosarito, a Mexican honky-tonk tourist trap in Baja California. They were kept there until July 4, when they were delivered to San Diego by boat and distributed to their buyers, including Vinitsky, who claimed his two "purchases."

The Komisaruks, Mezheritsky, and Vinitsky were caught in May 2001 and are serving long sentences in U.S. federal prison.

In October, I met Nicole, a young Russian woman who had been trafficked into Mexico by a different network. "I wanted to get out of Moscow, and they told me the Mexican border was like a freeway," said Nicole, who is now twenty-five. We were sitting at a cafe on the Sunset Strip in Los Angeles, and she was telling me the story of her narrow escape from sex slavery—she was taken by immigration officers when her traffickers were trying to smuggle her over the border from Tijuana. She still seemed fearful of being discovered by the trafficking ring and didn't want even her initials to appear in print. (Nicole is a name she adopted after coming to the U.S.)

Two years ago, afraid for her life after her boyfriend was gunned down in Moscow in an organized-crime-related shootout, she found herself across a cafe table in Moscow from a man named Alex, who explained how he could save her by smuggling her into the U.S. Once she agreed, Nicole said, Alex told her that if she didn't show up at the airport, "'I'll find you and cut your head off.' Russians do not play around. In Moscow you can get a bullet in your head just for fun."

Donna M. Hughes, a professor of women's studies at the University of Rhode Island and an expert on sex trafficking, says that prostitution barely existed twelve years ago in the Soviet Union. "It was suppressed by political structures. All the women had jobs." But in the first years after the collapse of Soviet Communism, poverty in the former Soviet states soared. Young women—many of them college-educated and married—became easy believers in Hollywood-generated images of swaying palm trees in L.A. "A few of them have an idea that prostitution might be involved," Hughes says. "But their idea of prostitution is *Pretty Woman*, which is one of the most popular films in Ukraine and Russia. They're thinking, This may not be so bad."

The girls' first contacts are usually with what appear to be legitimate travel agencies. According to prosecutors, the Komisaruk/Mezheritsky ring in Ukraine worked with two such agencies in Kiev, Art Life International and Svit Tours. The helpful agents at Svit and Art Life explained to the girls that the best way to get into the U.S. was through Mexico, which they portrayed as a short walk or boat ride from the American dream. Oblivious and full of hope, the girls get on planes to Europe and then on to Mexico.

Every day, flights from Paris, London, and Amsterdam arrive at Mexico City's international airport carrying groups of these girls, sometimes as many as seven at a time, according to two Mexico City immigration officers I spoke with (and who asked to remain anonymous). One of them told me that officials at the airport—who cooperate with Mexico's federal preventive police (PFP)—work with the traffickers and "direct airlines to park at certain gates. Officials go to the aircraft. They know the seat numbers. While passengers come off, they take the girls to an office, where officials will 'process' them."

Magdalena Carral, Mexico's commissioner of the National Institute of Migration, the government agency that controls migration issues at all airports, seaports and land entries into Mexico, told me: "Everything happens at the airport. We are giving a big fight to have better control of the airport. Corruption does not leave tracks, and sometimes we cannot track it. Six months ago we changed the three main officials at the airport. But it's a daily fight. These networks are very powerful and dangerous."

But Mexico is not merely a way station en route to the U.S. for third-country traffickers, like the Eastern European rings. It is also a vast source of even younger and more cheaply acquired girls for sexual servitude in the United States. While European traffickers tend to dupe their victims into boarding one-way flights to Mexico to their own captivity, Mexican traffickers rely on the charm and brute force of "Los Lenones," tightly organized associations of pimps, according to Roberto Caballero, an officer with the PFP. Although hundreds of "popcorn traffickers"—individuals who take control of one or two girls—work the margins, Caballero said, at least 15 major trafficking organizations and 120 associated factions tracked by the PFP operate as wholesalers: collecting human merchandise and taking orders from safe houses and brothels in the major sex-trafficking hubs in New York, Los Angeles, Atlanta, and Chicago.

Like the Sicilian Mafia, Los Lenones are based on family hierarchies, Caballero explained. The father controls the organization and the money, while the sons and their male cousins hunt, kidnap, and entrap victims. The boys leave school at twelve and are given one or two girls their age to rape and pimp out to begin their training, which emphasizes the arts of kidnapping and seduction. Throughout the rural and suburban towns from southern Mexico to the U.S. border, along what traffickers call the Via Lactea, or Milky Way, the agents of Los Lenones troll the bus stations and factories and school dances where under-age girls gather, work, and socialize. They first ply the girls like prospective lovers, buying them meals and desserts, promising affection and then marriage. Then the men describe rumors they've heard about America, about the promise of jobs and schools. Sometimes the girls are easy prey. Most of them already dream of El Norte. But the theater often ends as soon as the agent has the girl alone, when he beats her, drugs her, or simply forces her into a waiting car.

The majority of Los Lenones—80 percent of them, Caballero says—are based in Tenancingo, a charmless suburb an hour's drive south of Mexico City. Before I left Mexico City for Tenancingo in October, I was warned by Mexican and U.S. officials that the traffickers there are protected by the local police, and that the town is designed to discourage outsiders, with mazelike streets and only two closely watched entrances. The last time the federal police went there to investigate the disappearance of a local girl, their vehicle was surrounded, and the officers were intimidated into leaving. I traveled in a bulletproof Suburban with well-armed federales and an Immigration and Customs Enforcement agent.

On the way, we stopped at a gas station, where I met the parents of a girl from Tenancingo who was reportedly abducted in August 2000. The girl, Suri, is now twenty. Her mother told me that there were witnesses who saw her being forced into a car on the way home from work at a local factory. No one called the police. Suri's mother recited the names of daughters of a number of her friends who have also been taken: "Minerva, Sylvia, Carmen," she said in a monotone, as if the list went on and on.

Just two days earlier, her parents heard from Suri (they call her by her nickname) for the first time since she disappeared. "She's in Queens, New York," the mother told me breathlessly. "She said she was being kept in a house watched by Colombians. She said they take her by car every day to work in a brothel. I was crying on the phone, 'When are you coming back, when are you coming back?'" The mother looked at me helplessly; the father stared blankly into the distance. Then the mother sobered. "My daughter said: 'I'm too far away. I don't know when I'm coming back.'" Before she hung up, Suri told her mother: "Don't cry. I'll escape soon. And don't talk to anyone."

Sex-trafficking victims widely believe that if they talk, they or someone they love will be killed. And their fear is not unfounded, since the tentacles of the trafficking rings reach back into the girls' hometowns, and local law enforcement is often complicit in the sex trade.

One officer in the PFP's anti-trafficking division told me that ten high-level officials in the state of Sonora share a $200,000 weekly payoff from traffickers, a gargantuan sum of money for Mexico. The officer told me with a frozen smile that he was powerless to do anything about it.

"Some officials are not only on the organization's payroll, they are key players in the organization," an official at the U.S. Embassy in Mexico City told me. "Corruption is the most important reason these networks are so successful."

Nicolas Suarez, the PFP's coordinator of intelligence, sounded fatalistic about corruption when I spoke to him in Mexico City in September. "We have that cancer, corruption," he told me with a shrug. "But it exists in every country. In every house there is a devil."

The U.S. Embassy official told me: "Mexican officials see sex trafficking as a U.S. problem. If there wasn't such a large demand, then people—trafficking victims and migrants alike—wouldn't be going up there."

When I asked Magdalena Carral, the Mexican commissioner of migration, about these accusations, she said that she didn't know anything about Los Lenones or sex trafficking in Tenancingo. But she conceded: "There is an investigation against some officials accused of cooperating with these trafficking networks nationwide. Sonora is one of those places." She added, "We are determined not to allow any kind of corruption in this administration, not the smallest kind."

Gary Haugen, president of the International Justice Mission, an organization based in Arlington, Va., that fights sexual exploitation in South Asia and Southeast Asia, says: "Sex trafficking isn't a poverty issue but a law-enforcement issue. You can only carry out this trade at significant levels with the cooperation of local law enforcement. In the developing world the police are not seen as a solution for anything. You don't run to the police; you run from the police."

BREAKING THE GIRLS IN

Once the Mexican traffickers abduct or seduce the women and young girls, it's not other men who first indoctrinate them into sexual slavery but other women. The victims and officials I spoke to all emphasized this fact as crucial to the trafficking rings' success. "Women are the principals," Caballero, the Mexican federal preventive police officer, told me. "The victims are put under the influence of the mothers, who handle them and beat them. Then they give the girls to the men to beat and rape into submission." Traffickers understand that because women can more easily gain the trust of young girls, they can more easily crush them. "Men are the customers and controllers, but within most trafficking organizations themselves, women are the operators," Haugen says. "Women are the ones who exert violent force and psychological torture."

This mirrors the tactics of the Eastern European rings. "Mexican pimps have learned a lot from European traffickers," said Claudia, a former prostitute and madam in her late forties, whom I met in Tepito, Mexico City's vast and lethal ghetto. "The Europeans not only gather girls but put older women in the same houses," she told me. "They get younger and older women emotionally attached. They're transported together, survive together."

The traffickers' harvest is innocence. Before young women and girls are taken to the United States, their captors want to obliterate their sexual inexperience while preserving its appearance. For the Eastern European girls, this "preparation" generally happens in Ensenada, a seaside tourist town in Baja California, a region in Mexico settled by Russian immigrants, or Tijuana, where Nicole, the Russian woman I met in Los Angeles, was taken along with four other girls when she arrived in Mexico. The young women are typically kept in locked-down, gated villas in groups of sixteen to twenty. The girls are provided with all-American clothing—Levi's and baseball caps. They learn to say, "U.S. citizen." They are also sexually brutalized. Nicole told me that the day she arrived in Tijuana, three of her traveling companions were "tried out" locally. The education lasts for days and sometimes weeks.

For the Mexican girls abducted by Los Lenones, the process of breaking them in often begins on Calle Santo Tomas, a filthy narrow street in La Merced, a dangerous and raucous ghetto in Mexico City. Santo Tomas has been a place for low-end prostitution since before Spain's conquest of Mexico in the sixteenth century. But beginning in the early nineties, it became an important training ground for under-age girls and young women on their way into sexual bondage in the United States. When I first visited Santo Tomas, in late September, I found 150 young women walking a slow-motion parabola among 300 or 400 men. It was a balmy night, and the air was heavy with the smell of barbecue and gasoline. Two dead dogs were splayed over the curb just beyond where the girls struck casual poses in stilettos and spray-on-tight neon vinyl and satin or skimpy leopard-patterned outfits. Some of the girls looked as young as twelve. Their faces betrayed no emotion. Many wore pendants of the grim reaper around their necks and made hissing sounds; this, I was told, was part of a ritual to ward off bad energy. The men, who were there to rent or just gaze, didn't speak. From the tables of a shabby cafe mid-block, other men—also Mexicans, but more neatly dressed—sat scrutinizing the girls as at an auction. These were buyers and renters with an interest in the youngest and best looking. They nodded to the girls they wanted and then followed them past a guard in a Yan-kees baseball cap through a tin doorway.

Inside, the girls braced the men before a statue of St. Jude, the patron saint of lost causes, and patted them down for weapons. Then the girls genuflected to the stone-faced saint and led the men to the back, grabbing a condom and roll of toilet paper on the way. They pointed to a block of ice in a tub in lieu of a urinal. Beyond a blue hallway the air went sour, like old onions; there were thirty stalls curtained off by blue fabric, every one in use. Fifteen minutes of straightforward intercourse with the girl's clothes left on cost fifty pesos, or about $4.50. For $4.50 more, the dress was lifted. For another $4.50, the bra would be taken off. Oral sex was $4.50; "acrobatic positions" were $1.80 each. Despite the dozens of people and the various exertions in this room, there were only the sounds of zippers and shoes. There was no human noise at all.

Most of the girls on Santo Tomas would have sex with twenty to thirty men a day; they would do this seven days a week usually for weeks but sometimes for months before they were "ready" for the United States. If they refused, they would be beaten and sometimes killed. They would be told that if they tried to escape, one of their family members, who usually had no idea where they were, would be beaten or killed. Working at the brutalizing pace of twenty men per day, a girl could earn her captors as much as $2,000 a week. In the U.S., that same girl could bring in perhaps $30,000 per week.

In Europe, girls and women trafficked for the sex trade gain in value the closer they get to their destinations. According to Iana Matei, who operates Reaching Out, a Romanian rescue organization, a Romanian or Moldovan girl can be sold to her first transporter—who she may or may not know has taken her captive—for as little as $60, then for $500 to the next. Eventually she can be sold for $2,500 to the organization that will ultimately control and rent her for sex for tens of thousands of dollars a week. (Though the Moldovan and Romanian organizations typically smuggle girls to Western Europe and not the United States, they are, Matei says, closely allied with Russian and Ukrainian networks that do.)

Jonathan M. Winer, deputy assistant secretary of state for international law enforcement in the Clinton administration, says, "The girls are worth a penny or a ruble in their home village, and suddenly they're worth hundreds and thousands somewhere else."

CROSSING THE BORDER

In November, I followed by helicopter the twelve-foot-high sheet-metal fence that represents the U.S.-Mexico boundary from Imperial Beach, Calif., south of San Diego, fourteen miles across the gritty warrens and havoc of Tijuana into the barren hills of Tecate. The fence drops off abruptly at Colonia Nido de las Aguilas, a dry riverbed that straddles the border. Four hundred square miles of bone-dry, barren hills stretch out on the U.S. side. I hovered over the end of the fence with Lester McDaniel, a special agent with Immigration and Customs Enforcement. On the U.S. side, J-E-S-U-S was spelled out in rocks ten feet high across a steep hillside. A fifteen-foot white wooden cross rose from the peak. It is here that thousands of girls and young women—most of them Mexican and many of them straight from Calle Santo Tomas—are taken every year, mostly between January and August, the dry season. Coyotes—or smugglers—subcontracted exclusively by sex traffickers sometimes trudge the girls up to the cross and let them pray, then herd them into the hills northward.

A few miles east, we picked up a deeply grooved trail at the fence and followed it for miles into the hills until it plunged into a deep isolated ravine called Cottonwood Canyon. A Ukrainian sex-trafficking ring force-marches young women through here, McDaniel told me. In high heels and seductive clothing, the young women trek twelve miles to Highway 94, where panel trucks sit waiting. McDaniel listed the perils: rattlesnakes, dehydration, and hypothermia. He failed to mention the traffickers' bullets should the women try to escape.

"If a girl tries to run, she's killed and becomes just one more woman in the desert," says Marisa B. Ugarte, director of the Bilateral Safety Corridor Coalition, a San Diego organization that coordinates rescue efforts for trafficking victims on both sides of the border. "But if she keeps going north, she reaches the Gates of Hell."

One girl who was trafficked back and forth across that border repeatedly was Andrea. "Andrea" is just one name she was given by her traffickers and clients; she doesn't know her real name. She was born in the United States and sold or abandoned here—at about four years old, she says—by a woman who may have been her mother. (She is now in her early to mid-twenties; she doesn't know for sure.) She says that she spent approximately the next twelve years as the captive of a sex-trafficking ring that operated on both sides of the Mexican border. Because of the threat of retribution from her former captors, who are believed to be still at large, an organization that rescues and counsels trafficking victims and former prostitutes arranged for me to meet Andrea in October at a secret location in the United States.

In a series of excruciating conversations, Andrea explained to me how the trafficking ring that kept her worked, moving young girls (and boys too) back and forth over the border, selling nights and weekends with them mostly to American men. She said that the ring imported—both through abduction and outright purchase—toddlers, children, and teenagers into the U.S. from many countries.

"The border is very busy, lots of stuff moving back and forth," she said. "Say you needed to get some kids. This guy would offer a woman a lot of money, and she'd take birth certificates from the U.S.—from Puerto Rican children or darker-skinned children—and then she would go into Mexico through Tijuana. Then she'd drive to Juárez"—across the Mexican border from El Paso, Tex.—"and then they'd go shopping. I was taken with them once. We went to this house that had a goat in the front yard and came out with a four-year-old boy." She remembers the boy costing around five hundred dollars (she said that many poor parents were told that their children would go to adoption agencies and on to better lives in America). "When we crossed the border at Juárez, all the border guards wanted to see was a birth certificate for the dark-skinned kids."

Andrea continued: "There would be a truck waiting for us at the Mexico border, and those trucks you don't want to ride in. Those trucks are closed. They had spots where there would be transfers, the rest stops and truck stops on the freeways in the U.S. One person would walk you into the bathroom, and then another person would take you out of the bathroom and take you to a different vehicle."

Andrea told me she was transported to Juárez dozens of times. During one visit, when she was about seven years old, the trafficker took her to the Radisson Casa Grande Hotel, where there was a john waiting in a room. The john was an older American man, and he read Bible passages to her before and after having sex with her. Andrea described other rooms she remembered in other hotels in Mexico: the Howard Johnson in León, the Crowne Plaza in Guadalajara. She remembers most of all the ceiling patterns. "When I was taken to Mexico, I knew things were going to be different," she said. The "customers" were American businessmen. "The men who went there had higher positions, had more to lose if they were caught doing these things on the other side of the border. I was told my purpose was to keep these men from abusing their own kids." Later she told me: "The white kids you could beat but you couldn't mark. But with Mexican kids you could do whatever you wanted. They're untraceable. You lose nothing by killing them."

Then she and the other children and teenagers in this cell were walked back across the border to El Paso by the traffickers. "The border guards talked to you like, 'Did you have fun in Mexico?' And you answered exactly what you were told, 'Yeah, I had fun.' Runners moved the harder-to-place kids, the darker or not-quite-as-well-behaved kids, kids that hadn't been broken yet."

Another trafficking victim I met, a young woman named Montserrat, was taken to the United States from Veracruz, Mexico, six years ago, at age thirteen. (Montserrat is her nickname.) "I was going to work in America," she told me. "I wanted to go to school there, have an apartment and a red Mercedes Benz." Montserrat's trafficker, who called himself Alejandro, took her to Sonora, across the Mexican border from Douglas, Ariz., where she joined a group of a dozen other teenage girls, all with the same dream of a better life. They were from Chiapas, Guatemala, Oaxaca—everywhere, she said.

The group was marched twelve hours through the desert, just a few of the thousands of Mexicans who bolted for America that night along the 2,000 miles of border. Cars were waiting at a fixed spot on the other side. Alejandro directed her to a Nissan and drove her and a few others to a house she said she thought was in Phoenix, the home of a white American family. "It looked like America," she told me. "I ate chicken. The family ignored me, watched TV. I thought the worst part was behind me."

IN THE UNITED STATES: HIDING IN PLAIN SIGHT

A week after Montserrat was taken across the border, she said, she and half a dozen other girls were loaded into a windowless van. "Alejandro dropped off girls at gas stations as we drove, wherever there were minimarkets," Montserrat told me. At each drop-off there was somebody waiting. Sometimes a girl would be escorted to the bathroom, never to return to the van. They drove twenty-four hours a day. "As the girls were leaving, being let out the back, all of them fourteen or fifteen years old, I felt confident," Montserrat said. We were talking in Mexico City, where she has been since she escaped from her trafficker four years ago. She's now nineteen, and shy with her body but direct with her gaze, which is flat and unemotional. "I didn't know the real reason they were disappearing," she said. "They were going to a better life."

Eventually, only Montserrat and one other girl remained. Outside, the air had turned frigid, and there was snow on the ground. It was night when the van stopped at a gas station. A man was waiting. Montserrat's friend hopped out the back, gleeful. "She said goodbye, I'll see you tomorrow," Montserrat recalled. "I never saw her again."

After leaving the gas station, Alejandro drove Montserrat to an apartment. A couple of weeks later he took her to a Dollarstore. "He bought me makeup," Montserrat told me. "He chose a short dress and a halter top, both black. I asked him why the clothes. He said it was for a party the owner of the apartment was having. He bought me underwear. Then I started to worry." When they arrived at the apartment, Alejandro left, saying he was coming back. But another man appeared at the door. "The man said he'd already paid and I had to do whatever he said," Montserrat said. "When he said he already paid, I knew why I was there. I was crushed."

Montserrat said that she didn't leave that apartment for the next three months, then for nine months after that, Alejandro regularly took her in and out of the apartment for appointments with various johns.

Sex trafficking is one of the few human rights violations that rely on exposure: victims have to be available, displayed, delivered, and returned. Girls were shuttled in open cars between the Plainfield, N.J., stash house and other locations in northern New Jersey like Elizabeth and Union City. Suri told her mother that she was being driven in a black town car—just one of hundreds of black town cars traversing New York City at any time—from her stash house in Queens to places where she was forced to have sex. A Russian ring drove women between various Brooklyn apartments and strip clubs in New Jersey. Andrea named trading hubs at highway rest stops in Deming, N.M.; Kingman, Ariz.; Boulder City, Nev.; and Glendale, Calif. Glendale, Andrea said, was a fork in the road; from there, vehicles went either north to San Jose or south toward San Diego. The traffickers drugged them for travel, she said. "When they fed you, you started falling asleep."

In the past several months, I have visited a number of addresses where trafficked girls and young women have reportedly ended up: besides the house in Plainfield, N.J., there is a row house on Fifty-first Avenue in the Corona section of Queens, which has been identified to Mexican federal preventive police by escaped trafficking victims. There is the apartment at Barrington Plaza in the tony Westwood section of Los Angeles, one place that some of the Komisaruk/Mezheritsky ring's trafficking victims ended up, according to Daniel Saunders, the assistant U.S. attorney who prosecuted the ring. And there's a house on Massachusetts Avenue in Vista, Calif., a San Diego suburb, which was pointed out to me by a San Diego sheriff. These places all have at least one thing in common: they are camouflaged by their normal, middle-class surroundings.

"This is not narco-traffic secrecy," says Sharon B. Cohn, director of anti-trafficking operations for the International Justice Mission. "These are not people kidnapped and held for ransom, but women and children sold every single day. If they're hidden, their keepers don't make money."

IJM's president, Gary Haugen, says: "It's the easiest kind of crime in the world to spot. Men look for it all day, every day."

But border agents and local policemen usually don't know trafficking when they see it. The operating assumption among American police departments is that women who sell their bodies do so by choice, and undocumented foreign women who sell their bodies are not only prostitutes (that is, voluntary sex workers) but also trespassers on U.S. soil. No Department of Justice attorney or police vice squad officer I spoke with in Los Angeles—one of the country's busiest thoroughfares for forced sex traffic—considers sex trafficking in the U.S. a serious problem, or a priority. A teenage girl arrested on Sunset Strip for solicitation, or a group of Russian sex workers arrested in a brothel raid in the San Fernando Valley, are automatically heaped onto a pile of workaday vice arrests.

The U.S. now offers 5,000 visas a year to trafficking victims to allow them to apply for residency. And there's faint hope among sex-trafficking experts that the Bush administration's recent proposal on Mexican immigration, if enacted, could have some positive effect on sex traffic into the U.S., by sheltering potential witnesses. "If illegal immigrants who have information about victims have a chance at legal status in this country, they might feel secure enough to come forward," says John Miller of the State Department. But ambiguities still dominate on the front lines—the borders and the streets of urban America—where sex trafficking will always look a lot like prostitution.

"It's not a particularly complicated thing," says Sharon Cohn of International Justice Mission. "Sex trafficking gets thrown into issues of intimacy and vice, but it's a major crime. It's purely profit and pleasure, and greed and lust, and it's right under homicide."

IMPRISONMENT AND SUBMISSION

The basement, Andrea said, held as many as sixteen children and teenagers of different ethnicities. She remembers that it was underneath a house in an upper-middle-class neighborhood on the West Coast. Throughout much of her captivity, this basement was where she was kept when she wasn't working. "There was lots of scrawling on the walls," she said. "The other kids drew stick figures, daisies, teddy bears. This Mexican boy would draw a house with sunshine. We each had a mat."

Andrea paused. "But nothing happens to you in the basement," she continued. "You just had to worry about when the door opened."

She explained: "They would call you out of the basement, and you'd get a bath and you'd get a dress, and if your dress was yellow you were probably going to Disneyland." She said they used color coding to make transactions safer for the traffickers and the clients. "At Disneyland there would be people doing drop-offs and pickups for kids. It's a big open area full of kids, and nobody pays attention to nobody. They would kind of quietly say, 'Go over to that person,' and you would just slip your hand into theirs and say, 'I was looking for you, Daddy.' Then that person would move off with one or two or three of us."

Her account reminded me—painfully—of the legend of the Pied Piper of Hamelin. In the story, a piper shows up and asks for 1,000 guilders for ridding the town of a plague of rats. Playing his pipe, he lures all the rats into the River Weser, where they drown. But Hamelin's mayor refuses to pay him. The piper goes back into the streets and again starts to play his music. This time "all the little boys and girls, with rosy cheeks and flaxen curls, and sparkling eyes and teeth like pearls" follow him out of town and into the hills. The piper leads the children to a mountainside, where a portal opens. The children follow him in, the cave closes and Hamelin's children— all but one, too lame to keep up—are never seen again.

Montserrat said that she was moved around a lot and often didn't know where she was. She recalled that she was in Detroit for two months before she realized that she was in "the city where cars are made," because the door to the apartment Alejandro kept her in was locked from the outside. She says she was forced to service at least two men a night, and sometimes more. She watched through the windows as neighborhood children played outside. Emotionally, she slowly dissolved. Later, Alejandro moved her to Portland, Ore., where once a week he worked her out of a strip club. In all that time she had exactly one night off; Alejandro took her to see *Scary Movie 2*.

All the girls I spoke to said that their captors were both psychologically and physically abusive. Andrea told me that she and the other children she was held with were frequently beaten to keep them off-balance and obedient. Sometimes they were videotaped while being forced to have sex with adults or one another. Often, she said, she was asked to play roles: the therapist's patient or the obedient daughter. Her cell of sex traffickers offered three age ranges of sex partners—toddler to age four, five to twelve, and teens—as well as what she called a "damage group." "In the damage group they can hit you or do anything they wanted," she explained. "Though sex always hurts when you are little, so it's always violent, everything was much more painful once you were placed in the damage group.

"They'd get you hungry then to train you" to have oral sex, she said. "They'd put honey on a man. For the littlest kids, you had to learn not to gag. And they would push things in you so you would open up better. We learned responses. Like if they wanted us to be sultry or sexy or scared. Most of them wanted you scared. When I got older I'd teach the younger kids how to float away so things didn't hurt."

Kevin Bales of Free the Slaves says: "The physical path of a person being trafficked includes stages of degradation of a person's mental state. A victim gets deprived of food, gets hungry, a little dizzy and sleep-deprived. She begins to break down; she can't think for herself. Then take away her travel documents, and you've made her stateless. Then layer on physical violence, and she begins to follow orders. Then add a foreign culture and language, and she's trapped."

Then add one more layer: a sex-trafficking victim's belief that her family is being tracked as collateral for her body. All sex-trafficking operations, whether Mexican, Ukrainian or Thai, are vast criminal underworlds with roots and branches that reach back to the countries, towns and neighborhoods of their victims.

"There's a vast misunderstanding of what coercion is, of how little it takes to make someone a slave," Gary Haugen of International Justice Mission said. "The destruction of dignity and sense of self, these girls' sense of resignation. . . ." He didn't finish the sentence.

In Tijuana in November, I met with Mamacita, a Mexican trafficking-victim-turned-madam, who used to oversee a stash house for sex slaves in San Diego. Mamacita (who goes by a nickname) was full of regret and worry. She left San Diego three years ago, but she says that the trafficking ring, run by three violent Mexican brothers, is still in operation. "The girls can't leave," Mamacita said. "They're always being watched. They lock them into apartments. The fear is unbelievable. They can't talk to anyone. They are always hungry, pale, always shaking and cold. But they never complain. If they do, they'll be beaten or killed."

In Vista, Calif., I followed a pickup truck driven by a San Diego sheriff's deputy named Rick Castro. We wound past a tidy suburban downtown, a supermall, and the usual hometown franchises. We stopped alongside the San Luis Rey River, across the street from a Baptist church, a strawberry farm, and a municipal ballfield.

A neat subdivision and cycling path ran along the opposite bank. The San Luis Rey was mostly dry, filled now with an impenetrable jungle of fifteen-foot-high bamboolike reeds. As Castro and I started down a well-worn path into the thicket, he told me about the time he first heard about this place, in October 2001. A local health care worker had heard rumors about Mexican immigrants using the reeds for sex and came down to offer condoms and advice. She found more than four hundred men and fifty young women between twelve and fifteen dressed in tight clothing and high heels. There was a separate group of a dozen girls no more than eleven or twelve wearing white communion dresses. "The girls huddled in a circle for protection," Castro told me, "and had big eyes like terrified deer."

I followed Castro into the riverbed, and only fifty yards from the road we found a confounding warren of more than thirty roomlike caves carved into the reeds. It was a sunny morning, but the light in there was refracted, dreary and basementlike. The ground in each was a squalid nest of mud, tamped leaves, condom wrappers, clumps of toilet paper, and magazines. Soiled underwear was strewn here and there, plastic garbage bags jury-rigged through the reeds in lieu of walls. One of the caves' inhabitants had hung old CDs on the tips of branches, like Christmas ornaments. It looked vaguely like a recent massacre site. It was eight in the morning, but the girls could begin arriving any minute. Castro told me how it works: the girls are dropped off at the ballfield, then herded through a drainage sluice under the road into the riverbed. Vans shuttle the men from a 7-Eleven a mile away. The girls are forced to turn fifteen tricks in five hours in the mud. The johns pay fifteen dollars and get ten minutes. It is in nearly every respect a perfect extension of Calle Santo Tomas in Mexico City. Except that this is what some of those girls are training for.

If anything, the women I talked to said that the sex in the U.S. is even rougher than what the girls face on Calle Santo Tomas. Rosario, a woman I met in Mexico City, who had been trafficked to New York and held captive for a number of years, said: "In America we had 'special jobs.' Oral sex, anal sex, often with many men. Sex is now more adventurous, harder." She said that she believed younger foreign girls were in demand in the U.S. because of an increased appetite for more aggressive, dangerous sex. Traffickers need younger and younger girls, she suggested, simply because they are more pliable. In Eastern Europe, too, the typical age of sex-trafficking victims is plummeting; according to Matei of Reaching Out, while most girls used to be in their late teens and twenties, thirteen-year-olds are now far from unusual.

Immigration and Customs Enforcement agents at the Cyber Crimes Center in Fairfax, Va., are finding that when it comes to sex, what was once considered abnormal is now the norm. They are tracking a clear spike in the demand for harder-core pornography on the Internet. "We've become desensitized by the soft stuff; now we need a harder and harder hit," says ICE Special Agent Perry Woo. Cybernetworks like

KaZaA and Morpheus—through which you can download and trade images and videos—have become the Mexican border of virtual sexual exploitation. I had heard of one Web site that supposedly offered sex slaves for purchase to individuals. The ICE agents hadn't heard of it. Special Agent Don Daufenbach, ICE's manager for undercover operations, brought it up on a screen. A hush came over the room as the agents leaned forward, clearly disturbed. "That sure looks like the real thing," Daufenbach said. There were streams of Web pages of thumbnail images of young women of every ethnicity in obvious distress, bound, gagged, contorted. The agents in the room pointed out probable injuries from torture. Cyberauctions for some of the women were in progress; one had exceeded $300,000. "With new Internet technology," Woo said, "pornography is becoming more pervasive. With Web cams we're seeing more live molestation of children." One of ICE's recent successes, Operation Hamlet, broke up a ring of adults who traded images and videos of themselves forcing sex on their own young children.

But the supply of cheap girls and young women to feed the global appetite appears to be limitless. And it's possible that the crimes committed against them in the U.S. cut deeper than elsewhere, precisely because so many of them are snared by the glittery promise of an America that turns out to be not their salvation but their place of destruction.

ENDGAME

Typically, a young trafficking victim in the U.S. lasts in the system for two to four years. After that, Bales says: "She may be killed in the brothel. She may be dumped and deported. Probably least likely is that she will take part in the prosecution of the people that enslaved her."

Who can expect a young woman trafficked into the U.S., trapped in a foreign culture, perhaps unable to speak English, physically and emotionally abused and perhaps drug-addicted, to ask for help from a police officer, who more likely than not will look at her as a criminal and an illegal alien? Even Andrea, who was born in the United States and spoke English, says she never thought of escaping, "because what's out there? What's out there was scarier. We had customers who were police, so you were not going to go talk to a cop. We had this customer from Nevada who was a child psychologist, so you're not going to go talk to a social worker. So who are you going to talk to?"

And if the girls are lucky enough to escape, there's often nowhere for them to go. "The families don't want them back," Sister Veronica, a nun who helps run a rescue mission for trafficked prostitutes in an old church in Mexico City, told me. "They're shunned."

When I first met her, Andrea told me: "We're way too damaged to give back. A lot of these children never wanted to see their parents again after a while, because what do you tell your parents? What are you going to say? You're no good."

CORRECTION

February 8, 2004: An article on January 25 about sexual slavery referred erroneously to the film *Scary Movie 2*. A Mexican woman who was being held as a sex slave in the United States could not have been taken to see it by her captor; by the time the movie came out in 2001, she had already escaped and returned to Mexico.

Editors' Note, February 15, 2004: "The Girls Next Door," an article about the importing of women and girls to the United States for sexual slavery, has generated much discussion since it appeared in

The Times Magazine on January 25. In response to questions from readers and other publications about sources and accuracy, the magazine has carried out a thorough review of the article.

On the issue of sources, the writer, Peter Landesman, conducted more than forty-five interviews, including many with high-ranking federal officials, law enforcement officers, and representatives of human rights organizations. Four sources insisted on anonymity to protect their professional positions. A magazine fact checker also interviewed all relevant sources, many of them both before and after publication. Some readers have questioned the figure of 10,000 enforced prostitutes brought into this country each year. The source of that number is Kevin Bales, recommended to the magazine by Human Rights Watch as the best authority on the extent of enforced prostitution in the United States, who based his estimates on State Department documents, arrest and prosecution records, and information from nearly fifty social service agencies.

In the course of this review, several errors were discovered in specific details. One, an erroneous reference to the release date of *Scary Movie 2*, was corrected in the magazine last Sunday.

On the question whether women imported through Cottonwood Canyon, Calif., could have been wearing high heels, the original source, when pressed, acknowledged that his information was hearsay. The article should not have specified what the women were wearing, and the anecdote should have been related in the past tense, since the trafficking ring was broken up in 2001.

The woman in her twenties known to her traffickers as Andrea recalled an incorrect name for the hotel to which she was taken in Juárez, Mexico. The Radisson Casa Grande had not yet opened when she escaped from her captors.

After the article was published, the writer made an impromptu comment in a radio interview, noting that Andrea has multiple-personality disorder. The magazine editors did not learn of her illness before publication. Andrea's account of her years in slavery remained consistent over two and a half years of psychotherapy. Her therapist says that her illness has no effect on the accuracy of her memory. Her hours-long interview with the author, recorded on tape, is lucid and consistent.

An independent expert consulted by the magazine, Dr. Leonard Shengold, who has written books and papers about child abuse and the reliability and unreliability of memory, affirms that a diagnosis of multiple-personality disorder is not inconsistent with accurate memories of childhood abuse. Because multiple-personality disorder has been associated with false memory, however, the diagnosis should have been cited in the article.

The magazine's cover showed a nineteen-year-old nicknamed Montserrat, who escaped from a trafficker four years ago. An insignia on her school uniform had been retouched out of the picture to shield her whereabouts. The change violated *The Times*'s policy against altering photographs.

You've Got Tail

While the Rise of Internet Dating May Have Brought About a New Era of Sexual Freedom, Most Sites Still Cling to at Least the Pretense of Courtship. Not This One.

By Amy Sohn

New York magazine / May 26, 2003

Not all single people are looking to settle down, and the ones who aren't have finally found their heaven: the Casual Encounters page of online bulletin board Craigslist. If Missed Connections is the side of the dance floor where the wallflowers stare moony-eyed at the popular crowd, then Casual Encounters is the dank, smoky basement where the druggies and sluts party till dawn. Casual Encounters users post ads seeking sex, usually that same day, with come-ons like LET'S GET NAKED IN W'BURG or MUTUAL J/O TO STR8 PORN. Despite all the risks of trolling for sex on the Internet—disease, violence, a spouse who hacks into your e-mail—fans say they're thrilled, relieved to have found a place where a paramour can be at your door in less time than the Shun Lee delivery guy.

Craigslist launched Casual Encounters in New York in April 2002, sensing that people looking for a quick fix needed a haven. "We only introduce new categories when we guess there's a critical mass for them," says founder Craig Newmark. "A lot of people are a lot more interested in something casual than I ever imagined," he says. "And that's okay with me as long as no one gets hurt. Unless they want to be."

Judging by the numbers, interest is soaring. The monthly postings in New York have gone from about 1,000 in April 2002 to 14,400 in March, and the monthly page views have reached 3.2 million.

Not surprisingly, over three quarters of the posts in New York on a recent day were "m4w," men seeking women, with the next most popular group "m4m" (about 10 percent). Until recently, many of the female posters used phrases like "sensual massage" and "happy ending" to indicate that they wanted quid for the pro. In response to repeated complaints that the site was being corrupted (even sex maniacs have limits), Craigslist started a category last month called Erotic Services, for professionals and the men who love them.

Now most of the female posters are "civilians." Debbie, thirty-three, has slept with a few guys she's met on Casual Encounters and likes the efficiency. "It's the lazy man's bar," she says. "I can come home, put my feet up on the couch, go through a couple ads, and have someone in my house shortly. I answered one guy because he was eight blocks from my apartment looking for company, he sent me a photo, and was really cute! Those are the things that matter, that someone's close to you and cute."

Does she feel unsafe with strange men in her apartment? "I have dogs," she says.

She describes herself as "not the most beautiful woman in the world," but says she never had trouble getting laid the old-fashioned way. What she likes about CE is that people's motives are on the table. "What's more hurtful is when you think someone wants more than sex and then you find out they don't."

She's been surprised by how normal the interludes seem. "The guys will come over and have a drink and sit and talk. It's not as awkward as you would expect. And except for the fact that I'll come home late and have casual sex with men I met on the Internet, I'm relatively normal, too."

Lee, twenty-four, a production assistant, began browsing CE posts last summer. One day he saw a post from a woman in the music industry who was looking for a friend. He works at MTV and thought she could be a good contact. She sent a photo, and though he didn't have one, she suggested they meet at Hooters. After beer and chicken wings, they went for a walk in Central Park and wound up on the stage of the Delacorte, where, he says, "it became a stereo-typical casual encounter."

He's met four other women on CE, though Shakespeare in the Park's the only one he slept with. One time after posting an ad, he got a few e-mails from a woman named Adrienne. He gave her his phone number and a little while later it rang. "It was a guy. I asked who it was, and he said, 'I'm Adrian.' I said, 'Oh. I was expecting someone female.' He said, 'I'm bisexual, I hope you're not offended by that.' I told him I was looking for a woman, and he said, 'Well, you should at least give it a try.' I said, 'I'm sorry, my door doesn't swing that way.'"

Neil, a fifty-four-year-old divorced father, first used Craigslist to sell an old Mac. After he posted, he started reading Missed Connections and Casual Encounters for the fun of it. One night he spotted an ad marked "w4m" in which the poster expressed a desire for oral sex and nothing more, and he saw that she lived not far from him, just outside the city. They exchanged photos, and he was happy to find she was attractive and over forty.

Over the next few days, they exchanged explicit e-mails. "She was very clear that all she wanted to do was have cunnilingus performed. I said I had to have kissing too, and she said she wasn't sure. The e-mails were whimsical, humorous, and sexual." They spoke on the phone and arranged to meet at a cocktail lounge. He requested she not wear underwear. She obliged.

"She was smart, charming, and gorgeous," he says. "After drinks, we went to the car. There was a lot of heavy touching, and there were orgasms involved." They've gone out twice since then. "I have yet to do what she asked, but only because it's not that easy in a car."

When Neil asked why she agreed to meet him, she told him he was among the first responders. His proximity helped, too. "She had answered a few others, and they had turned out to be jerks, but the thing that really interested her was that I lived so close. I told her I thought she was brave, and she said she based it on instinct." He thinks they'll continue to see each other, though neither is looking for a relationship.

Neil partied a lot in the eighties, and even went to Plato's Retreat a few times, but says this casual encounter was very different. "We are both adventurous and cosmopolitan people, but we are not people who are living on the edge. We have responsible lives, we did this, and it was fun. We're not wild. She's a single working woman, and I'm a single working father of two."

Do his kids know he's dating someone he met in a place called Casual Encounters? "They know I met her on the Internet," he says. "To them, it's totally normal."

from *Skipping Towards Gomorrah*

By Dan Savage

The sexually liberated student putting herself through college working as an escort has become something of a cliché. The old prostitute stereotype—a drug addiction, tenth-grade education, track marks, bad skin, a dozen STDs, an abusive boyfriend—has been replaced by this newer, more user-friendly stereotype. Patronizing a prostitute seems a little less opportunistic if your money is helping to put someone through school, which will ultimately get her out of the business altogether. So I was a little disappointed to find that Emily, the New York City escort I rented my first night in town, was not a film student at Columbia or getting her master's in social work at New York University. She was, Emily said, "just a ho."

"I find that putting-myself-through-college line tedious," said Tracy Quan, author of the novel *Diary of a Manhattan Call Girl*, and a member of Prostitutes of New York (PONY), an advocacy group that is seeking to decriminalize prostitution. "Most of the pros I've known were not going to college," said Quan. "Most of the pros are materialistic, very attractive girls who liked to shop. Girls putting themselves through Columbia don't make very good prostitutes.

They're usually badly groomed, they don't know how to dress, they don't really like what they're doing. The people who are really good at this are the ones who decide to make it their career."

Emily was definitely making it her career. A college dropout from New Mexico, Emily got into the business after she followed her rock-star-wannabe boyfriend to New York City. Her boyfriend's band broke up shortly after they arrived in New York in 1997, and she refused to return to New Mexico with him. Emily had fallen in love with the city and couldn't imagine living anywhere else ever again. When he went back to New Mexico, she stayed behind in New York, and within a few months she was working full-time as an escort.

"It was the only way I could afford the rent on the studio apartment we used to share," Emily told me over cocktails in the crowded bar of a crowded hipster hotel. "Once he moved, I had to make a lot of money or get a roommate, and I didn't want a roommate."

Emily didn't work for an agency, she didn't have a pimp, she wasn't a streetwalker, and she didn't work in a brothel. Instead, Emily paid a friend to maintain a Web site for her, which is where I found her. In my hotel room, the day I arrived in New York, I plugged in my laptop computer and logged on to my Internet service provider. Then I typed "Manhattan," "Female," and "Escort" into a search engine. I had somewhere in the neighborhood of fifteen thousand Web sites to choose from, and I spent some time surfing around before I found Emily's Web site. Her site had a few pictures, some tasteful nude shots, and a cell-phone number. I liked Emily's pictures: she didn't have big hair, wasn't wearing a ton of makeup, and didn't look like someone escorting out of desperation or against her will. There was also a disclaimer: "What my clients buy is my time," it said. "If anything happens during our time together, we're just two consenting adults with a professional relationship who happened to hit it off. It happens in offices and at workplaces all over the country every day."

Emily was expensive, however. She charged five hundred dollars an hour with a three-hour minimum. Why so expensive?

"I'm beautiful and charming and fun," her bio read. "You probably pay at least that much to talk to your lawyer. And you're lawyer isn't nearly as beautiful. Or fun . . ."

I called Emily, expecting to leave a message on an answering machine, so I was a bit flustered when Emily answered the phone. For some reason I was worried that Emily might not see me if she realized I wasn't interested in her for the same reasons her other clients were. I didn't want to have sex with Emily; I really did just want to buy her time. I was looking for an escort, not a euphemism.

"Is it okay if we just go out and have dinner, see a show? And nothing else happens?" I asked.

"We don't have to do anything you don't want to, Dan," she said in a soothing voice. "Is this your first time using a service like this?"

"Yes," I said.

"You should know that the time we spend together is your special time," Emily said. "I'm there for you. Things can go just as slow or just as fast as you want them to. Nothing has to happen." She asked for my first and last name and the name of my hotel; then she hung up and called me back at my hotel to make sure I was really a guest. That's when she reminded me that her time cost five hundred dollars an hour. She would also be happy to make dinner reservations at a nice place near my hotel, if I didn't have a place picked out already. I told her to go ahead and make a reservation.

"I'll meet you in the bar in the lobby of your hotel at six," she said. "Does that sound good?"

That sounded fine.

"If we meet and I'm not quite what you wanted," she said in an I've-said-this-a-thousand-times tone of voice, "you don't have to pay me. Cab fare back home would be nice, but it's not necessary." If I wasn't into her, I should say so within ten minutes, and she would leave, and there would be no hard feelings on her end. If I made her uncomfortable, or my personal hygiene was poor, she would say so within ten minutes, and she asked that there be no hard feelings on my end. If I wanted her to join me for dinner, I would need to hand her an envelope with $1,500 dollars in it for the first three hours. If I didn't have cash, she could take a credit card but would have to do it now, over the phone, and the charge would have to be approved before she came to the hotel. If things didn't work out, all but fifty dollars of the charge would be removed from my Visa bill.

Before we got off the phone, Emily asked what I would be wearing. I was confused. Did it matter what I was wearing? I'd seen her picture, so I knew what she looked like. I'd be able to spot her in the bar—

"I only ask because you said you want to go out to dinner and a show," Emily explained. "If you're in jeans and a sweatshirt and I show up looking like I'm on my way to the Golden Globes, we're going to make a pretty conspicuous couple. And if you're in a suit, you don't want me showing up looking like I'm ready to go clubbing."

I told Emily that I would be wearing what I've been wearing all of my life—jeans, a T-shirt, tennis shoes, and a jeans jacket.

"I'll dress down," she said. "See you in the lobby bar at six."

I almost fainted when Emily walked into the lobby two hours later.

The hotel's bar was, surprisingly enough, overrun with businessmen and hipsters, and I decided to wait for Emily in the lobby instead. I was sitting in a ridiculous oversize chair just outside the bar when she came through the doors. She was a stunningly beautiful woman—the pictures on her Web site didn't do her justice—with nary a track mark in sight. Emily's legs were longer than the Oscars. She was wearing jeans and a tasteful little top held up by spaghetti straps, and carrying a metallic silver jeans jacket. The jacket sounds trashy on the page, but in person it was just the right amount of flash. She looked like Cameron Diaz on her way to a club, which is to say, Emily was a total fucking knockout—a steal at five hundred dollars an hour.

I didn't wait for the ten minutes to pass; I handed her the envelope with fifteen one-hundred-dollar bills in it, which she tucked into the pocket of her jeans jacket, which I had to compliment her on.

Talk about your New York miracles—I'd been in town for less than four hours, and a beautiful woman had just been delivered to my hotel. If I were straight, this would have been the night of my life.

"Let's get a drink," Emily said, strolling into the bar.

I didn't go to New York City simply to sin and to defy Osama bin Laden and his Islamo-fascist pals. I was also in New York because Jerry Falwell pisses me off.

Falwell's comments after the terrorist attacks made me angry, and I wasn't alone; Falwell caught hell for his remarks, even from good ol' Diane Sawyer on *Good Morning America*. On some level, though, I was secretly thrilled by Falwell's remarks. By attempting to pin the blame for the attacks of September 11 on the American Civil Liberties Union, abortion-rights groups, pagans, gay men and lesbians, and federal judges, Falwell not only exposed himself for what he was (hateful, divisive, mean-spirited), but he also exposed Christian fundamentalism for what it is (hateful, divisive, mean-spirited). Thanks to Falwell, millions of Americans realized that Christian fundamentalists hate all the same things about the United States that the Islamic fundamentalists hate: liberated women, sexual freedom, secular culture, fundamental human rights. After Falwell opened his fat trap on the *700 Club,* people in the political center had to admit that the Falwells and Robertsons were, as John McCain dubbed them during the Republican primaries in 2000, "agents of intolerance." (McCain was slammed by the media for that bit of straight talk.)

After September 11, reasonable Americans could no longer pretend that all men of faith were harmless do-gooders. The nineteen hijackers were men of faith, and in their own twisted minds, they meant well—they thought they were doing God's work, just as Falwell thinks he's doing God's work. Osama bin Laden, if he's still alive somewhere, is a man of faith. John Walker, aka the American Taliban, is a man of faith.

Maddeningly, right-wing pundits have attempted to paint Walker, a religious conservative, as a hot-tubbing Marin County, California, liberal. "We need to execute people like John Walker in order to physically intimidate liberals, by making them realize that they can be killed, too. Otherwise they will turn out to be outright traitors." That comment by psychoconservative writer, commentator, and supposed "babe" Ann Coulter was greeted with cheers at the Conservative Political Action Conference in Washington, D.C., in February of 2002.

Fascist isn't a word that I toss around lightly—I can't stand lefties who cry fascist every time a Republican or a police officer enters the room—but that's the only word that accurately describes Coulter's politics. What's revealing about her comments and the comments of so many other right-wing pundits is their burning desire to convince us that Walker is some sort of liberal. Excuse me, but Walker didn't embrace the Marin County's live-and-let-live liberalism. Walker rejected Marin County's liberal ethos in favor of an intolerant, ranting, raving "faith." What's more, Walker and his co-religionists hate all the same things Falwell hates: liberated women, secular culture, homosexuals, religious freedom.

In the case of both Walker and Falwell—and in the case of September 11—faith wasn't the solution to the problem, faith was and is the problem. "If we believe absurdities," Voltaire said, "we will commit atrocities." On September 11, Islamo-fascists, heads stuffed with absurdities, committed the most appalling atrocities. It was religious fanaticism that brought down the World Trade Center, not secularism, and a murderous intolerance inflamed by hate-mongering clerics. Falwell did a real public service by reminding Americans immediately after the attacks that the Islamic world doesn't have a monopoly on religious hatred and fanaticism, nor does the Islamic world have a monopoly on hateful clerics.

It isn't just religious fanaticism that drives young Islamic males to become suicide bombers. It's also sex—or the want of it.

"In the sight of Allah, the ones who died are the lucky ones," a Pakistani Muslim told the *New York Times* in reference to the September 11 terrorists. "They have gone to paradise now, with all the pleasures they have been promised in the Koran. Now they will have girls, and wine, and music, and all the things forbidden to them here on earth. Now they will be happy, as we who remain can never be on earth."

One of the unexamined aspects of the September 11 attacks was the role that sexual deprivation played in turning young men into mass murderers. Fifteen of the nineteen hijackers on September 11 came from Saudi Arabia, "a theocratic kingdom that bans dating, cinemas, concert halls, discotheques, clubs, theaters, and political organizations," the *New York Times* reported. In Saudi Arabia, "religion and tradition prohibit unmarried men and women from mixing." Is it any wonder that a certain number of young men in places like Saudi Arabia—where all educational system is all Islam, all the time—will resent people who enjoy all the things that their religion and government forbid?

Like the puritan haunted by the fear that somewhere, someone is happy, the Islamo-fascist is haunted by the fear that somewhere, someone is enjoying the lap dances and the dates and the discos and everything else that his religion forbids him—at least until he gets to heaven. Once he gets to heaven, *then* he can have all the lap dances and dates and black-eyed virgins he can handle, on just one little condition: He has to die a martyr, which he can do by blowing himself up in an Israeli pizza parlor or flying a plane into the World Trade Center.

"The fundamentalist seeks to bring down a great deal more than buildings," Salman Rushdie wrote in the *Washington Post* on October 2, 2001. "Such people are against, to offer just a brief list, freedom of speech, a multi-party political system, universal adult suffrage, accountable government, Jews, homosexuals, women's rights, pluralism, secularism, short skirts, dancing, beardlessness, evolution theory, sex. . . ." The Islamic fundamentalists, Rushdie continued, don't think Westerners believe in anything. "To prove him wrong, we must first know he is wrong. We must agree on what matters: kissing in public places, bacon sandwiches, disagreements, cutting-edge fashion, literature, generosity, water, a more equitable distribution of the world's resources, movies, music, freedom of thought, beauty, love. These will be our weapons."

Reading Rushdie's comments after September 11 inspired me.

Fuck Falwell, fuck Coulter, fuck bin Laden, fuck Walker, fuck fundamentalism, fuck Islamo-Fascism, and fuck plain ol' Fascism. Committing the sin of anger in New York City would be easy— much easier than it had been in Texas. Blasting away at paper targets at the Bullet Trap in Plano didn't make me feel angry; if I committed a single sin at the Bullet Trap it was probably the sin of pride. I couldn't wait to get home and show my friends what a good shot I was, or to indulge my newfound skill at a slightly closer-to-home shooting range. (Have I mentioned what a good shot Paul, my instructor, thought I was?) In New York City, however, I had anger down.

"Why, I wondered, were not more of us angry [after the attacks on September 11]?" William Bennett asked in his quickie post-9/11 book, *Why We Fight: Moral Clarity and the War on Terrorism.* "Why did so many, especially the county's elite, seem to back away from any hint of righteous anger?"

Huh? Why weren't more of us angry? Everyone I knew was angry, and everywhere I went I met angry people. But according to Bennett, only a small number of right-thinking conservatives could see that the War on Terrorism was necessary and just. In the same essay in which he dubbed Bennett, Bork, and Buchanan "scolds," Andrew Sullivan expressed frustration with the right's inability to take yes for an answer. "As the country becomes more conservative," Sullivan wrote, "the right sees liberalism everywhere."

In *Why We Fight,* William J. Bennett can't bring himself to take yes for an answer. There's a reason peace rallies after September 11 were sparsely attended. The overwhelming majority of Americans agreed with Bill Bennett. We said yes. But Bennett and his fellow scolds could only see a resolve-sapping pacifism stoked by leftie cultural critics. Admittedly, some of what the left pumped out immediately after

September 11 was idiotic, just as the comments of Jerry Falwell and Pat Robertson were idiotic. Americans were not, however, led down the primrose path by Susan Sontag, Katha Pollitt, and Edward Said. Thoughtful, angry lefties were marching in lockstep with Christopher Hitchens, not Noam Chomsky. We wanted to bomb bin Laden with bombs, and not, as Toni Morrison suggested, love.

"Little schoolchildren in our country are routinely taught to believe that America represents but one of many cultures [and] that there is no such thing as a better or worse society," Bennett fumes at the end of *Why We Fight*. Even Americans who believe Western society and culture is superior to that of, say, Saudi Arabia are afraid to speak up, "[because] saying so can get you into trouble."

Hell, Bill, I'll speak up: Western culture—liberal democracy, representative government, universal human rights—is superior to Saudi culture. Far superior. Personally, I would rather live in a country where I can buy a drink, kiss a guy, and rent a hooker without risking a public beheading—and like the overwhelming majority of Americans after September 11, I was angry at the people who wanted to take those things away from me, be they Bennett's enemy bin Laden or Bennett's buddy Jerry Falwell.

I had never been out on an adult-style date with a woman before. When I was growing up in Chicago, I dated some girls under duress, but those dates didn't take place in hipster bars and expensive restaurants. We were teenagers on the north side of Chicago in the mid-eighties, so our dates took place in bowling alleys and fast-food restaurants. I felt awkward on those teenage dates because I was dating them only so I could tell my friends and family that I had been on a date with a girl. With Emily I felt awkward because I wasn't worthy. Even if I had played her particular sport, she was still way out of my league.

It was a little after six o'clock when we arrived at the bar, in a short lull between after-work drinkers and the early evening partiers. Emily and I found a couple of seats together at the bar. There were a lot of men in the bar around my age, and these men looked at me—me in my jeans and T-shirt and tennis shoes—and quickly concluded that I wasn't worthy. What was an incredibly beautiful woman like Emily doing out on a date with a schmo like me? If I were a few decades older, and wearing a suit, like most of Emily's customers, they would have assumed she was attracted to older, more powerful men (or attracted to their money), and therefore not a woman they had any chance of getting for themselves. But since she was with me, a poorly dressed guy around their age, the men in the bar assumed they all had a shot. Not only did they have a shot, but I had a woman I clearly didn't deserve, and they would be doing her a favor by taking her from me.

I could sense the envy emanating from the clumps of youngish men in their business suits, ties loosened or hanging out of their suit jacket pockets. It was fun to be envied, but there was an undercurrent of—well, of violence. Here and there in the bar the men were glaring at me, as if I had something that belonged to them, which in a way I did.

Emily and I were talking about New York—about the attacks, what else—when one of the other men in the bar decided to do something about his envy. He strolled up to us and stood right behind our bar stools until we turned and looked at him.

"How are you guys doing tonight?" he asked. He was a good-looking guy, bigger than I was. He had a big smile but very small teeth, and his smile exposed two parallel lines of healthy, bright pink gums. He introduced himself and then asked me who I was.

"Are you this lovely lady's big brother?" Jim said. "Or are you her coworker?"

Jim laughed. Loud. The big brother/coworker question was supposed to be a joke, I guess. Emily laughed, but her laugh began after his did and ended before. She was being polite, deferential, upbeat.

"No, we're on a date," she said, gesturing towards me but—hey!—beaming at Jim!

Jim looked me up and down; then he looked back at Emily. "Where you from?" he said, turning to me.

"Seattle," I said.

"Shit, I thought all the dot-com boys had gone broke!" He laughed and put his hand on the bar between me and Emily, separating us. Then he turned his back to me. "Those guys didn't know how to run a business, and they never knew how to dress," he said, laughing his loud, mean laugh.

"He's probably spending the last of his stock options to take someone like you out on a date." Then he handed Emily his card. "Give me a call if things don't work out with the Microsofty here."

He stared at me when he called me a softy, smiling his big gummy smile. I think he wanted me to hit him. His gummy smile said, "I'm picking up on your date right in front of you, and what are you going to do about it?" He was clearly an alpha-male type, and I suppose he expected me to challenge him for alpha position, which I refused to do. I like to think of myself as an alpha male—all men do, don't they?—but I wasn't up for getting into a fistfight over a *woman*. Now, if he had attempted to steal my collection of show tune CDs, well, then I would've laid him flat. But Emily? He could take her off my hands for fifteen hundred bucks.

Jim lingered for a second, looking at me. I grinned at him, playing dumb. If he wanted to have a fistfight, he would have to throw the first punch. He gave me an angry, imploring look. It was as if he thought I was doing something wrong by not holding up my end of the deal. He seemed to think I was obligated to hit him so that he could hit me and win the girl.

"Let's go get something to eat," Emily said, taking my hand. Turning to Jim, she said, "It was great to meet you."

"Give me a call sometime," Jim said to Emily. "See you around, softy."

Emily had made reservations at a restaurant a block from the hotel.

"It's my favorite restaurant," she said. "I'm sure you'll love it."

Emily's favorite restaurant was also one of New York City's more expensive restaurants—and it was on me, of course; high-priced call girls don't go dutch. While we ate, I couldn't help but contemplate the sinfulness of paying someone five hundred dollars an hour to eat incredibly expensive food in her favorite restaurant. What sin is this? I wondered to myself while we ate small rounds of goat cheese that cost more than twenty-five dollars each. Was it greed on Emily's part for making reservations in such a pricey place? Was she getting a kickback from the restaurant? Or was it gluttony, even with tiny portions? Later in the evening, the same thoughts would flit through my head as we sat watching a hit show that's almost impossible to get tickets to—a show I would wind up paying Emily five hundred dollars an hour to watch. What sin is this? Greed on her part? Or stupidity on mine?

During the walk to the restaurant, I confessed everything—writer, doin' research, not interested in "hitting it off"—because my pride wouldn't allow me to let Emily think I was a coward. I didn't want her to think what I'd done in the bar, or hadn't done in the bar, made me somehow less of a man. I wasn't afraid of Jim, I lied. I was taking her to dinner and a show to pick her brain, not her booty, and anyway I wasn't the kind of guy who gets into drunken fistfights over women. Emily nodded. She'd picked up on that the moment we met in the lobby.

"Usually when I meet a man at his hotel the first thing out of his mouth isn't, 'Wow, I *totally* love your jacket.' "

While she would normally shoot down any guy who tried to pick her up when she was with a client ("Clients appreciate that"), Emily thought the guy was pretty cute, she liked aggressive men, and she didn't think it would bother me. After all, I liked her jacket.

The restaurant she took me to was one of those hushed places, where the tables are incredibly close together, making it nearly impossible to have a private conversation; it was the kind of restaurant where white, well-off New Yorkers gather to discuss the cartoons in that week's issue of *The New Yorker.* The food was tremendous, and we ordered quite a lot of it; yes, this was definitely gluttony. There were only four other couples in the restaurant the night we went, and we were off in a corner by ourselves, which made it possible for me and Emily to talk shop.

"Business has been way off," Emily confided. "Not for the twenty-dollar blow-job crowd—their clients are local. But the vast majority of my clients are rich businessmen from out of town or overseas. They haven't been coming to New York City, obviously, so for me business is way, way down. It's been hard."

While Emily's business may have been down after September 11, PONY's Quan said that wasn't necessarily the case for other New York City prostitutes.

"I don't know very many prostitutes who rely very much on tourists for their income," said Quan. "Anyone who makes their living as a prostitute is looking to have regular clients, who tend to be local. Tourists are not regular clients. When people are being tourists, they're often traveling with someone, like their family. That doesn't make seeing a prostitute very easy."

Business travelers, however, do make good clients. "Business travel was way off after September 11," said Quan, "and prostitutes who do most of their trade with business travelers were losing money. Higher-end, three- and four-hundred-dollar-an-hour prostitutes had the most to lose. I also know some people who had clients that died on September 11."

Emily's business was gone, she said, because before September 11 she had carved out a niche serving Japanese and Taiwanese businessmen ("They adore—and will pay a lot for—tall blondes!"), and they weren't coming to town. She had an established group of regular clients, and she had stopped advertising her services. A few weeks after September 11, she was forced to put her Web site back up.

"I needed to get some new clients," she said, "some men who didn't have to fly to the city to see me."

Emily was everything she claimed to be in her Web site—beautiful, fun, charming, sexy. Emily wasn't a student, however, and this came as a shock to me. I was so invested in the paying-my-way-through-college-escort stereotype that I assumed Emily was doing postgraduate work somewhere or other.

"How long do you plan to keep doing this?" I asked. "If you're not going to school, what do you plan on doing when you get out of this line of work?"

Emily set her spoon down—we were working on desserts by this point—and shot me a disapproving look.

"Why would I get out of this line of work?" she said. "I'm making good money, and I live really well in the greatest city on earth. I work a few hours a night, three or four nights a week, and I have the rest of my time to myself."

"But you won't always make good money doing this," I replied. "Gravity comes for everyone."

She shrugged, then cracked her lavender crème brûlée with her spoon. In the first two years she was escorting, Emily sank every cent into a two-bedroom condo, which she now owned outright.

"Whatever happens, I'll always have a place to live."

What will she do for income when she gets older?

"I don't know. Maybe I'll do domination work," she said. "I'll set up a dungeon in my extra bedroom. There's good money in that, and you can do that until you're fifty."

"So you're happy doing what you're doing indefinitely?"

"I'm a ho. I like being a ho. Are you happy doing what you're doing indefinitely?"

"Yeah, but I don't have to see people naked or—"

"Or what?"

"I don't have to have sex with people I'm not attracted to."

"You're beginning to annoy me a little," Emily said, smiling at me, a singsong lilt in her voice. "I just want to get that on the table. I mean, do you know how many married women have sex with someone they're not attracted to every time they have sex with the husband? And what makes you think I automatically have sex with people?"

"Uh, the naked pictures? The hints on your Web site?"

"I don't have sex with anyone I don't want to have sex with. Men buy my time, that's all, and what—"

"—what happens between two consenting adults is perfectly legal."

"If I'm with a man I find attractive, something might happen. If I'm not attracted to him, nothing happens."

"Don't the guys expect it, though? Don't they get angry if you don't put out?"

"I guess you could say I'm attracted to a lot of different kinds of men. I would do you, for instance, even though you're not really my type."

"Well, if you had a dick," I said, "I'd definitely be into you."

"Thanks, I wouldn't be into you in a nonprofessional context," Emily continued, turning the spoon. She cocked her head to one side and squinted at me, as if she were trying to picture me naked. "No, I'm very much into muscular men, especially men who are at least a few inches taller than I am. That's what I love, and it's hard to find."

How big? How muscular?

"I like that classic V shape, a lot of muscle, no facial hair. Big, ripped guys, without an ounce of fat, but a little rough around the edges. The guy I moved here with looked like Henry Rollins. He thought he was Henry Rollins, too, but he only looked like him. That's my type. My current boyfriend is six-six and all muscle."

I asked Emily if her boyfriend minded the line of work she was in. She shrugged as she scooped up the last of her crème brûlée with her spoon.

"Why should he mind?" Emily said. "He's in the business himself."

It was almost midnight when the show ended. Emily walked me back to my hotel, and thanked me for dinner and the show. Then she informed me I owed her another fifteen hundred dollars, since we'd been together six hours. We had to leave the hotel to find a cash machine. I had hoped Emily might not charge me for the three hours we spent watching a hit show, but times were tight. ("I promise to put your money into my IRA," Emily joked, "so that you don't have to worry about me when I'm old.") By the time I got back up to my room, I had calculated just how much money I'd dropped into New York City's battered economy since arriving in the city eight hours earlier: $500 for the hotel room, $200 for theater tickets, $200 for

dinner, $40 for drinks in the bar, $30 for a cab from the airport; and
$3,000 for Emily—$3,970 total. I didn't pay any state or local sales
taxes on most of the money, since the lion's share of it went to
Emily, and Emily is officially part of the underground economy. But
the money I gave her had to surface sooner or later. When Emily
spent my $3,000 on food, clothes, and her condo's monthly dues,
she would be paying taxes.

When I got up to my room after saying good-bye to Emily and
three thousand of my publisher's dollars, I opened up my laptop
computer and began to search for Emily's boyfriend.

During intermission at the theater, I pumped Emily for info about
her boyfriend. I was fascinated by the concept of coming to New
York and renting both halves of a straight couple. They had been
seeing each other for a little more than a year, Emily told me. He was
six feet six, white, with dark black hair and blue eyes, and he com-
peted in "natural" body-building contests (no steroids).

"Are his clients women?" I asked.

Emily looked at me like I was from Mars.

"Brad does gay work," she said. "I wouldn't want him seeing
women. Anyway, there's no money in women." Her boyfriend wasn't
bi, she explained. He was a straight guy and a body builder who
made money letting gay men worship his body—but that's all. Just
worship, no sex.

"The gay guys he sees usually just beat off while they're with him,"
Emily said. "He poses, flexes. He's huge. Two hundred and forty
pounds, all muscle," said Emily. "All he does is muscle worship. Gay
guys pay him to let them feel his muscles, kiss his biceps, his calves.
That's all he does with them. No sex whatsoever."

Emily and Brad met through a friend, a gay neighbor of Emily's
who was a regular client of Brad's. As a loyal customer over a period

of years, Richard had come to know Brad pretty well. Richard paid
Brad two hundred dollars a week for the privilege of washing his
gym clothes by hand; with Brad dropping by once or twice a week
to drop off and pick up his gym clothes, he and Richard had
become friendly. When Emily moved into the condo next door, she
also got to know Richard. Soon they were friends, and in their conversations about men Richard discovered that he and Emily shared a
passion for big, muscular guys. Richard didn't know that Emily was
an escort when he threw a small party in his apartment with the sole
purpose of introducing Emily and Brad. The couple didn't find out
they were both escorts until a few months into the relationship.
Another New York City miracle: A boy escort and a girl escort are
set up on a blind date by a gay male client of the boy escort—it
sounds like Nora Ephron's next movie. Brad eventually moved in
with Emily, and as a token of appreciation, Brad no longer charged
Richard for the honor of washing his gym clothes.

I wasn't really into muscle guys, but the idea of renting the
boyfriend of the escort I'd been with all night, well, it was too deli-
cious to pass up. If Brad was anything like Emily—who was beautiful and, once I stopped trying to be her career counselor, charming
and delightful—I wanted to get to know him. And who knows?
Maybe I was into muscle guys and I didn't know it. ("It's not until
you run your hands over someone supersized that you can appreciate
how wonderful all that flesh feels," the FA at the NAAFA convention
told me.) Since I've always been into skinny, bookish guys, I'd never
really had cause to run my hands over a guy with a lot of muscles.
Maybe an hour with Brad would change my mind.

It took a couple of hours, but I finally found an ad for a guy who
fit Brad's description on a male escort Web site: "Live your fantasy.
6'6", 240 lbs. ripped. I'm the straight guy at the gym you're always

staring at. Massive, rock-hard, ripped abs, huge guns. Model looks, great face. $200 IN/$250 OUT. Muscle worship only. No sex." I called and left a message. Early the next morning I got a call from Brad. He had an hour free late Saturday night. If I wanted the "in" price, I would have to go to his apartment, or he would come "out" to my hotel for $250.

Halfway through my weekend in New York City, I'd managed to commit five of the seven deadly sins. Anger, as I said, was easy; it was the reason I came to New York. Greed was taken care of by Emily's outrageously high fees. (Although I will admit that Emily was better looking than my lawyer, as advertised.) Gluttony was the outrageously expensive meal with Emily; envy in the form of the reaction of Jim, the man in the bar who wanted to get into a fistfight and run off with my very expensive date. Pride was my feeble attempt to explain to Emily why I didn't punch Jim in the bar, and lust, well, that would be taken care of by Brad, who would be coming to my hotel room late Saturday night.

I had just one sin left to tackle before Brad came by and took care of lust: sloth. I took a nap after Brad called, and that might have counted towards sloth, but napping did nothing to pump money into New York City's battered economy. I would have to be more proactively slothful. So I got up, got dressed, and headed down to the East Village to kill some time and score myself some of that leafy, green sloth the kids like so much.

I have a friend who lives on East Twelfth and Avenue A, and I often stay at his place when I come to New York. Walking around his neighborhood, men mutter "weed, weed," under their breath at passersby.

It was dark when I got to the East Village, and as I walked by Tompkins Square Park, a black guy in a satin Yankees jacket and an

FDNY baseball hat walked past me muttering, "weed, weed, weed." I'd never said anything but "no, thanks," to weed mutterers before, so I wasn't sure how to initiate or close the sale. In fact, as I walked around the park, I found myself dwelling on the fact that I had never once purchased pot in my life. To satisfy my rather minimal need for pot, I had always relied on the kindness of a few potheaded friends, all of whom seemed more than happy to give me marijuana for free. I think my potheaded friends are amused by how little it takes to get me high; again, I didn't start smoking pot until I was in my thirties, and I've never smoked enough to develop much tolerance for the stuff. I wondered for a moment if I might get arrested buying pot on the streets of New York. Then I figured that New York City's police department had better things to do right now than come between New York City's potheads and their pursuit of happiness.

"I'd like some weed," I said to the man in the baseball jacket. He looked at me, long and hard.

I began to panic. Did I say the right thing? What if he was a cop? What if I said the wrong thing and he decided to gun me down, drug-deal-gone-bad style?

"How much you want?" the man finally said.

I had planned to spend three hundred dollars on pot—I intended to get New York City's underground economy roaring!—but being a novice pot buyer, I didn't anticipate the reaction my request would get.

"Three hundred dollars' worth," I said.

"What you need so much for?" the mutterer said, looking pissed. "You a cop?"

"No," I said, "not a cop. You a cop?"

"No, I'm not a cop. What you need so much for? You settin' me up?"

Ah, I got it. If I was a cop, and I could get him to sell me a *lot* of pot, he might get sent away for a long stretch of time.

"I . . . uh . . . just need a lot of pot. I'm buying it for my friends. And me. They smoke a lot of pot, you see, so I need to get . . . a . . . lot."

"You a cop," the mutterer said, "you a damn cop."

The mutterer walked around the corner, off Avenue A, and onto East Fourteenth Street. I thought the deal was off and was about to split when the mutterer looked over at me and said, "You buying pot or not?" I walked around the corner. He asked me to show him the money. I pulled three hundred-dollar bills out of my pocket.

"You not a cop?" he asked again.

"Not a cop."

"How much you want?" he asked. I was confused by the question; hadn't I already indicated to the gentleman that I required three hundred dollars of his finest marijuana? In my confusion, I said the wrong thing:

"How much pot can I get for three hundred dollars?"

In retrospect, my mistake was so frigging obvious it makes my head hurt. I basically told the pot dealer that I had no idea how much pot three hundred dollars buys. Now he knew that I didn't know what I was doing. Since the sale of marijuana isn't regulated by the New York City Department of Consumer Fraud, Weights and Measures Division, I would have no one to complain to if he fleeced me.

"Okay," he said, "three hundred dollar' worth." He made a show of taking three bags of pot out of his pocket. He held out his left hand. I handed him three hundred dollars; he handed me the three bags of pot.

At my friend's apartment ten minutes later, I pulled out my three "hundred-dollar" bags of pot. I'd been had, Sean laughed. His friendly neighborhood pot dealer charged me three hundred dollars for three twenty-five-dollar bags of pot. I didn't feel like getting high (I didn't want to be fucked up when I met Brad at my hotel), and I told Sean that I would leave it all for him on one condition: He had to smoke a little of my very expensive pot, just to test it out. I wanted to know if I'd been completely had; I was overcharged, and I could live with that. But was it pot at least?

Sean smoked some in a little pipe, then sat back in his chair at his kitchen table and waited a minute or two. Then he smiled.

"Good news. This is *excellent* pot," Sean said. "You may have been overcharged, but you weren't ripped off."

Apparently some dealers by the park keep pot in one pocket to sell to locals and bags of chopped-up bay leaves in another to sell to tourists.

"They figure half the tourists don't know what pot looks like, and he's never going to see them again anyway," Sean said. "He probably sold you the real stuff because he thought he might see you again. So look at it this way: You got ripped off, but at least the guy who ripped you off didn't think you were a tourist. He thought he might see you again. He thought you were a New Yorker. Isn't that worth the extra two hundred twenty-five dollars?"

"Look at these muscles, faggot," Brad said, one hand on the back of my head. "Faggot, look at these muscles. You could never have muscles like this. No faggot could. Yeah, you're a fucking faggot. I'm a man. A real man. You? You're a faggot. Faggot. Faggot."

Brad was slowly dragging my face across his massive chest as he called me a faggot, moving my face into one armpit, then onto his biceps, down his side, across his abs, and back to his other armpit. Then he ran my face through the whole upper-body circuit again. Brad was everything Emily told me he was—huge, gorgeous, a little rough—and while his demeaning you're-a-fucking-faggot rap probably qualified as a hate crime in New York City, the tone of his voice was oddly tender. He murmured the insults as if they were sweet nothings, which to some of his clients they no doubt were.

Brad didn't want to meet in the lobby; he preferred to come right to my room. I tried to watch some television while I waited for Brad to come to my room, but I couldn't concentrate on *Saturday Night Live.* (Tina Fey rules.) My heart jumped out of my chest when Brad knocked on the door. He told me to leave the money on the table by the bed, which I did, and he smiled and said hello as he came into the room. I expected him to pick up the money right away, but he didn't seem to notice it sitting on the nightstand. He was wearing black sweats, a black T-shirt, and a pair of running shoes, and his black hair was a little longer than it looked in his pictures. He walked to the middle of the room, looked out the window, then turned around and pulled his shirt over his head, tossing it on the end of the bed. He stood there for a second, letting me take him in, all rippling shoulder muscles, abs, and pecs. He slapped his abs with his hands and then held his hands out, palms up, as if to say, "Solid, huh?" I was transfixed—but not by lust, unfortunately. Brad was about as far from my type as men get; I like slightly sissy guys. Brad, towering over me, was none of those things. He was massive, a human SUV.

Brad reminded me that he was straight, and that he only did muscle worship. Then he asked me what I wanted to do—and he called me *dude.*

Oops. I didn't have a game plan. All I really wanted to do was meet Emily's great big boyfriend, pump a little money into New York City's underground economy, and piss off a few fundamentalists. I was satisfied just to see him with his shirt off. But he was mine for an hour, and I had to fill the time, so I explained that all my boyfriends had been shorter than I was and skinnier than I was, which was true. Then I lied and told Brad that I was curious what a big, muscular body felt like. I didn't want to get naked, I said, I just wanted to run my hands over him.

"Mostly," I said, "I just want to feel you up, I guess. I've never really worshiped muscles, so I'm not sure how that's done. Is it okay if I just feel them?"

"It's your hour, dude," said Brad. "I just came from the gym. I can take a quick shower if you like, and you can watch. Some guys like that; we can even shower together. Or if you like, we can do this with me all sweaty. Your call, dude."

I hesitated.

"It's good, clean sweat, dude. I don't smoke or drink, so my sweat is clean. Dudes tell me all the time that they dig it."

I opted to watch him take a shower, hoping it would kill fifteen or twenty minutes. He looked amazing naked, and I was amazed that this sort of beauty could be ordered up to my hotel room like a bucket of ice. He was one of those body builders with hugely broad shoulders but a very narrow waist. Like Emily, breathtaking. Richard deserves all the dirty laundry he can handle for bringing these two young people together.

Unfortunately, Brad was in and out of the shower in about five minutes. He invited me to dry him off. I demurred. I plopped down on the end of the bed, and when Brad came out of the bathroom he was wearing a clean pair of underwear. He walked to the edge of the bed, stood right in front of me, and began to flex and pose.

"Come on," he said. "Feel my body, dude. You know you want to."

Actually, I didn't want to—but I didn't want Brad to know that I didn't want to, so I began running my hands over him. He was male, and he was beautiful, but he was so far from my type that running my hands over his chest and shoulders and arms wasn't having much of an effect on me. Brad felt like an enormous armoire that someone had stretched turkey skin over, popped in the oven and roasted to a golden brown. I wasn't turned off, but I wasn't turned on. I was thinking to myself, Shit, do I really have to stand here like an idiot running my hands over this guy for the next fifty minutes?

I broke the law pumping money into New York City's underground economy. What I did with Emily probably wasn't illegal, but what I did with Brad—or what Brad was about to do to me, I should say—definitely was. There were 2,598 arrests made for prostitution in New York City in 1998, according to the New York State Uniform Crime Report. The average big-city police department spends 213 workhours a day enforcing laws against prostitution. In Los Angeles in 1993, one city official estimated that the ineffective enforcement of his city's prostitution laws was costing the city $100 million a year. In the city where I live, the police department seems much more interested in setting up prostitution stings than catching violent criminals. And why not? "You get up in a penthouse at Caesar's Palace," Las Vegas vice cop told the *Vancouver Sun*, "with six naked women frolicking in the room and then say 'Hey, baby, you're busted!' " Compared to regular police work, "busting prostitutes is fun."

The urge to alter consciousness is as old as humanity itself, as Salim Muwakkil points out, and so, too, is buying and selling sex. Prostitution has been and always will be with us, so, the only rational argument about prostitution is not, "Shall we allow it or ban it?" but "How shall we make this thing that we can't stop less harmful and less dangerous for all involved?" Every problem moralists and virtuecrats cite as an argument for keeping prostitution illegal—violence, disease, child prostitution—is a problem that is either created or made worse by keeping prostitution illegal.

In Australia, where brothels are legal, a street hooker is eighty times more likely to have an STD than a woman who works in a brothel. In the Netherlands, where prostitution is legal, the rate of STDs among prostitutes is no higher than the rate of STDs in the general population. Edinburgh, Scotland, decriminalized prostitution, which is now permitted in public baths, which are licensed and regulated as places of "public entertainment." Streetwalking is permitted on particular streets in Edinburgh where hookers have plied their trade for centuries. After decriminalization, prostitution did not expand into other areas, as some predicted, and the health, social, and crime problems associated with prostitution actually decreased.

The owners of licensed bathhouses in Edinburgh are required to keep drugs out to hold on to their licenses, and they can't abuse or exploit the women who work in them very easily since those women can now take their complaints to the police without fear of being arrested themselves. In the areas where streetwalking is allowed, there's a policewoman on duty who works with the girls; as a result, prostitutes are subjected to much less violence in Edinburgh than they are in Glasgow, where it remains illegal.

Following Edinburgh's example, England is moving towards legalization, as is Germany. Even the Jesuit magazine *La Civiltà Cattolica* has come out in favor of decriminalizing and regulating brothels, which were closed in Italy in 1958.

"Dude, what gives?" Brad asked, breaking out of his pose.

What gives?

"You a cop, dude?"

This was the second time tonight that someone asked me if I was cop, and I laughed, further killing the mood Brad was trying to create. I had to explain to Brad that I laughed because I didn't think I looked much like a New York City cop.

"I'm sorry," I said, "I'm just not sure what I was supposed to be doing. I've never done this muscle-worship stuff before."

"Tell you what, dude," Brad said. "I'll take the lead. I'll do what most guys like, all right?"

All right.

"I'm going to be a little rough with you, okay?"

Okay.

That's when Brad grabbed the back of my neck and began steering my face around his upper body and calling me faggot. (It was better than being called dude.) Brad's body hair must have been thick and black, like the hair on his head, because there was stubble all over his body, and after my face took a few spins around his torso, I had a nasty whisker burn.

"You know what I want you to do, faggot?" Brad said, pulling my face out of his armpit.

"Uh . . . no, what do you want me to do?"

Brad wrapped his arm around my head, and holding on to my hair pulled my face up to his while at the same time flexing his biceps, which pressed into my jaw.

"I want you to get down on the floor and kiss my feet." Okay . . .

"And I want you to call me a god, you faggot, while you kiss my fucking feet," Brad said, still holding my face up to his.

"Okay," I said, thinking, Okay . . . just . . . let . . . me . . . go . . . and . . . I'll . . . do . . . it. . . .

He pulled my face away from his and, keeping hold of the back of my neck, pushed me all the way down on the floor. I kissed his feet. I called him a god—ah, so this must be muscle *worship*, I thought to myself. Now I get it. Brad was aggressive, just like Emily liked her men. I wasn't embarrassed about worshiping Brad, or kissing his feet, although it's a little embarrassing to reread this story up to this point—and we're not even to the really weird stuff yet.

When I sat back on my legs and looked up at Brad, he had an erection, which was a lot more than I had. Brad looked down at me— way down—and smirked. Then he pulled his dick out of his underwear, whispered *faggot*, closed his eyes, and began to beat off.

This is some fucked-up shit, I thought to myself, and I was momentarily overwhelmed by feelings of guilt. It was less than a month since the attacks, and not fifty blocks away they were still pulling bodies out of the wreckage of the World Trade Center, and here I was goofing around in a hotel room with a big, straight, body-building, object-of-muscle-worship escort. It felt—oh, I dunno— somehow disrespectful. But all Brad was doing was what the president asked us all to do—go about our business. Maybe if this scene were turning me on, I thought, maybe if running my hands over the flesh of someone who looked like Brad were my favorite thing, I would've gotten turned on and, like all turned-on people, I might have forgotten about everything else in the world for the duration of our time together. If this scene with Brad represented "getting back to normal" to me, maybe it wouldn't feel so wrong.

But was it wrong? People all over the country were having "terror sex," as the papers dubbed it, hooking up with strangers in bars and going back to their apartments. Churches also filled up in the days immediately after the attacks, but so did bars and nightclubs. ("I believe that Americans are a virtuous people," wrote Ken Connor, president of the Family Research Council, in Reverend Moon's the

Washington Times. "Our nation uniquely aspires to virtue. It is our national purpose and has been since its founding. This is why, since that terrible Tuesday morning, we Americans have returned to our foundational virtues [and] filled our churches.") Two months later, however, church attendance was back down to its pre–September 11 levels, but terror sex was stilt roaring. In February of 2002, *USA Today* reported under the headline, SKIN AND SIN ARE IN! that floor shows featuring naked women were returning to the stages in Las Vegas. Clearly the triumphalism of the virtuecrats and the scolds and conservative pundits after September 11 was premature. We were at war, it was a just war, and we were winning that war. But the nation wasn't being remade in the image of the Family Research Council.

I also wasn't the only tourist in New York City checking out the men on the weekend of October 5 through 7. While I cavorted in New York with Emily and Brad, 972 tourists from Oregon were in New York to show their support for the city. Nancy and Ken Bush (no relation to the Bushes of D.C., Maine, Florida, and Texas) came to New York on the "Flight for Freedom" tour organized by an Oregon travel agency, and they didn't sit around their hotel room feeling glum—that wasn't what Mayor Giuliani and Senator Schumer wanted them to do.

"We were frustrated by the attacks and wanted to do something to help," Nancy Bush told a reporter from the *New York Daily News.* What did they do? Nancy went shopping, went out to dinner, and caught a performance of *The Full Monty,* the Broadway musical about a troupe of male strippers. If Nancy Bush could come to New York to check out a half a dozen naked guys and feel patriotic about it, why shouldn't I feel patriotic about renting Brad?

"Kiss my feet, faggot," Brad said, bringing his right foot up to my neck, and using it to push my head down to his left foot. "Kiss my fucking feet, faggot. Faggot. Faggot."

I can take a hint. I went back to kissing Brad's feet. I was fully clothed, but Brad wasn't, having kicked off his underwear by this point. You notice strange things when you're waiting for someone else to finish up. While I was kissing Brad's feet, I noticed that there were little copper-colored dots in the royal-blue carpet. Then I noticed a quarter on the floor under the desk. Kissing Brad's right foot, I noticed he had stubble on his big toe. Apparently he shaved his toes, just like he shaved his chest, arms, and stomach. Then I kissed his left foot and—hey, what do you know!—his right big toe had about three dozen long, black hairs on it. One shaved toe, one nonshaved toe. Weird.

"Faggot," Brad said, breathing pretty heavily. "You're a faggot. What are you, faggot?"

"I'm a faggot?" I said, thinking, You're the one beating off, and I'm the faggot?

"That's right, you're a faggot. And what am I?"

"You're a god." You're beating off, and you're a god.

"That's right, I'm a—"

And Brad came.

There was an awkward pause. Brad stood there, breathing and shivering. I didn't know what I was supposed to do. Could I get up now? Or was I supposed to wait for permission to stop kissing his feet? Since Brad was so much bigger than I was, I decided to stay down on the floor until he gave me further orders.

"Hey, dude, thanks," Brad finally said, stepping back and pulling his foot out from under my face. "You can get up."

I walked to the bathroom and got Brad a towel so he could clean off his abs. Brad asked if I wanted to get off, and I took a pass. What I wanted to do, I said, was ask him a few quick questions.

"Fire away, dude."

First, what's with the unshaved right toe? Brad laughed and explained that he has a client who pays him for the honor of shaving his body. This particular client likes to leave the hair on one of Brad's toes so that he can fantasize about how different Brad's body would look if it wasn't kept shaved.

Listening to this, I had a you've-got-to-be-kidding look on my face.

"Dude, I know, it's freaky. But it pays the rent. That's not even the strangest guy I see," he said. "My next-door neighbor used to pay me to let him do my laundry. I see another guy who pays me to watch his TV and ignore him and drink his beer, only he wants me to walk up to him every once in a while and punch him in the stomach as hard as I can. This is a freaky business."

Okay, speaking of freaky: I'm the gay client, you're the straight escort. You had an orgasm, I didn't. Why were you turned on by what we were doing?

"It's a trip, dude." Brad laughed. "I didn't dig it at first, guys worshiping me. Ninety percent of the guys I see want me to call 'em fags and kiss my feet and call me a god. After a while, I don't know, it started to turn me on. I mean, there's another man kissing my feet. Some other guy is so intimidated by my body that he'll do whatever I tell him to. I guess humiliating other guys makes me horny."

Brad suddenly reminded me of Jim, the man in the bar the night before, the alpha male who tried to pick up Emily right in front of me. He was definitely straight, but he seemed to enjoy humiliating other men. Renting Emily allowed me to commit two of the seven deadly sins, gluttony and greed, and I had planned on renting Brad so that I could commit the sin of lust. It seemed ironic that it was Brad, a man who is about ten thousand times better looking than I am, who committed the sin of lust in my hotel room. Oh, I had sinned; by kissing Brad's feet and calling him a god, I had inspired a kind of semidetached lust in his heart, making myself the occasion of sin. He didn't lust after me; he was straight, after all. What turned him on, what he lusted after, wasn't who I was but what I was doing.

Brad was dressed now and heading out to see another client.

"He's a regular," Brad said.

Anything freaky?

"No," Brad said, "not really. Pretty much what we just did."

Brad walked to the door, snagging the money from the nightstand on his way. He tucked the money into a pocket on the side of his gym bag, and then turned to face me.

"Last chance for a feel, dude," he said, holding his arms out, smiling.

I wish I could write something like, "I took a pass," or, "Having learned so much about myself already, I didn't feel the need to further violate Brad," or "I looked at Brad and said, 'STOP CALLING ME "DUDE," YOU FUCKING MEATHEAD!' " Sad to say, I wanted my money's worth, and I figured I wasn't going to have the chance to run my hands over someone who looked like Brad ever again, so . . . I copped one last feel. It actually felt better to run my hands over his body with his clothes on; I couldn't feel the stubble on his chest and stomach, and he wasn't tensing his muscles, which made him feel a little more like a human being and less like an armoire.

I removed my hands from the nice man and thanked him for his time.

Brad opened the door and stepped into the hall. "See you around, faggot," he said, winking. Then he turned and walked down the hall towards the elevators. After I shut the door, I lay down on the bed and looked at the clock. Brad had been in my room for almost two hours. I was touched. While Emily had insisted I pay her to eat dinner and watch a play, Brad was too much a gentleman to insist that I pay him to have an orgasm.

Okay, *now* I was completely sinned out. I'd done my patriotic duty, and all I wanted now was a little legitimate room service. I found the menu in my room and ordered myself a bacon sandwich. As I lay in yet another hotel room looking out my window at yet another American Gomorrah, it occurred to me for the first time that there was a Bible in every hotel room I'd stayed in while I ran around sinning my brains out, thoughtfully provided by the Gideon Society.

Somehow despite the biblical reference in the title of this book and, of course, the book that inspired it[1] (I wanna give a shout out to my homey Bobby Bork), and despite all the reading I was doing while I worked on this book (I may be the only unreformed sinner in America who has plowed through the complete works of Messrs. Bork, Bennett, and Buchanan), I hadn't thought to sit down and reread the biblical story of Sodom and Gomorrah. I went to my nightstand, opened the drawer, and pulled out a familiar looking Gideon Bible, with its red cover and gold embossing.

The story of the destruction of Sodom and Gomorrah, "the cities of the plain," appears in Genesis chapters 18 and 19. Biblical scholars who aren't grinding the Bible-as-word-of-God ax theorize that the story of the destruction of two cities most likely derives from a pre-Israelite folk tale, perhaps recalling a volcanic catastrophe. Or, shit, maybe the same aliens who built the pyramids nuked the place. Who knows? In early Jewish and early Christian literature, Sodom and Gomorrah are held up as examples of sin and the destructive wrath of God. The story in Genesis takes place in the city of Sodom, but we never get to go inside Gomorrah, so we don't know if Gomorrah had a lot of trendy cafés, a lively performance art scene, and an alternative weekly newspaper—all features of our modern American Gomorrahs. The Bible doesn't have a lot to say about Sodom either, only that the city had "gates."

So what exactly were the people of Gomorrah up to? We first hear about the rumors of their sinfulness in Genesis 18.20, when God says to Abraham, "How great is the outcry against Sodom and Gomorrah and how very grave their sin!" The Hebrew word translated as "sin" is *z'aqa* which implies violence or injustice, not sexual depravity.

Still, when two angels visit Lot in Sodom—Lot being Sodom's only stand-up guy—a crowd gathers outside Lot's home: "The men of Sodom, both old and young, all the people from every quarter, surrounded the house." The men of Sodom wanted to "know" the angels, and Lot refused to hand God's messengers over to the men of Sodom. Instead Lot offered them his daughters: "I have two daughters who have not known a man; please, let me bring them out to you, and you may do to them as you wish; only do nothing to these men." (Lot may have been the only decent guy in Sodom, but I can't imagine he was ever named Father of the Year.) The fact that *all* the men of Sodom demanded that Lot release the two angels to them emphasizes the collective guilt of the entire city.

Here's an interesting fact: Nowhere in the story of the destruction of Sodom and Gomorrah are the men of Gomorrah mentioned. They don't crowd around Lot's house, demanding to "know" the visiting angels. Maybe there was a pride parade in Gomorrah that night—or a rap concert or a swingers' convention or a riverboat casino was opening—and the men of Gomorrah couldn't tear themselves away. On this point, the Bible is silent.

While the men of Gomorrah were up to God only knows what (and God, the Bible's author, isn't telling), it's clear that the men of Sodom wanted to subject the strangers at Lot's place to a mob rape. Many scholars believe that the account emphasizes the social aspect of the sin of Sodom, rather than the sexual aspect. The men of Sodom desired to humiliate and dehumanize the strangers, not enjoy sexual pleasure with them. The men of Sodom were breaking the sacred law of hospitality, since the angels are Lot's guests, and a good host isn't supposed to let his guests come to harm. (Lot's daughters, on the other hand . . .) Since the men of Sodom are such pricks, God decides to destroy both cities, "raining brimstone and fire on Sodom and Gomorrah, from the Lord out of his heavens."

By no stretch of the imagination is the United States of America "slouching towards Gomorrah." We may have a lot of those trendy cafés, performance art spaces, gay bars, and alternative weekly news-papers, and while we tolerate a huge number of things specifically forbidden in the Bible (shellfish, bacon, cheeseburgers, leg-shaving, divorce, adulterers, uncircumcised males, gays and lesbians, and so on), we *don't* tolerate the kind of mob violence that any unbiased reading of the Sodom and Gomorrah story reveals to be God's beef with the citizens of those doomed cities. The sinners of Sodom and Gomorrah, unlike modern American sinners, weren't content to sin with other sinners and leave virtuous Lot and his virtuous daughters and those virtuous angels the hell out of it. The men of Sodom sought to impose their sinful ways on Lot's guests, to violate and humiliate them, to "know" them in the biblical sense. (Picture an episode of HBO's *Oz* crossed with CBS's *Touched by an Angel*.) The people of Sodom and Gomorrah went from tolerably wicked in God's eyes to I'm-going-to-nuke-this-place wicked when they attempted to force their sins down the throats (or up the butts) of unwilling participants. (If the men of Sodom had contented themselves with raping Lot's virgin daughters, God might have spared the place.) While the men of Sodom and Gomorrah (and the children and women, too, I assume, since God destroyed them along with any unborn children the women were carrying at the time) were sinful, it wasn't until they tried to impose their sins on others that God pressed the button.

As I said at the beginning of this book, modern American sinners don't attempt to impose their sinful ways on their fellow Americans. We may do things that are injurious to ourselves—eat too much, gamble too much, fuck too much, shoot too much—but if it makes us happy, that's our right, and, remember, we were endowed with that right by our Creator, and our founding fathers saw fit to enshrine that right in our nation's founding document. Anyone who strives to deprive his or her fellow Americans of their right to pursue happiness is not only violating the original intent of founding fathers, *but also flying in the face of God.* (Take that, Alan Keyes!) As much as it annoys the virtuecrats and talk-show moralists, the American sinners have the same rights to life, liberty, and the pursuit of happiness as any other American. Bork, Bennett, and Buchanan are free to believe that our pursuit of happiness is sinful, just as we are free to believe that their virtues are vastly overrated.

Unlike Andrew Sullivan, I'm not convinced that the paleoconservative scolds are on their way out. Indeed, I think they're going to be with us for a long, long time. As I write these words, Patrick Buchanan's *Death of the West* remains on the *New York Times* bestseller lists, and books by his fellow scolds dot Amazon.com's Top 100 list. There are apparently a huge number of Americans, registered Republicans all, who never seem to tire of being told that they live in a morally bankrupt shithole; these people will keep American virtuecrats and scolds in book deals and speaking gigs for the rest of their natural lives. Isn't it odd how the same conservatives who complain about "blame America first" lefties never challenge the "nothing nice to say about America" paleoconservatives?

Books by virtuecrats and scolds go on for three or four hundred pages about what a shithole this country is—this Gomorrah, this moral sewer, this dismal state, these morally collapsed United States—but they all end with a paragraph or two of uplift. Bork, Bennett, and Buchanan all hold out hope at the end of their books. If she heeds the call of the virtuecrats and the scolds, America can right herself: ". . . The blessings of marriage and family life are indeed recoverable," Bennett writes at the end of *The Broken Hearth*. "If we do our part, there is reason to hope that those blessings may yet again be ours."

"We have so much to be thankful for," Buchanan writes at the end of *Death of the West*. "And while no one can deny the coarseness of her manners, the decadence of her culture, or the sickness in her soul, America is still a country worth fighting for and the last best hope of earth."

"We have allowed [our nation] to be severely damaged," Bork writes at the end of *Slouching Towards Gomorrah*, "but perhaps not beyond repair. As we approach the desolate and sordid precincts, the pessimism of the intellect tells us that Gomorrah is our probable destination. What is left to us is a determination not to accept that fate and the courage to resist it. . . ."

Like Bork, Bennett, and Buchanan, I'd like to end with a few hopeful words. Unlike Bork, Bennett, and Buchanan, I'm not tacking a few hopeful words onto the end of four hundred pages of "this place sucks," "moral sewer," "slouching towards Gomorrah," or "what a dump." I don't think my country is a shithole. Indeed, I agree with Buchanan that America is the "last best hope of earth," and, like Bennett, I believe the United States is worth fighting for—these United States—not some 1950s era dream of the United States. The country worth fighting for is the big, messy, complicated, diverse, fascinating place the United States is right now. What makes the United States the envy of the world (besides Hooters and Krispy Kremes, of course) is that this is a nation where full citizenship has nothing to do with race, religion, sex, political persuasion or, yes, personal virtue. Good or bad, religious or irreligious, male or female, left or right, of color or washed out—we're all Americans.

This is a country where the culture evolves and remains vibrant because people are free to challenge the existing order. The right to life, liberty, and the pursuit of happiness means that each of us is free to go our own way, even if the ways some of us may choose to go seem sinful or shocking to some of our fellow citizens. America is at its best when our freedom to go our own way is restricted only when, as Thomas Jefferson said, "[our] acts are injurious to others."

So like Bork, Bennett, and Buchanan, I have hope. I hope that people who disagree with the scolds and the virtuecrats will go right on ignoring them; I hope that our drug laws will one day be changed to reflect reality; I hope that more people who want to cheat on their spouses will do so with their spouses' permission; and I hope to one day spot Bill O'Reilly at a gay pride parade in heels and a bra. I hope that Americans who find happiness in sinful pursuits will always be able to exercise their God-given right to gamble, swing, smoke, eat, shoot, march, spend, and procure. And I hope that the Borks, Bennetts, and Buchanans will one day recognize that their right to pursue happiness as they define it is not threatened by the right of their fellow Americans to pursue happiness as we define it. It's a big country, after all, with plenty of room for saints and sinners alike.

DAN SAVAGE

I. Here's my brother Bill on the title: The source for Bork's title is probably as much Joan Didion's *Slouching Towards Bethlehem* as it is Didion's course, W. B. Yeats's poem "The Second Coming," which includes this line: "And what rough beast, its hour come round at last. Slouches towards Bethlehem to be born?" Didion's book of essays on the cultural revolutions of the sixties uses this phrase because of the sense people had that the world was changing, and Bork, by shifting the tile to another less happy city, implies that America is changing for the worse.

But all of this imagery is profoundly un-American if you look at its roots. Yeats believed things were going to hell in a handbasket because he thought history was cyclical, and at the end of our current 2,000-year-cycle we'd be plunged into a new dark age. His evidence for this coming dark age was the decline of the aristocratic order of the world, particularly his Anglo-Irish ascendancy, as Irish Catholics ousted the British. So when this phrase gets used by folks who claim to be all-American, they're really showing up their inborn elitism. Just as the Borks of the world seem not to have read the Sodom and Gomorrah story, they haven't read the poem they're alluding to either.

226

The Expurgation of Pleasure

By Judith Levine
from *Harmful to Minors*

> It is dangerous to suggest to children, as certain books do,
> that there is any pleasurable sensation resulting from
> manual manipulation of the organs, for the force of sug-
> gestion or curiosity has led some children to experiment
> with themselves until they formed the habit.
>
> —Maurice Bigelow, *Sex-Education* (1916)

In 1989, reviewing the definitions of healthy teenage sexuality that
she had collected from hundreds of professionals over the years, the
veteran progressive sex educator Peggy Brick noticed "a profound
gap in adult thinking about adolescent sexuality. Several concepts
central to human sexuality [were] missing," she said, "notably
pleasure, sexual satisfaction and gratification, and orgasm. Even
adults who discount the usefulness of 'just say no' are unlikely to
advocate good sex for teens."[1] In 1994, SIECUS reported that fewer
than one in ten courses mentioned anything about sexual behavior,
and only 12 percent of sex-ed curricula "suppl[ied] any positive
information about sexuality" at all.[2]

Around the same time as Brick was lamenting the arid state of sex educators' thinking, sociologist Michelle Fine was observing it in practice in city high schools. Struck, too, by what wasn't there, Fine wrote an article in the *Harvard Educational Review* called "Sexuality, Schooling, and Adolescent Females: The Missing Discourse of Female Desire." The piece showed how the official line of sex ed was that girls want love but they'd rather not have sex, and that they consent to sex only as a ruse to attain love. Because this quest was presumed to put girls at risk of exploitation by callow boys and caddish men, classroom conversation concerned itself exclusively with female victimization, sexual violence, and personal morality. On the rare occasion female desire did come up, it was only a "whisper" emerging from the girls as "an interruption of the ongoing [official] conversation."[3] Symptomatic of the problem it was critiquing, for years Fine's article remained the only citation on the subject of desire in the sex-educational literature.

Nothing much has changed in a decade. While desire swirls around teens in every aspect of the popular culture and social life, in the public school curricula it is still a "hidden" discourse. But this hiding, paradoxically, makes desire very much the subject of sex education. Any half-awake student knows what to infer from all those lessons about chlamydia and early fatherhood: desire and pleasure are dangerous and teens must learn how to keep them resolutely at bay.

A near-universal classroom exercise consists of students "brainstorming" the reasons kids might have sex ("Uh . . . to get a better grade in biology?"). Almost every curriculum includes a printed list of such reasons, similar to that of "Will Power/Won't Power," the Girls Incorporated's abstinence-plus program for girls twelve to fourteen. Whereas the abstinence-only curricula recognize only reprobate reasons for sex, "Will Power" offers motivations both authorized and condemned: "to communicate warm, loving feelings in a relationship; to keep from being lonely; to get affection; to show independence by rebelling against parents, teachers or other authority figures; to hold on to a relationship; to show that they are 'grown up'; to become a parent; to satisfy curiosity."[4] Not on this list or almost any other: to have pleasure.

While these texts teach that sex is compelled by emotional need and social pressure, the body they represent is that of puberty and reproduction—one of sprouting hair, overactive oil ducts, egg-shedding uteruses, and wiggling zygotes. In them, physical desire is an animal response to increased hormone production and the species' imperative to preserve itself; at the same time, it is represented as an intellectual and emotional response to powerful propaganda: MTV made me do it. The closest the texts come to recognizing the body of longing and sensation is to deem "sexual feelings" and "curiosity" natural or normal (a small minority tell students that some people are attracted to people of the same sex, usually leaving it to the students to decide whether such a taste is natural or normal). But the ways such feelings might be experienced physically are rarely described; they remain elusive, almost metaphysical. The deletions create a bizarrely disjoint sense of sexuality's relationship to the body. A student might know what ejaculation is and be able to catalogue the sexually transmitted bugs that can lurk in semen but never have discussed orgasm in class. She may come away expert in the workings of the vas deferens, yet ignorant of the clitoris.

Curiously, while most curricula overlook desire or pleasure as a reason to have sex, and while the physical signs of desire are rarely addressed, all classes supply students with a repertoire of "refusal skills" and "delaying tactics" to combat the urge, along with plenty of time to rehearse them in structured role playing. (These tactics don't inspire much confidence in this skeptical observer. ETR's

"Reducing the Risk," for example, suggests chewing a cough drop to prevent deep kissing and, to cool down a heated moment, leaping up to exclaim, "Wow, look at the time!")[5] Desire, when acknowledged, is as often as not someone else's or that of the crowd, which seeks not pleasure but, rather, conformity. "Peer pressure" is uniformly high on the list of reasons to have sex.

As for gender, the abstinence-only curricula continue to exhibit what Michelle Fine described a decade ago: the peer doing the pressuring is male; the refuser-delayer is female. Some mainstream publishers set out to fix this bias in the 1990s. "Reducing the Risk," for instance, employs a novel approach: it names one of its fictional couples Lee and Lee, who evince no obvious gender traits and take turns aggressing and thwarting aggression. In Lee and Lee, the ideology of chastity has trumped women's liberation. Now, boys are expected to desire as little as girls.

"THE SEX ACT"

If the focus of abstinence-based education is the risks of pregnancy and disease, it makes sense that the sexual behavior students learn about is the one that carries the most risk: intercourse, which, unless specified otherwise, means penile-vaginal intercourse. Many of the abstinence-onlys assiduously exclude specifying otherwise. I attended meetings in the late 1990s of a New York City Board of Education committee packed with conservatives by Republican mayor Rudolph Giuliani and charged with revising a sex-ed curriculum authored by the previous, Democratic administration. A large part of one session was devoted to striking the words *vaginal, anal,* and *oral* wherever they appeared modifying *intercourse* in the text. Said one board member, who identified himself as a father, "We don't have to give children any more ideas than they already have."

For educators with a conservative agenda, teaching that sex means heterosexual intercourse is part of the point. For straight unmarried boys and girls, according to them, anything more than holding hands is treacherous and sinful; homosexuality is beyond consideration. (Even for married folk, sex beyond intercourse can be dicey. In their megaseller *The Act of Marriage*, fundamentalist Christian marriage counselors Tim and Beverly LaHaye caution that a vibrator "creates an erotic sensation that no human on earth can equal," putting a woman who gets used to one at risk of finding her "major motivation to marry . . . destroyed." They also warn that the jury is still out on the potential dangers of oral sex.)[6]

For the comprehensives, as we saw in the previous chapter, the censorship of classroom conversation is not deliberate in this way. It represents for some instructors a resigned surrender to pressure from the opposition (the banishment of Surgeon General Joycelyn Elders, for suggesting that masturbation might be discussed in the classroom, stands as a sort of cautionary parable). For others, the shrinking repertoire of topics they are willing to discuss signals a gradual, not-so-conscious absorption of the values behind that conservative pressure. In either case, though, the abstinence-plusers haven't given in all the way. They don't foment fear of all sex or try to persuade kids that sex is a privilege of married couples, like the joint income-tax return and the preprandial martini. In abstinence-plus programs, *abstinence* means refraining from risky behavior, which is to say from intercourse.

That said, abstinence-plusers don't spend much time, if any, discussing the more sophisticated aspects of lovemaking (say, a hand job), because, ironically, a straightforward conversation about a hand job can get a teacher into more trouble than talking about the Good Housekeeping-approved must-to-avoid, even though the former has far less potential of getting its practitioners into serious trouble. The easily inferred message: hand jobs are as illicit as intercourse. Throughout the 1980s and 1990s the comprehensive curricula featured recitals of what sex therapists call outercourse, but most such lists were vague, dull, and short. One suggested to students only that they "explore a wide range of ways to express love and sexual feelings," excluding going all the way. Romantic practices were often specified, such as sending billets-doux. But more clearly erotic pursuits, even hands-off practices like talking dirty on the phone or masturbating in front of a partner, were not.

Erotic creativity in educational writers is decidedly not rewarded in the abstinence era. The author of the first version of a 1997 Planned Parenthood pamphlet entitled *Birth Control Choices for Teens* was brave enough to inventory, under "Outercourse," reading erotica, fantasizing, role play, masks, and sex toys (with the warning to keep them clean and cover them with condoms). But, even though the brochure would not necessarily be used in the public schools, these suggestions were too hot for the organization to handle, and the pamphlet was revised to omit them, leaving only the more staid options of masturbation, erotic massage, and body rubbing. Then, according to a source at Planned Parenthood, the warehoused originals were burned.

Even progressive educators can unwittingly find themselves endorsing intercourse as *the* sex act. Teacher Joan Rappaport, who led a wide-ranging series of discussions called "Adolescent Issues" at a Manhattan private school, was mystified when she heard the course evaluations of her middle schoolers. When asked what they'd learned, said Rappaport, "one girl said, 'Basically, like, *Don't have sex.*'" The other kids concurred. Rappaport spent a weekend contemplating how a program that treated sexuality in a balanced,

tolerant, and, she thought, enthusiastic way could have metamor-
phosed into "just say no."

Finally, she figured it out. "You know," she said, "we talk a lot
about AIDS and STDs, we talk about emotions and sexual identities, about different kinds of families, about, well, most everything.
We say masturbation is normal and they shouldn't be ashamed or
worried about it. And yes, we do discourage intercourse. But we
never, ever talk about masturbation as *pleasure* or any other ways of
having sexual pleasure."

Now, American sex ed was never conceived as erotic training.
Quite the contrary: Most in the field today and in the past have presumed that kids get more than enough of that. These people view
the classroom experience as an antidote to the "oversexualizing"
commercial media and a coercive peer culture; their own role is as an
advocate of informed forethought against the merchants of impul-
siveness and of the soberer pleasures of childhood, such as sports
and friendship, against the premature pull of genital sex. It is the rare
pedagogue who breaks out. The week after that revealing review,
Rappaport gave her sixth-grade girls an assignment: "Go home and
find your clitorises." The teacher, who was then the mother of two
teenage boys, chuckled recalling her students' shocked faces and also
understood the hazards of what she'd done: "If I were in a public
school, they'd have fired me."

In the end, while the abstinence-plus teachers do not impose the
Right's embargo on talking about sex outside heterosexual monoga-
mous marriage, their focus on intercourse as *the* verboten act, coupled with the bowdlerization of nonpenetrative sexual experiences,
has an ironic and ultimately harmful effect. Much as they try to
*de*emphasize intercourse, it comes to take up the whole picture. The
infinitive *to have sex* is restored by default to the exact meaning it has

long held for American kids (and presidents)—that is, what the penis does inside the vagina.[7] "To kids, 'to have sex' means 'to have intercourse,'" Rappaport reflected, echoing what many other teachers told me. "So when we say 'Don't have intercourse' and leave out the rest, it's as if the rest doesn't exist. What they get is, 'Don't have sex.'"

When curriculum writers started to comprehend this confusion, they inserted exercises in which students would discuss just what abstinence means. But the main message, planted deep in the vernacular, endures. A Minneapolis sex educator paraphrased his students' definition of abstinence this way: "We did the things with our hands and our mouths and the trapeze and the pony—but we didn't have sex."

In representing intercourse as the ultimate—and, by implication, uniquely "normal"—sexual experience, educators do more than increase the odds their students will have mediocre sex until they stumble upon some other source of erotic enlightenment. Consciously or not, they also communicate the assumptions that sex is primarily heterosexual and reproductive and, above all, that it is always perilous.

Such uninformed sex, moreover, is perilous. "When adults deny the full range of human sexual expression and regard only intercourse as 'sex,' students are denied an important educational opportunity," wrote the sex educator Mary Krueger in 1993. "Many young people believe there is no acceptable form of sexual behavior other than intercourse. Operating under that assumption, students may put themselves at risk from unwanted pregnancy or sexually transmitted disease by engaging in intercourse when less risky sexual behavior would have been equally fulfilling."[8] In *Fatal Advice,* the author and AIDS activist Cindy Patton agreed strenuously. The dissemination of information crucial to containing the AIDS epidemic among young people was "made virtually impossible by the restrictions that prevented the discussion of condoms or instruction in non-intercourse forms of sex," she wrote.[9] By 2001, the omissions in abstinence-only education seem to have left a fair number of teens with the impression that anal intercourse carries no risk. The practice, at any rate, appears to be more common than in previous generations, especially in communities that attach a high value to vaginal virginity and among young urban gay men, an alarming number of whom report practicing the riskiest act, unprotected anal intercourse.[10] Such "prevention" of sex prevents real prevention: of disease. As a result, young people are dying.

BAD SEX

The Minneapolis student playing with the pony and the trapeze suggested what the findings of scant behavioral research show. Sexual experience, in kind, frequency, and age of engagement, differs according to a youngster's race and class, as well as her gender and whether she lives in the city or the country. But it can be generally said that fear of AIDS is increasing the incidence of nonpenetrative sexual practices among teens and preteens. By the preteen years, most children have started pursuing eroticized romances. In 1997, a quarter of fourteen-year-old boys said they had touched a girl's vulva, and 85 percent of teenagers had kissed somebody romantically. Almost a third of high schoolers in one California study had masturbated someone else, and a quarter to a half engaged in heterosexual fellatio or cunnilingus. Although they admit to a dearth of statistical data, some social scientists believe that journalists are overestimating the amount of oral sex among teens, especially young teens.[11]

In addition to what kids are doing, though, equally interesting is what the things they are doing mean to them. Whereas their parents' generation tended to regard oral sex as more intimate than inter-course, many kids see it the other way around. One fourteen-year-old boy told a reporter that intercourse implied a "real commitment," but oral sex didn't necessarily mean a relationship at all.[12]

With all that touching and sucking, are youngsters having sexual pleasure, even if their teachers neglect to mention it? That's hard to know. For, while evaluators of sex education programs can measure the impact of contraceptive instruction on birth-control practices or exposure to HIV-transmission information on condom use, they rarely ask the kinds of questions that would help them assess the effect of schoolhouse prudery (or *Buffy the Vampire Slayer*, for that matter) on how sex *feels* to young people sensually or emotionally.

Research on the quality of youths' sexual experience is virtually nonexistent. Getting funding to ask adults about their sexual attitudes or behavior is hard enough; asking minors the same questions is nigh on illegal. Congress has repeatedly blocked surveys of young people that mention oral sex.[13] Imagine what it would be to apply to the National Institutes of Health to find out about sixteen-year-olds' fantasies, their desires, their arousal or orgasm? That, in the eyes of many influential Congress members, would border on sexual abuse.

Still, there's no reason to believe kids are different from adults in this regard. Under the best of circumstances, pleasure takes practice. And sexual ignorance, coupled with sexual guilt perpetrated by parents, clergy, teachers, and public-service announcements, contributes to crummy sex, and to all the emotional "harms" with which the abstinence-only educators impugn adolescent sexual activity. Said sexologist Leonore Tiefer, "It is impossible to separate issues of coercion and consent, regret, neurosis, harm, or abuse from a culture in which there is no sex education."

Some people I've talked with conjecture that current teen sex might be worse than that in previous generations. The stock explanation is confusion: the media say, "Just do it"; school says, "Just say no." My own feeling is, it's more complicated. For one thing, popular culture is nothing if not eclectic in its sexual messages. On one channel the boys in *Queer as Folk* are buggering each other at the back of the disco; on another, the characters can't escape the surveillance of angels. Ally McBeal spends half her day in orgasmic fantasies about her clients and the other half being seduced by her law partners, yet she becomes apoplectic when her roommate sleeps with a man on the first date. The only consistent media message—about hamburgers, headache relief, or a high return on investments—is get it fast. Americans of all generations expect immediate gratification of desire, for everything.

This demand to have it all right now may be a leftover from a Sixties culture of unapologetic hedonism. But that culture offered the tools and some instruction in the art and craft of immediate and long-lasting pleasure: drugs, leisure time, and a widespread popular education in sexual technique, from erotic massage to the clitoral orgasm. In one sense, these cultural and erotic changes have taken permanent hold; just peruse the self-help shelves if you don't think so (not to mention the pornography shelves in any small-town video rental store). But the reveling in excess that characterized that era has turned to penitence. The Right indicts the counterculture as the handbasket in which we are all being carried to hell, and everyone else nods in sheepish assent. A result: Young people probably feel the sexual urgency their parents felt at their age.[14] But since they get little true pleasure instruction from any source, they are less likely to find gratification.

Although many "sexually active" youngsters actually have intercourse only intermittently, anecdotal evidence suggests that when intercourse is possible, it happens fast, and oral sex is an equally hasty affair. "We used to do all this slow kissy, touchy stuff," a seventeen-year-old who had recently lost her virginity told me. "But now it's like, the minute we start, he's looking for that condom." (At least he's looking for that condom. While 75 percent of teens use a condom their first time, only 60 percent say they use them regularly.) Long Island, New York, middle school guidance counselor Deb Rakowsky asked one ninth-grade girl what sex was to her. "It's, like, the boy puts it in you and moves around for about three minutes," she replied. How does it feel to you? The girl shrugged. "If that's her idea of sex," Rakowsky told me, "I think it's pretty sad."

REGRET

Of at least one phenomenon we have plenty of evidence: kids are having sex they don't want, and the ones who say they don't want it tend to be girls. In the late 1980s, the prominent sex educator Marian Howard announced that the greatest wish expressed by the eighth-grade girls entering her Atlanta sexuality-ed program was to learn how to say no without hurting a boy's feelings. In the two decades that have followed, study after study has been released demonstrating that girls are having sex they don't want, that girls who feel good about themselves don't have sex, and that girls who have had sex don't feel good about themselves. In the mid-1990s, it was reported that one in four teenage girls said she'd been abused or forced to have sex on a date.[15]

Girls are indisputably the more frequent victims of sexual exploitation and violence. But the gender assumptions articulated by Fine play not only into young people's feelings about themselves and sex but also subtly into the ways these research data are obtained and interpreted. One way gender biases are smuggled into research is under cover of a study's definitions, or lack thereof. In one of the above studies, conducted by the prestigious Commonwealth Fund, the questionnaire the girls answered did not define "abuse" at all. The other, from the highly respected Alan Guttmacher Institute, described abuse as "when someone in your family or someone else touches you in a sexual way in a place you did not want to be touched, or does something to you sexually which they shouldn't have done."[16] These studies, in other words, left about an acre of space for unarticulated cultural assumptions to creep in, both the subjects' assumptions and their interpreters'.

If girls are not supposed to feel desire and are charged with guarding the sexual gates, were Marian Howard's students able to conjure any self-respecting, self-protective self-image besides saying no? What, to the Guttmacher respondents, was "something . . . they shouldn't have done"? Nancy D. Kellogg, at the pediatrics department at the University of Texas, San Antonio, has pointed out that teenagers may use the term *abuse* for wanted but illegal sex, such as that between an adolescent girl and an adult man.[17] Or might these girls desire to be touched by a boy but worry that if it comes to intercourse he won't put on a condom? If he forces her anyway, it is rape. But fearing the consequences of arousal is not the same as not wanting to be touched.

In 2000, a poll of five hundred twelve- to seventeen-year-olds conducted by the National Campaign to Prevent Teen Pregnancy found that nearly two-thirds of those who had "had sex" wished they had waited (the report used the unclear terms *had sex* and *sexually active*). Of the girls, 72 percent had regrets, compared with 55 percent of the boys. More than three-quarters of the respondents thought teens should not be "sexually active" until after high school.[18] A spokesperson for the campaign said the poll was evidence that "many teens are taking a more cautious attitude toward having sex."[19] If a cautious attitude were all, and if caution were to translate to safer sex, that would be great. But these data reveal more than caution; they reveal shame. Teens get the message that the sex they are having is wrong, and whenever they have it, at whatever age, it's too early.

The findings inspire many troubling questions. Are these expressed feelings akin to "postabortion syndrome," a second-thought sadness brought on not necessarily by the experience itself but by the barrage of scolding messages from teachers, parents, and media? And why do girls feel them more than boys do? Again, might this be related to the still-thriving double standard? How much of that sexual regret is really about romantic disappointment? Might real pleasure, in a sex-positive atmosphere, balance or even outweigh regret over the loss of love? Even if the sex isn't satisfying, Thompson has found, a young person may look back on the experience with happiness, pride, or secret rebellious glee. But my instinct is, bad sex is more likely to leave bad feelings.

If nothing else, the blank spaces in these data remind us that most pencil-and-paper tests reveal only the slimmest minimum about sexuality. As for informing us about desire or pleasure, that shrug of Deb Rakowsky's student may be as eloquent as all the statistics we have.

The banishment of desire and pleasure is not exclusive to the sex education classroom, of course. As we've seen in the first half of *Harmful to Minors*, the notion that youthful sexuality is a problem pervades our thinking in all arenas. If images of desire appear in the media, critics call them brainwashing. In the family and between people of different ages, sizes, or social positions, sex is always thought of as coercion and abuse. At best, youthful sex is a regrettable mistake; at worst it is a pathology, a tragedy, or a crime. In the secular language of public health, engaging in sex is a "risk behavior," like binge drinking or anorexia. In religion, it is temptation and a sin.

All the while, from the political right to the left, adults call child sexuality normal. What's abnormal, or unhealthful, is acting on it. In "responsible" circles, it is nearly verboten to suggest that youthful sex can be benign—and heretical to call it a good thing. When Naomi Wolf, in her otherwise rather pursed-lipped book on teen sex, *Promiscuities,* endorsed erotic education and offered a few cross-cultural examples of same, reviewers ridiculed her. As you may remember from the introduction to *Harmful to Minors,* an erstwhile editor of this book—the liberal, highly educated mother of a grade-school boy—thought it wise to hold off using the word *pleasure* as far into the text as possible or eschew it altogether.

In the end, there is something giddily utopian in thinking about sexual pleasure when danger and fear loom. But idealism is just the start. How can we be both realistic and idealistic about sex? With toddlers, children, or adolescents, how can we be protective but not intrusive, instructive but not preachy, serious but not grim, playful but not frivolous? Part II will suggest some ways of rethinking our approaches to kids' sexuality and offer some examples of sensible practice by educators, parents, and friends of youth, practice that is based on a simple belief: erotic pleasure is a gift and can be a positive joy to people at every age.

---

1. Peggy Brick, "Toward a Positive Approach to Adolescent Sexuality," *SIECUS Report* 17 (May–June 1989): 3.
2. *Guidelines for Comprehensive Sexuality Education,* 1.
3. Michelle Fine, "Sexuality, Schooling, and Adolescent Females: The Missing Discourse of Desire," *Harvard Educational Review* 58 (1988): 33.

4. Girls Incorporated, Will Power/Won't Power: A Sexuality Education Program for Girls Ages 12–14 (Indianapolis: Girls Inc., 1998), V-12.

5. Richard P. Barth, *Reducing the Risk: Building Skills to Prevent Pregnancy, STD, and HIV*, 3d ed. (Santa Cruz, Calif.: ETR Associates, 1996), 89.

6. Tim LaHaye and Beverly LaHaye, *The Act of Marriage: The Beauty of Sexual Love* (Grand Rapids, Mich.: Zondervan, 1976), 289–90.

7. This was the definition given by the majority in Stephanie A. Sanders and June Machover Reinisch's "Would You Say You 'Had Sex' If . . . ?" *Journal of the American Medical Association* 281 (January 20, 1999): 275–77. See also Lisa Remez, "Oral Sex among Adolescents: Is It Sex or Is It Abstinence?" Alan Guttmacher Institute, Special Report 32, November–December 2000.

8. Mary M. Krueger, "Everyone Is an Exception: Assumptions to Avoid in the Sex Education Classroom," *Family Life Educator* (Fall 1993).

9. Cindy Patton, *Fatal Advice: How Safe-Sex Education Went Wrong* (Durham, N.C.: Duke University Press, 1996), 34.

10. The National Survey of Adolescent Males Ages 15 to 19, conducted in 1995 and published in 2000, found that one in ten had experienced anal sex. Tamar Lewin, "Survey Shows Sex Practices of Boys," *New York Times*, December 19, 2000. In one San Francisco survey of seventeen- to nineteen-year-old men who have sex with men, 28 percent had had unprotected anal sex, the behavior carrying the highest risk for HIV transmission. U.S. Conference of Mayors, "Safer Sex Relapse: A Contemporary Challenge," *AIDS Information Exchange* 11, no. 4 (1994): 1–8.

11. On the masturbation datum, see Krueger, "Everyone Is an Exception." On the oral sex datum, see Susan Newcomer and J. Richard Udry, "Oral Sex in an Adolescent Population," *Archives of Sexual Behavior* 14 (1985): 41–46. In another survey, of more than two thousand Los Angeles high school "virgins" in 1996, about a third of both boys and girls had masturbated or been masturbated by a heterosexual partner; about a tenth had engaged in fellatio to ejaculation or cunnilingus, with boys and girls more or less equally on the receiving end. Homosexual behavior was rarely reported among these kids, but 1 percent reported heterosexual anal intercourse. Mark A. Schuster, Robert M. Bell, and David E. Kanouse, "The Sexual Practices of Adolescent Virgins: Genital Sexual Activities of High School Students Who Have Never Had Vaginal Intercourse," *American Journal of Public Health* 86 (1996): 1570–76. Remez ("Sex among Adolescents") provides a good review of the scant literature on noncoital adolescent sexual behavior. She also suggests that the incidence and prevalence of fellatio probably far outweigh cunnilingus among teens. Many teens who have had oral sex have not had vaginal intercourse. One of Remez's sources guesses that "for around 25 percent of the kids who have had any kind of intimate sexual activity, that activity is oral sex, not intercourse."

12. Tamar Lewin, "Teen-Agers Alter Sexual Practices, Thinking Risks Will Be Avoided," *New York Times*, April 5, 1997, 8.

13. "Research Critical to Protecting Young People from Disease Blocked by Congress," Advocates for Youth, press release, December 19, 2000.

14. See Thompson, *Going All the Way*; and, e.g., Deborah L. Tolman, "Daring to Desire: Culture and the Bodies of Adolescent Girls," in *Sexual Cultures and the Construction of Adolescent Identities*, ed. Irvine, 250–84.

15. Tamar Lewin, "Sexual Abuse Tied to 1 in 4 Girls in Teens," *New York Times*, October 1, 1997.

16. Lewin, "Sexual Abuse Tied to 1 in 4 Girls."

17. Nancy D. Kellogg, "Unwanted and Illegal Sexual Experiences in Childhood and Adolescence," *Child Abuse and Neglect* 19 (1995): 1457–68.

18. *Not Just Another Thing to Do: Teens Talk about Sex, Regret, and the Influence of Their Parents* (Washington, D.C.: National Campaign to Prevent Teen Pregnancy, 2000), 6–7.

19. "Many Teens Regret Having Sex," National Campaign to Prevent Teen Pregnancy, press release, June 30, 2000.

from *Against Love*

By Laura Kipnis

Imagine the most efficient kind of social control possible. It wouldn't be a soldier on every corner—too expensive, too crass. Wouldn't the most elegant means of producing acquiescence be to somehow transplant those social controls so seamlessly into the guise of individual needs that the difference between them dissolved? And here we have the distinguishing political feature of the liberal democracies: their efficiency at turning out character types who identify so completely with society's agenda for them that they volunteer their very beings to the cause. But . . . *how* would such a feat be accomplished? *What* mysterious force or mind-altering substance could compel an entire population into such total social integration without them even noticing it happening, or uttering the tiniest peep of protest?

What if it could be accomplished through *love?* If love, that fathomless, many-splendored thing, that most mutable yet least escapable of all human experiences, that which leads the soul forward toward wisdom and beauty, were also the special potion through which renunciation could, paradoxically, be achieved? The paradox being that falling in love is the nearest most of us come to glimpsing Utopia in our lifetimes (with sex and drugs as fallbacks), and harnessing our most Utopian inclinations to the project of social control would be quite a singular achievement in the annals of modern population management. Like soma in *Brave New World*, it's the perfect drug. "Euphoric, narcotic, pleasantly hallucinant," as one character describes it. "All the advantages of Christianity and alcohol; none of their defects," quips another.

Powerful, mind-altering Utopian substances do tend to be subject to social regulation in industrialized societies (as with sex and drugs): we like to worry about whether people will make wise use of these things. What if they impede productivity! So we make them scarce and shroud them in prohibitions, thus reinforcing their danger, along with the justification for social controls.

Clearly love is subject to just as much regulation as any powerful pleasure-inducing substance, if not more. Whether or not we fancy that we love as we please—free as the birds and butterflies—an endless quantity of social instruction exists to tell us what it is, and what to do with it, and how, and when. And tell us, and tell us: the quantity of advice on the subject of how to love properly is almost as infinite as the sanctioned forms it takes are limited. Love's proper denouement, matrimony, is also, of course, the social form regulated by the state, which refashions itself as benevolent pharmacist, doling out the addictive substance in licensed doses. (It could always be worse: the other junkies are forced to huddle outside neighborhood clinics in the cold for their little paper cups; love at least gets treated with a little more pomp and ceremony.) Of course, no one is physically held down and forced to swallow vows, and not all those who love acquire the proper licenses to do so, but what a remarkable compliance rate is nevertheless achieved. Why bother to make marriage compulsory when informal compulsions work so well that even gays—once such paragons of unregulated sexuality, once so contemptuous of whitebread hetero lifestyles—are now demanding state regulation too? What about re-envisioning the form; rethinking the premises? What about just insisting that social resources and privileges not be allocated on the basis of marital status? No, let's *demand regulation!* (Not that it's particularly easy to re-envision anything when these intersections of love and acquiescence are the very backbone of the modern self, when every iota of self-worth and identity hinge on them, along with insurance benefits.)

So, here you are, gay or straight, guy or gal, with matrimony—or some functional equivalent—achieved, domestication complete, steadfastly pledged and declawed. A housetrained kitten. But wait: what's that nagging little voice at the edge of your well-being, the one that refuses to shut up, even when jabbed with the usual doses of shame. The one that says: "Isn't there supposed to be something more?" Well maybe there is, but don't go getting any ideas because an elaborate domestic security apparatus is on standby, ready to stomp the life out of them before they can breed—stomp them dead like the filthy homewrecking cockroaches they are.

Sure, we all understand jealousy. All precarious regimes are inherently insecure, casting watchful eyes on a citizenry's fidelity, ready to spring into action should anything threaten the exclusivity of those bonds. Every government knows that good intelligence props up its rule, so it's best to figure you're always being watched—you never know exactly from where, but a file is being compiled. Like seasoned FBI agents, longtime partners learn to play both sides of the good cop/bad cop routine. *"Just tell me, I promise I'll understand. . . . You did WHAT?!"* Once suspicions are aroused, the crisis alarm starts shrilling, at which point any tactics are justified to ensure your loyalty. Since anything can arouse suspicion, "preventative domestic policing" will always be an option: loyalty tests, trick questions, psychological torture, and carefully placed body blows that leave no visible marks. (Private detectives are also an option, or if you like, a Manhattan company called Check-a-Mate will send out attractive sexual decoys to see if your mate will go for the bait, then issue a full report.)*

Sure, easy to feel sympathetic to wronged partners: humiliated, undesired, getting fat, deserving better. The question of why someone cheats on you or leaves you can never be adequately explained. ("Intimacy issues," no doubt.) Realizing that people are talking, that friends knew and you didn't, that someone else has been poaching in your pasture and stealing what is by law yours is a special circle of hell. And even if you don't much want to have sex with the mate anymore, it's a little galling that someone else does. (Though this knowledge sometimes sparks a belated resurgence of desire: the suspicion-ridden marriage bed can be a pretty steamy place.)

But here's a question for you spouse-detectives as you're combing through credit card receipts, or cracking e-mail passwords, or perfecting the art of noiselessly lifting up phone extensions, counting condoms or checking the diaphragm case: What are you hoping to find? If you're looking, you basically know the answer, right? And if you don't find anything this time, are you willing to declare the

---

* Or consider the possibilities opened up by new technologies. A web site called Adulteryandcheating.com counsels tactics like satellite tracking and cyber-spying to nab cheating partners; spy equipment stores are also promoting new keystroke capture programs as a surveillance system for suspicious spouses, which, once installed on a home computer, will record your partner's e-mail exchanges and Web site visits for your later review.

matter settled? Hardly! Suspicion is addictive, sometimes even grat-
ifying. After all, rectitude is on your side, and you want those promises kept, damn it. You want those vows *obeyed.* You want security, and
of course you want love—since don't we all? But you'll settle for
obedience, and, when all else fails, ultimatums might work. But it's
not as though you don't know when you're being lied to—though
what constitutes "knowing" and "not knowing" in this regard could
fill another book—and having transformed yourself into a one-
person citizen-surveillance unit, how can you not hate the mate for
forcing you to act with such a lack of dignity?

Here we come to the weak link in the security-state model of
longterm coupledom: desire. It's ineradicable. It's roving and
inchoate, we're inherently desiring creatures, and sometimes desire
just won't take no for an answer, particularly when some beguiling
and potentially available love-object hoves into your sight lines,
making you feel what you'd forgotten how to feel, which is *alive,*
even though you're supposed to be channeling all such affective
capacities into the "appropriate" venues, and everything (Social
Stability! The National Fabric! Being a Good Person!) hinges on
making sure that you do. But renunciation chafes, particularly
when the quantities demanded begin to exceed the amount of
gratification achieved, for instance when basic monogamy evolves,
as it inevitably does under such conditions, into *surplus monogamy:*
enforced compliance rather than a free expression of desire. (Or
"repressive satisfaction" in Marcuse's still handy and stinging
phrase.) The problem is that maybe we're really *not* such acquies-
cent worker bees in our desires, and maybe there actually *isn't* consent about being reduced to the means to an end, especially when
the end is an overused platitude about the social fabric, whatever
that is. Meaning what?—that we'll all just churn out the proper

emotions to uphold calcified social structures like cows produce milk, like machines spit out O-rings?

But start thinking like that, and who knows what can happen? And that's the problem with dissatisfaction—it gives people "ideas." Even critical ideas. First a glimmering, then an urge, then a transient desire, soon a nascent thought: "Maybe there's something else." Recall that the whole bothersome business with labor unions and workers demanding things like shorter workdays started out in the same way: a few troublemakers got fed up about being treated like machines, word spread, and pretty soon there was a whole move-ment. "Wanting more" is a step on the way to a political idea, or so say political theorists, and ideas can have a way of turning them-selves into demands. In fact, "wanting more" is the simple basis of all Utopian thinking, according to philosopher Ernst Bloch. "Philosophies of Utopia begin at home," Bloch liked to say—found in the smallest sensations of pleasure and fun, or even in daydreams, exactly because they reject inhibitions and daily drudgery. Utopi-anism always manages to find an outlet too, operating in disguise when necessary, turning up in all sorts of far-flung places. Or right under our noses, because utopianism is an aspect of anything that opens up the possibilities for different ways of thinking about the world. For madcap Utopian Bloch, the most tragic form of loss wasn't the loss of security, it was the loss of the capacity to imagine that things could be different.

And for us? If philosophies of utopia begin at home, if utopianism is buried deep in those small, lived epiphanies of pleasure, in sensa-tions of desire, and fun, and play, in love, in transgression, in the rejection of drudgery and work, well . . . no one *works* at adultery, do they? If this makes it a personal lab experiment in reconfiguring the love-to-work ratio, or a makeshift overhaul of the gratification-to-

renunciation social equation, then it's also a test run for the most verboten fly-in-the-ointment question of all: *"Could things be different?"*
No, it may not be particularly thought-out, or even articulable, but
really, what else is behind these furtive little fantasies and small acts of
resistance—playing around, acting out, chasing inchoate desires and
longings—but trying to catch fleeting glimpses of what "something
else" could feel like. (Not that anyone here is endorsing adultery!
After all, it hardly needs endorsements, it's doing quite well on its
own. New recruits are signing up by the minute.)

Sure, adulterers behave badly. Deception rules this land, self-
deception included. Not knowing what you're doing risks bad faith,
and living exclusively in the present, and leaving sodden emotional
disasters strewn behind. But note the charges typically leveled against
the adulterer: "immaturity" (failure to demonstrate the requisite
degree of civilized repression); "selfishness" (failure to work for the
collective good—a somewhat selectively imposed requirement in
corporate America); "boorishness" (failure to achieve proper class
behavior). Or the extra fillip of moral trumping: "People will get
hurt!" (Though amputated desires hurt too.) True, typically in out-
bursts of mass dissatisfaction—strikes, rebellions, sedition, coups—
people sometimes get hurt: beware of sharp rocks and flying debris.
But if adultery summons all the shaming languages of bad citizenship, it also indicates the extent to which domestic coupledom is the
boot camp for compliant citizenship, a training ground for gluey resignation and immobility. The partner plays drill sergeant and anything short of a full salute to existing conditions is an invitation to
the stockades—or even a dishonorable discharge.

Still, conflicted desires and divided loyalties don't present a pretty
picture when seen up close: the broken promises, the free-range seduc-
tiveness, the emotional unreliability, all perched a little precariously on

that chronic dissatisfaction, crashing up against the rocky shoals of desperation. Ambivalence, universal though it may be, isn't much fun for anyone. (Least of all when you're on the receiving end. Deceived partners everywhere: our sympathies.) Ambivalence may fade into resignation, and given a high enough tolerance for swallowing things, this is supposed to count as a happy ending. But ambivalence is also just another way of saying that we social citizens have a constitutive lack of skill at changing things. Understandably—who gets any training at this? Even when not entirely resigned to the social institutions we're handed, who has a clue how to remake them, and why commit to them if there could be something better? Unfortunately, "something better" is also an idea so derided it's virtually prohibited entry to consciousness, and consequently available primarily in dreamlike states: romantic love and private Utopian experiments like adultery (or secondhand, in popular fantasy genres like romance and myth). But after all, we don't make history under conditions of our own choosing, and private life is pretty much all we have to work with when it comes to social experiments in our part of the world these days, where consumer durables and new technologies come equipped with planned obsolescence. A word to the wise. Before signing up for the thrill ride of adultery, let's all be aware that passionate love involves alarmingly high degrees of misrecognition in even the best of cases (that poignant Freudian paradigm), which means that we players in the adultery drama will be especially beset, madly flinging ourselves down uncharted paths in states of severe aporia, the impediments to self-knowledge joined at the hip to the lures of disavowal. All of us risk drowning in those swirling tidal waves of emotion and lust, cramped up and overwhelmed, having thought ourselves shrewd and agile enough to surf the crest despite the posted danger signs. You may say you're not going to get in too deep, you may say you just want to have fun, but before you know it you're flattened by a crashing wave from nowhere and left gasping for air with a mouthful of sand. (Translation: you're in love, or you're in lust, and not with your mate, and your life feels out of control, and maybe you've been waiting your whole life to feel this way about someone, which means you're in big trouble.)

So watch out, baby—a few missteps, a couple of late-night declarations, and everything could be up for grabs. What started as a fling has somehow turned serious; the supplement has started to supersede the thing that needed supplementing. Perhaps unplanned exposures have forced things into the open, or those "contradictions" of yours have started announcing themselves in some unpleasant somatic form that eventually can't be ignored. Insomnia. Migraines. Cold sores. Digestive ailments. Heart palpitations. Sexual difficulties. (Sometimes bodies just won't play along, even when instructed otherwise). Choices will need to be made. Choices that you, with your terminal ambivalence and industrial-strength guilt are not capable of making. Antacids aren't working. Work is suffering. The shrink just says, "What do you think?" Love is the drug; love is the trap; love is the way we have of forgetting the question. Using love to escape love, groping for love outside the home to assuage the letdowns of love at home . . . —it's kind of like smoking and wearing a nicotine patch at the same time: two delivery systems for an addictive chemical substance that feels vitally necessary to your well-being at the moment, even if likely to wreak unknown havoc in the deepest fibers of your being at some unspecified future date.

The best polemic against love would mimic in prose the erratic and overheated behavior of its hapless practitioners: the rushes and excesses, the inconsistent behavior and inchoate longings, the moment-by-moment vacillations between self-doubt (*"What am I doing?"*) and utter certainty (*"You're the one"*), all in quest of something utterly unknown. It would replicate in form the impediments and trade-offs and fumbling around, all the things felt but not entirely known, and the tension of being caught in-between—between mates and lovers or between rival ways of telling this conflicted tale, each beckoning with its own sultry and alluring vocabulary: social theory and love affairs, Marx and Freud, Utopia and pragmatics, parody and sentimentality. "Just pick one and settle down already," you can hear people saying. But what if you keep finding yourself looking "elsewhere" as much as you tell yourself not to, and that this is really no way to act? Yes, just like all you adultery clowns out there tripping over your big floppy shoes and chasing improbable fulfillment, knowing it has the whiff of a doomed undertaking and making up the rules as you go along, we polemicists too are propelled to (intellectual) promiscuity, rashness and blind risks and becoming the neighborhood pariah (or joke) just for thinking there could be reasons to experiment with reimagining things.

But to those feeling a little stultified and contemplating a spin down Reinvention Road: do weigh your options carefully. Don't forget that all outbreaks of love outside sanctioned venues still invite derisive epitaphs like "cheating" or "mid-life crisis," while those that play by the rules will be community-sanctified with champagne and gifts in the expensive over-rehearsed costume rituals of the wedding-industrial complex (its participants stiffly garbed in the manner of landed gentry from some non-existent epoch: clearly, playing out unnatural roles is structured into these initiation rites as a test of the participants' stamina for role-playing as a social enterprise, and a measure of their resolve and ability to keep doing so in perpetuity).

So consider this not just a polemic, but also an elegy: an elegy for all the adultery clowns crying on the inside, with our private experiments and ragtag Utopias. The elegiac mode traditionally allows a degree of immoderation, so please read on in an excessive and mournful spirit—or at least with some patience for the bad bargains and compensatory forms the discontented classes engineer for themselves in daily life. So many have met such dismal joyless fates, dutifully renouncing all excess desires, and along with them any hopes that the world could deliver more than it currently does—or could if anyone had the temerity to fight about it, and face down the company goons, then face down the ritual shaming, and last but not least the massive self-inflicted guilt shortly to follow.

But beware their seductive and dangerous lures too, those beguiling adulterers, dangerous as pirate ships lying in wait to cadge any unguarded troves of emotion and pleasure, promises brandished like a swashbuckler's sword, slicing through qualms like they were air. Was ever there a more seductive seducer—or a more captivating captor— than an emotionally starving human with potential ardor in sight? (*"Trust me, things will work out."*) But to all you temporary utopians and domestic escape artists who couldn't sustain your own wishes for more courageous selves or different futures or love on better terms, who could only filch a few brief moments of self-reinvention and fun before being drop-kicked, guilt-ridden and self-loathing, back to the household gulags, the compartmentalization, the slow death of "maturity" (because risking stagnation is obviously preferable to risking change in the prevailing emotional economy): we mourn your deaths. We leave immoderate bouquets at your gravesides.

The Naked and the Red

By Marc Cooper
The Nation / April 3, 2003

LAS VEGAS

A specter haunts Las Vegas: organized strippers. Behind this night-mare vision lurks Andrea Hackett, a former male factory-worker turned nude dancer. And the headlines Hackett's been making have nothing to do with her sex change. Here in Glitter Gulch that raises no more eyebrows than, say, a PTA president's divorce in Peoria.

No. Hackett's been the talk of the town because the lanky, blond-streaked forty-nine-year-old with a spectacular set of enameled fin-gernails has been frenetically trying to organize Vegas's thousands of strippers and nude dancers, launching them into a head-on battle royal against local government—and indirectly against the all-pow-erful corporate gambling interests that dominate this city's political life. "They wanted a fight," she says, unpacking a file of organiza-tional charts and strategy notes. "And now I'm giving it to them."

This unusually colorful episode of open class warfare erupted last summer when the Clark County commissioners voted five to one to heavily regulate the stripping and lap dancing that bring millions of tourists and conventioneers and many more of their dollars annually into Vegas's thirty-six "gentlemen's clubs" and provide income for 15,000 women dancers. (No one knows for sure, but the guess is that something like a million lap dances a year are performed in Vegas clubs at twenty-five bucks a pop or more.)

Like a Church Lady skit straight out of *SNL*, the county commissioners took a hands-on approach—excuse the pun—to defining what would now become a legal or illegal lap dance. In brief, a dancer would no longer be able to sit on a customer's genital area— i.e., his lap—more or less rendering the very essence of the dance impotent. Dancers could no longer solicit tips. Customers could offer them but were specifically barred from any longer performing the traditional gesture of placing currency in dancers' G-strings. "This was a declaration of war," Hackett huffs. "In short, they were outlawing lap dancing."

Before her sex-change operation in 1995, Hackett spent seventeen years working for Boeing in Seattle as a machinist and union activist. Now she drew upon her previous organizing experience to fight back. "I know I'm the only nude dancer in Vegas who went to Woodstock and who burned her draft card," she says. And for good measure, she adds, "I'm also a socialist."

Within days of the bill's passage, Hackett founded the Las Vegas Dancers Alliance, and by the end of the summer she had signed up nearly a thousand members. She now has "club reps"—sort of clandestine shop stewards—in about two-thirds of the dance establishments, and they are signing up about twenty-five new members a week. In addition to holding regular organizing meetings at the local library, Hackett's LVDA published a "Dancers Voter Guide" for the November 2002 election and conducted the first known voter-registration drive in history of nude and lap dancers. "We registered almost 500 new voters among the girls," she says proudly.

The LVDA has affiliated unofficially with almost fifty other groups, including the Sierra Club and the northern Nevada NAACP, that make up the Progressive Leadership Alliance of Nevada (PLAN), and Hackett has forged a close working relationship with the local ACLU. "She's got the energy of ten organizers and the skills to go along with it," says Paul Brown, southern Nevada director of PLAN. "The County Commission has set off a spark that has turned into a firestorm. This basically comes down to an important issue of labor practices." In the past few weeks Hackett has also met with state AFL-CIO officials and other union activists exploring affiliation. "Do we want to become a union?" she asks and then answers her own query. "Let's just say that all roads are leading to the same conclusion." One organizer for a major international industrial union who met with Hackett says his organization is looking seriously into some form of collaboration. "We'd love to have these dancers eventually in our union, and we're going to help out every way we can," he says.

Hackett and other local political observers agree that the crackdown on lap dancing can be traced to the economic squeeze the big Vegas casinos and hotels have been feeling since 2000. Business is only down 2 to 4 percent, but that's an ice-cold shower for an industry that has been spoiled by two decades of uninterrupted growth and profitability. To jack up the inflow of tourists, many of the casino resorts have been turning to racier floor shows, but they are still prohibited by state regulation from mixing gambling with strip or lap dancing. In the past few weeks all of America has been exposed to a new, sexually suggestive, multimillion-dollar TV ad campaign run by Vegas gambling and hotel interests promising "What happens here, stays here." Meanwhile, the mega-lit billboards atop the giant Vegas hotels are filled more and more with explicitly sexual lures.

• • •

The lap-dance clubs near the big hotels commit the cardinal sin of drawing guests off these resort properties and out of the casinos and pricey restaurants. And some of these clubs are very big businesses in themselves. The newly opened Sapphire Gentleman's Club is a $25 million investment that draws upon a pool of 6,000 dancers. In short, it seems the casinos have been using their political clout to shut down competition from the dance clubs. "This is life in the post-9/11 economic environment," says Hackett, sounding very much like a union economist. "It's all about the corporations shifting their revenue and profit stream away from gaming." Traditionally, the corporate owners of Vegas have made 60 to 70 percent of their profits from gambling and the rest from lodging, food, and entertainment. But at the recent "American Gaming Summit," the CEO of the powerhouse MGM Mirage boasted of how his corporation has managed to invert that formula.

Not everyone agrees with Hackett that the big casinos are the lone motivating force behind the lap-dance suppression. "No question that in the end this is about economics," says Gary Peck, executive director of the Nevada ACLU. But Peck thinks the pressure might also be coming from some of the bigger, politically connected dance clubs trying to squeeze out the smaller ones. He also argues that some of the county commissioners behind the ordinance have a less than healthy view of sex. "It's very difficult for me to delve into the heads of that crowd," he says with a laugh. "But I can certainly tell you they are obsessed with sex!" Of his alliance with Hackett, Peck says: "She's working with women who are working people and whose business is protected by the First Amendment. And that is where our interests and concerns coincide."

Hackett, meanwhile, has found fertile organizing territory among the dancers, who have also been feeling the economic pinch of the past two years. While in the salad days of the dot.com bubble a top dancer could count on maybe forty to fifty lap dances a night at twenty-five dollars each, today she is lucky to do ten. "You might think that's a lot of money either way," says Hackett. "But we are exploited by everybody." Vegas's exotic dancers are treated as "independent contractors" by club owners, meaning not only are they not on the payroll, thus receiving no benefits or insurance, but they have to pay the owners as much as $70 a night just for the right to perform. Then there are payoffs to the bouncers, the deejays, and sometimes even to the parking valets. And whatever money is generated by the dancers has to be split with the club owners, sometimes on a fifty-fifty basis.

The non-employee status of the dancers may eventually thwart unionization efforts, but in that case the LVDA could still exert influence as a "professional organization," perhaps on the model of the National Writers Union. The alliance is also close to concluding a deal with an insurance carrier so that dancer-members would be able to purchase healthcare at group rates. Once that deal is concluded, alliance membership could soar.

LVDA can already claim some partial victories. Vigorous lobbying, a few rallies and marches downtown, and oodles of local and even international publicity forced partial reversal of last summer's near-total ban on lap dancing. Some weeks ago Clark County officials amended the ordinance so that G-string tipping would once again be allowed. Hackett's group has also convinced local county and city officials to put on the back burner proposals to impose a stiff registration and licensing tax on individual dancers. Nevertheless, there's been a marked increase in arrests and ticketing of dancers since last summer's law went into effect. "All that law has done is turn us into criminals," says Hackett. So she's moving ahead with a new project: sponsoring a countywide measure, known as the Protection of Dancing Initiative, that will impose standardized regulation of the industry and reverse the more draconian aspects of the recent legislation. "Call it Christmas for dancers," says Hackett. To qualify these measures for the ballot, thousands of voter signatures will have to be gathered in the next few months. Hackett is confident. "We've already lined up squads of volunteer signature gatherers," she says mischievously. "And they are all hardbodies," she says, using the industry term that refers to the youngest dancers, usually eighteen to twenty-one years old. "Now you tell me, honey," she says, "you think anyone walking the streets of Vegas is gonna say no to these girls?"

The signature campaign is now getting under way. But even before that, Hackett and her hardcore group of about fifty activists were already working around the clock, leafleting the dance clubs for new members, shopping around for union affiliation, and plotting out the initiative campaign.

By night Hackett is still dancing at the Deja Vu Showgirls club. By day she is putting the finishing touches on what she's calling her own "Politics of Dancing" educational course—designed, she says, to offer a quick political education to the average apolitical nineteen-year-old nude dancer. Hackett has already written a first primer. Skimming through the 7,500-word pamphlet, it's clear that the enforcers of decency at the County Commission and the casino interests behind them have taken on a formidable opponent. Hackett closes by saying she hopes her work can "help solidify the great natural allies of the American left and begin to heal the wounds inflicted by our natural enemies on the American right . . . the first basic facts to remember are these: There are far less rich people than poor people. And the rich generally want things to stay the way they are. The poor, by their very nature, want things to change, hopefully for the better."

Hackett has recently started working with a nucleus of nude dancers in Texas who are trying to organize. And eventually, she says, she'd like to have a national organization. "I've already got the name figured out. The United States Dancers Alliance. Or USDA," she says with a laugh, slapping her flank. "Get it?"

The Zipless Fallacy

By Erica Jong
Newsweek / June 30, 2003

"I was not against marriage. I believed in it, in fact. It was necessary to have one best friend in a hostile world . . . yet what about all those other longings which after a while, marriage did nothing much to appease?"—FEAR OF FLYING

When I published *Fear of Flying* in 1973, women were not supposed to publicly confess to sexual boredom in marriage. It was rampant, of course. But as I was to discover (to my horror), it is one thing to be a secret, silent adulterer and quite another to be an adulterer on paper—especially if you are a woman—and *Fear of Flying* humorously suggested that there might be sexual fantasies about other partners even within marriage. My novel was passed from hand to hand, read aloud in bed, pressed on boyfriends by girlfriends and on girlfriends by boyfriends. Analysts recommended it to their patients. Mothers kept it from their daughters—the best PR a book can have. *Fear of Flying* made its way in the world, and so did I.

Now, thirty years later, when every glossy mag promises to teach "101 Ways to Drive Him (or Her) Wild in Bed," you'd think that marriage would have evolved into something lusty and liberated. But no, we still hear that sex is dead, that exhaustion depletes libidos and that workaholic careers leave no time for connubial canoodling.

Is it true? Must we never hope for that zipless encounter in the five-star hotel with our beloved spouse, a bottle of Krug or Cristal and beluga caviar? The problem with Americans is that, unlike the French, we want all our emotional eggs in one basket. We crave passion, sex, friendship, and children all with the same partner. Can such miracles occur? And if they occur, how long can they last? Two years? Time to conceive the baby and swaddle it? Twenty years? Time to teach the baby (almost) civilized behavior?

Since passion is about fantasy and marriage is about reality, passion and marriage are the oddest of odd bedfellows. My own experience has been that passion ebbs and flows in marriage. It is far more dependent on romantic vacations and child-free weekends than we like to admit. And when we do check into a fancy hotel with our spouse, as the women's mags recommend, we're likely to start talking about whether the roof needs fixing or the car needs tuning. After all, marriage with work and children leaves little time for adult conversation. You might get to that hotel room in the sky and use the time just to converse with your spouse. And you might consider that a perfect evening.

Perhaps the problem is not in our marriages but in our expectations. In our post-sexual-revolution era, we expect carnality and familiarity wrapped up in the same shiny gift package. We would be much happier and much more fulfilled if we changed those unrealistic expectations. And our glossy mags would do well to stop teasing us while pretending to be helping us.

The truth is that ziplessness has always been a Platonic ideal rather than a daily reality. Yes, wild passionate sex exists. It can even exist in marriage. But it is occasional, not daily. And it is not the only thing that keeps people together. Talking and laughing keep couples together. Shared goals keep couples together. If this were not true, how would some couples survive illnesses, deaths of beloved family members, even holocausts? The pair bond is strong. We are pair-bonding creatures—like swans or geese. We can also be as promiscuous as baboons or bonobos. Those are the two extremes of human sexuality, and there are all gradations of chastity and sensuality in between. The glue that holds couples together consists of many things: laughter, companionship, tenderness—and sex. The busyness of marriage is real, but we also use it to protect us from raw intimacy, from having to be too open too much of the time. Pleasure is terrifying because it breaks down the boundaries between people. Embracing passion means living with fear. "Love is a breach in the walls, a broken gate," wrote the poet Rupert Brooke. "Love sells the proud heart's citadel to fate." Amen.

About the Contributors

Nina Bernstein is a reporter for the *New York Times*. She has won such awards as the Columbia Journalism School's Mike Berger Award and the George Polk Award for distinguished metropolitan coverage. In 1994 she was made an Alicia Patterson Fellow.

Susie Bright is the author or editor of over a dozen books including *Mommy's Little Girl, The Best American Erotica* series, the first three editions of *Herotica, Full Exposure,* and *The Sexual State of the Union.* She hosts the weekly audio show *In Bed with Susie Bright* on Audible.com. She lectures and performs at theaters and universities nationwide and currently lives in Northern California.

Alessandro Camon is a film producer living in Los Angeles. His recent work includes the films *Owning Mahowny, The Cooler,* and *Never Die Alone.*

Marc Cooper is a contributing editor to *The Nation*, the host of the syndicated *RadioNation*, and has covered politics and culture from across the U.S. and around the world for the last three decades. His writing has appeared in *Harper's*, *The New Yorker*, *Rolling Stone*, *Playboy*, and others. His books include *The Last Honest Place in America* and *Pinochet and Me*.

Benoit Denizet-Lewis is a contributing writer at *The New York Times Magazine* and a 2004 Alicia Patterson Fellow. Formerly a senior writer at *Boston* magazine and staff writer at the *San Francisco Chronicle*, his work has also appeared in *ESPN the Magazine*, *Spin*, *Out*, *Salon*, and *Jane*. He has received numerous journalism awards, including the Excellence in Journalism Award from the National Lesbian and Gay Journalists Association and the GLAAD award for magazine feature writing.

Samantha Dunn is the author of the novel *Failing Paris*, which was nominated for the PEN/West Award. She lives in Southern California.

Barbara Ehrenreich is a political essayist and social critic. She is the author or coauthor of twelve books, including *Nickel and Dimed*; *Fear of Falling: The Inner Life of the Middle Class*; and *Blood Rites: Origins and History of the Passions of War*. She has written for dozens of magazines, including *The Nation*, *The New Republic*, *Atlantic Monthly*, and *The New York Times Magazine*.

Niles Eldredge is a paleontologist and a curator at the American Museum of Natural History and the author of many books on evolutionary theory. He lives in New Jersey.

Steve Erickson is the author of numerous novels, including *The Sea Came in at Midnight*, *Days Between Stations*, *Rubicon Beach*, *Tours of the Black*

Clock, Arc d'X, and *Amnesiascope,* which have been published in ten languages throughout Europe and Asia. His work has appeared in such magazines and journals as *Esquire, Elle, Rolling Stone, Spin, San Francisco* magazine, *Conjunctions,* and *Salon.*

Mark Jacobson is a journalist and novelist. His recent books include the travelogue *12,000 Miles in the Nick of Time,* the saga of a trip around the world with his family, and the anthologies *American Monsters* (edited with Jack Newfield) and *The KGB Bar Nonfiction Reader,* a sampling of pieces from the long running salon. He lives in Brooklyn.

Erica Jong is the author of eight novels including *Fear of Flying; Sappho's Leap;* and *Fanny: Being the True History of the Adventures of Fanny Hackabout-Jones.* Several of her novels have been worldwide bestsellers. Her other books include the nonfiction works *Fear of Fifty: A Midlife Memoir, Witches,* and *What Do Women Want?* She lives in New York City and Connecticut.

Cole Kazdin is a writer in New York. His work appears regularly on Salon.com and in numerous other publications.

Laura Kipnis is a professor of media studies at Northwestern University. She has received fellowships and grants from the Guggenheim Foundation, the Rockefeller Foundation, and the National Endowment for the Arts. She has published numerous essays and articles on sexual politics and contemporary culture both here and abroad.

Peter Landesman is a journalist, novelist, and screenwriter. His nonfiction appears in *The New York Times Magazine, Atlantic Monthly,* and

The New Yorker. He received the 1996 American Association of Arts and Letters Best First Fiction Award for *The Raven.* His second novel, *Blood Acre,* is about the downward spiral of a corrupt attorney in New York City.

Judith Levine is a journalist and essayist who has written about sex, gender, and families for two decades. She is the author of two books published by Thunder's Mouth Press, *My Enemy, My Love,* and *Harmful to Minors,* winner of the *Los Angeles Times* Book Prize. She lives in Brooklyn and Vermont.

Chris O'Brien is a reporter at the *San Jose Mercury News.*

Camille Paglia is professor of humanities at the University of the Arts in Philadelphia. She is the author of three bestselling books, *Sexual Personae: Art and Decadence from Nefertiti to Emily Dickinson; Sex, Art and American Culture;* and *Vamps & Tramps: New Essays.* Her fourth book, a study of Alfred Hitchcock's *The Birds* has been published by the British Film Institute in its Film Classics series.

Esther Perel is on the faculties of the New York Medical Center Department of Psychiatry and the International Trauma Studies Program at New York University. She is in private practice in New York.

Neal Pollack is the author of *The Neal Pollack Anthology Of American Literature, Beneath The Axis Of Evil,* and *Never Mind the Pollacks,* as well as the singer for the Neal Pollack Invasion. He lives in Austin, Texas.

Katha Pollitt has been contributing to *The Nation* since 1980. Pollitt has written essays for *The New Yorker, Atlantic Monthly, The New Republic,*

Harper's, Mirabella, Mother Jones, and the *New York Times.* She has appeared on NPR's *Fresh Air* and *All Things Considered,* as well as *The McLaughlin Group, Dateline NBC,* CNN, and the BBC.

Dan Savage is the author of the nationally syndicated column "Savage Love" and the editor of *The Stranger,* His books include *Savage Love, The Kid,* and, most recently, *Skipping Towards Gomorrah.* He lives in Seattle, Washington.

Roger Scruton is among the most prominent contemporary English writers. A philosopher who was formerly a professor at Birkbeck College in London and at Boston University, he is now a freelance writer living in Wiltshire, England.

Ingrid Sischy is the editor in chief of *Interview* and a contributing editor to *Vanity Fair.*

Amy Sohn now writes the weekly "Naked City" column in *New York* magazine, in which she interviews ordinary and extraordinary New Yorkers about their love lives. She is the author of the novel *Run Catch Kiss* and the bestselling companion guide to television's *Sex and the City—Sex and the City: Kiss and Tell.* She grew up in Brooklyn, where she lives today.

Permissions

"Is the Pope Crazy?" by Katha Pollitt. Reprinted with permission from the November 3, 2003 issue of *The Nation*. For subscription information, call 1-800-33-8536. Portions of each week's *Nation* magazine can be accessed at http://www.thenation.com. ✢ "Letter to the Editor of *New York* Magazine" by Susie Bright. Copyright © 2003 by Susie Bright, used by arrangement with the author. ✢ "Where's Mae West When We Need Her?" by Camille Paglia and Ingrid Sischy. Copyright © 2003 Brant Publications. Originally published in *Interview* magazine, July 2003, Brant Publications, Inc. Used by permission of the authors. ✢ "The Prisoner of Sex.com" by Chris O'Brien. Copyright © 2003 by Chris O'Brien. Originally appeared in *Wired*, August 2003. Used by permission of the author. ✢ "The Forbidden Realm" by Steve Erickson. Copyright © 2003 by Steve Erickson. First appeared in *Los Angeles* magazine, July 2003. Reprinted by permission of Melanie Jackson Agency, LLC. ✢ "The Moral Birds and Bees" by Roger Scruton. Copyright © 2003 by National Review, Inc. Originally published in *National Review*, September 15, 2003. Reprinted by permission. ✢ "Might and Right in Colorado Springs" by Samantha Dunn. Copyright © 2003 by *Ms.* magazine. Originally published in *Ms.*, June 2003. Reprinted by permission of *Ms.* magazine. ✢ "Double Lives on the Down Low" by Benoit Denizet-Lewis. Copyright 2003 by Benoit Denizet-Lewis. Reprinted by permission. ✢ "Do Women Need Viagra?" by Barbara Ehrenreich. Copyright © 2003 by TIME Inc. Originally published in *Time*, January 19, 2003. Reprinted by permission. ✢ "Times Up" by Mark Jacobson. Copyright © 2003 by Mark Jacobson, used by arrangement with the author. ✢ "American Torture, American Porn" by Alessandro Camon. Copyright © 2004 by Salon.com. First appeared in *Salon.com* at www.salon.com. An online version remains in the Salon archives. Reprinted by permission. ✢ "In